MULTICULTURAL EDU[

JAMES A. BANKS, *Series Editor*

(continued)

TEACHING
for EQUITY in
COMPLEX TIMES

Negotiating Standards in a
High-Performing Bilingual School

Jamy Stillman
Lauren Anderson

with John Luciano Beltramo,
Kathryn Struthers, and Joyce Gomez-Najarro

TEACHERS COLLEGE PRESS

TEACHERS COLLEGE | COLUMBIA UNIVERSITY
NEW YORK AND LONDON

Published by Teachers College Press, 1234 Amsterdam Avenue, New York, NY 10027

Library of Congress Cataloging-in-Publication Data is available at loc.gov

ISBN 978-0-8077-5784-0 (paper)
ISBN 978-0-8077-5785-7 (hardcover)
ISBN 978-0-8077-7490-8 (ebook)

Printed on acid-free paper
Manufactured in the United States of America

24 23 22 21 20 19 18 17   8 7 6 5 4 3 2 1

*for all the teachers
and bilingual education advocates
helping to bend
that long arc
toward justice*

Contents

Series Foreword

This penetrating and discerning book is an ethnographic account and analysis by Stillman, Anderson, and associates of a high-performing bilingual charter school that the authors call "Playa." Playa has several distinguishing characteristics that make it a goldmine for the generation of ideas about the complex factors that influence the ways in which Common Core Standards and standards-based reform are implemented in the daily lives of schools and classrooms. Playa has a culture which values collaboration, the languages and cultures of Emergent Bilingual (EB) students, and high student expectations. The 10 focus teachers in this study embrace the major tenets of multicultural education, multilingualism, and critical pedagogy.

Equity is institutionalized within the school culture of Playa, which the authors refer to as "the Playa way." Playa teachers respect and try to incorporate the language and cultures of their students into their curriculum and pedagogy. Stillman, Anderson, and associates chronicle the ways in which Playa's teachers often find themselves in contradictory situations because of the ways in which they have to negotiate their high academic expectations for students, their principal's expectations, and the requirements of the Common Core State Standards. The authors detail how these difficult negotiations often caused Playa's teachers to make instructional decisions that resulted in one-size-fits-all approaches such as whole-class instruction that did not meet the individual needs of their students. The authors' insightful and thick ethnographic descriptions of the ways in which the teachers at Playa tried to make their beliefs consistent with their teaching practices and the challenges they faced in resolving these conundrums are compelling and unique contributions of this incisive and informative book.

The ways in which teachers negotiate and work to implement national standards in a high-performing bilingual school is a significant and timely topic because of the growing population of students from diverse language groups who are attending schools in the United States. Although students in the U. S. are becoming increasingly diverse, most of the nation's teachers are White, female, and monolingual. Race and institutionalized racism are significant factors that influence and mediate the interactions of students and teachers from different ethnic, language, and social-class groups (G. R. Howard, 2016; T. C. Howard, 2010; Leonardo, 2013). The growing income gap between adults (Stiglitz, 2012)—as well as between youth that are described by Putnam (2015) in *Our Kids: The American*

Dream in Crisis—is another significant reason why it is important to help teachers understand how variables such as race, class, and language influence classroom interactions and student learning and to comprehend the ways in which these variables influence student aspirations and academic engagement (Suárez-Orozco, Pimentel, & Martin, 2009).

American classrooms are experiencing the largest influx of immigrant students since the beginning of the 20th century. Approximately 21.5 million new immigrants—documented and undocumented—settled in the United States in the years from 2000 to 2015. Less than 10% came from nations in Europe. Most came from Mexico, nations in South Asia, East Asia, Latin America, the Caribbean, and Central America (Camarota, 2011, 2016). The influence of an increasingly diverse population on U.S. schools, colleges, and universities is and will continue to be enormous.

Schools in the United States are more diverse today than they have been since the early 1900s when a multitude of immigrants entered the United States from Southern, Central, and Eastern Europe. In 2014, the National Center for Education Statistics estimated that the percentage of students from ethnic minority groups made up more than 50% of the students in prekindergarten through 12th grade in public schools, an increase from 40% in 2001 (National Center for Education Statistics, 2014). Language and religious diversity is also increasing in the U.S. student population. The 2012 American Community Survey estimated that 21% of Americans aged 5 and above (61.9 million) spoke a language other than English at home (U.S. Census Bureau, 2012). Harvard professor Diana L. Eck (2001) calls the United States the "most religiously diverse nation on earth" (p. 4). Islam is now the fastest-growing religion in the United States, as well as in several European nations such as France, the United Kingdom, and the Netherlands (Banks, 2009; O'Brien, 2016).

The major purpose of the Multicultural Education Series is to provide pre-service educators, practicing educators, graduate students, scholars, and policy-makers with an interrelated and comprehensive set of books that summarizes and analyzes important research, theory, and practice related to the education of ethnic, racial, cultural, and linguistic groups in the United States and the education of mainstream students about diversity. The dimensions of multicultural education, developed by Banks (2004) and described in the *Handbook of Research on Multicultural Education* and in the *Encyclopedia of Diversity in Education* (Banks, 2012), provide the conceptual framework for the development of the publications in the Series. The dimensions are content integration, the knowledge construction process, prejudice reduction, equity pedagogy, and an empowering institutional culture and social structure. The books in the Multicultural Education Series provide research, theoretical, and practical knowledge about the behaviors and learning characteristics of students of color (Conchas & Vigil, 2012; Lee, 2007), language minority students (Gándara & Hopkins 2010; Valdés, 2001; Valdés, Capitelli, & Alvarez, 2011), low-income students (Cookson, 2013; Gorski, 2013), and other minoritized population groups, such as students who speak different varieties of English (Hudley & Mallinson, 2011), and LGBTQ youth (Mayo, 2014). Two other books in the Multicultural Education Series complement this book because they focus on national standards and standards-based reform, *Un-Standardizing Curriculum: Multicultural Teaching in the Standards-Based Classroom* by Sleeter and Flores Carmona (2017), and *Facing Accountability in Education: Democracy and Equity at Risk*, edited by Sleeter (2007).

One of the salient findings of the perceptive study reported in this book is that national standards have powerful and complex effects on the perceptions and behaviors of classroom teachers in part because of the strong influence they have on the culture of a school, including the behavior of the principal and the messages that he or she communicates to teachers. Stillman, Anderson, and associates describe how the national standards had problematic and negative effects on teachers because policy demands were an important factor that prevented them from engaging critically with the standards. Ironically, Playa's reputation as a school that exemplified the best practices in bilingual education also inhibited teachers from critically interacting with or attempting to deconstruct the national standards.

The findings reported in this readable and edifying book reveal that it is not sufficient for teachers in an era dominated by national standards to have commitments to multicultural teaching and a desire to help emergent bilingual students to experience academic success. They also need to work within a school and institutional culture that encourages and allows them to critically analyze and push back on standards that have adverse effects on the learning opportunities of bilingual students. The findings and analyses in this book can help visionary and committed teachers in schools serving bilingual students to construct and implement pedagogies that are consistent with their values and that will enhance the academic and social success of bilingual students. I hope this book will have the substantial influence and wide readership that it deserves.

—James A. Banks

REFERENCES

Banks, J. A. (2004). Multicultural education: Historical development, dimensions, and practice. In J. A. Banks & C. A. M. Banks (Eds.), *Handbook of research on multicultural education* (2nd ed., pp. 3–29). San Francisco, CA: Jossey-Bass.

Banks, J. A. (Ed.). (2009). *The Routledge international companion to multicultural education*. New York, NY & London, UK: Routledge.

Banks, J. A. (2012). Multicultural education: Dimensions of. In J. A. Banks (Ed.), *Encyclopedia of diversity in education* (vol. 3, pp. 1538–1547). Thousand Oaks, CA: Sage Publications.

Camarota, S. A. (2011, October). A *record-setting decade of immigration: 2000 to 2010*. Washington, DC: Center for Immigration Studies. Retrieved from http://cis.org/2000-2010-record-setting-decade-of-immigration

Camarota, S. A. (2016, June). *New data: Immigration surged in 2014 and 2015*. Washington, DC: Center for Immigration Studies. Retrieved from http://cis.org/New-Data Immigration-Surged-in-2014-and-2015

Conchas, G. Q., & Vigil, J. D. (2012). *Streetsmart schoolsmart: Urban poverty and the education of adolescent boys.* New York, NY: Teachers College Press.

Cookson, P. W., Jr. (2013). *Class rules: Exposing inequality in American high schools.* New York, NY: Teachers College Press.

Eck, D. L. (2001). *A new religious America: How a "Christian country" has become the world's most religiously diverse nation.* New York, NY: HarperSanFrancisco.

Gándara, P. & Hopkins, M. (Eds.). (2010). *Forbidden language: English language learners and restrictive language policies.* New York, NY: Teachers College Press.

Gorski, P. C. (2013). *Reaching and teaching students in poverty: Strategies for erasing the opportunity gap.* New York, NY: Teachers College Press.

Howard, G. R. (2016). *We can't teach what we don't know: White teachers, multiracial schools* (3rd ed.). New York, NY: Teachers College Press.

Howard, T. C. (2010). *Why race and culture matter in schools. Closing the achievement gap in America's classrooms.* New York, NY: Teachers College Press.

Hudley, A. H. C., & Mallinson, C. (2011). *Understanding language variation in U. S. Schools.* New York, NY: Teachers College Press.

Lee, C. D. (2007). *Culture, literacy, and learning: Taking bloom in the midst of the whirlwind.* New York, NY: Teachers College Press.

Leonardo, Z. (2013). *Race frameworks: A multidimensional theory of racism and education.* New York, NY: Teachers College Press.

Mayo, C. (2014). *LGBTQ youth and education: Policies and practices.* New York, NY: Teachers College Press.

National Center for Education Statistics. (2014). *The condition of education 2014.* Retrieved from http://nces.ed.gov/pubs2014/2014083.pdf

O'Brien, P. (2016). *The Muslim question in Europe: Political controversies and public philosophies.* Philadelphia, PA: Temple University Press.

Putnam, R. D (2015). *Our kids: The American dream in crisis.* New York, NY: Simon & Schuster.

Sleeter, C. E. (Ed.). (2007). *Facing accountability in education: Democracy and equity at risk.* New York, NY: Teachers College Press.

Sleeter, C. E., & Flores Carmona, J. (2017). *Un-standardizing curriculum: Multicultural teaching in the standards-based classroom* (2nd ed.). New York, NY: Teachers College Press.

Stiglitz, J. E. (2012). *The price of inequality: How today's divided society endangers our future.* New York, NY: Norton.

Suárez-Orozco, C., Pimentel, A., & Martin, M. (2009). The significance of relationships: Academic engagement and achievement among newcomer immigrant youth. *Teachers College Record, 111*(3), 712–749.

U.S. Census Bureau (2012). *Selected social characteristics in the United States: 2012 American Community Survey 1-year estimates.* Retrieved from http://factfinder2.census.gov/faces/tableservices/jsf/pages/productview.xhtml?pid=ACS_12_1YR_DP02&prodType=table

Valdés, G. (2001). *Learning and not learning English: Latino students in American schools.* New York, NY: Teachers College Press.

Valdés, G., Capitelli, S., & Alvarez, L. (2011). *Latino children learning English: Steps in the journey.* New York, NY: Teachers College Press.

Acknowledgments

This project would not have been possible without the support of numerous people. Most especially, we want to thank the amazing educators who volunteered to participate in our study. We will always be grateful for the opportunity to learn from such an accomplished, principled group. We remain inspired by their commitment to making the world a more just place for students like their own. We recognize the risks—especially in these times—that come with opening classroom doors to outsiders, the trust that teachers placed in us, and the responsibility that we have to write about their work truthfully and with care.

In addition, we are thankful for the Spencer Foundation's support of our project. Funding through the Small Research Grant Program enabled us to spend extensive time at our research site and to employ methods of inquiry that helped yield the study's most salient findings.

We also want to express our appreciation to the following people: first and foremost, our families, and particularly Chris, Charles, and Sasha, who kept life moving forward while we were away on data collection visits and who provided encouragement and unconditional love throughout, and our wonderful mentors and colleagues—most especially Jeannie Oakes, Christine Sleeter, Ken Zeichner, Sandy Grande, Etta Hollins, Kris Gutiérrez, Marjorie Faulstich-Orellana, Marleen Pugach, Tyrone Howard, Irene McGinty, Bernadette Anand, Nadeen Ruiz, José Cintrón, and Adele Arellano—who continue to inspire us, and whose wisdom we tried our best to draw on as we researched and wrote. While we are sure we fell short of their examples in myriad ways, we hope that in some places at least we have made them proud.

We additionally want to thank the editors and reviewers from *Teachers College Record* and *Voices from the Middle*, as well as the National Council of Teachers of English (NCTE), Literacy Research Association (LRA), and the Center for Advanced Research on Language Acquisition (CARLA) conference-goers who provided insightful feedback on preliminary analyses. Their feedback influenced us and helped us to improve what we have written here.

Finally, we'd like to express our heartfelt thanks to Dr. James Banks for including our book in his esteemed series; to Brian Ellerbeck and others at Teachers College Press, who were patient when life got in the way of initial deadlines; and to Brian Gibbs, who wrote a sweet and humbling Facebook comment that carried us through our final revisions.

To all of you, we vow to pay your generosity forward.

Introduction

In early 2012, we visited a school that was bucking national trends by support-ing predominantly Latinx[1] students, most of whom are also emergent bilinguals[2] (EBs), to develop as biliterate, socially conscious citizens, while also supporting them to achieve at high levels on traditional academic assessments. We were there to interview a few accomplished educators who had been recommended for in-clusion in the social justice–oriented foundations textbook that we were revising. Unprompted, the teachers began discussing the Common Core State Standards (CCSS), elsewhere the subject of heated debate. They spoke with agency and opti-mism about their plans for CCSS implementation, which they viewed as an oppor-tunity to build on their school's success, improve their own practice, and deepen their students' learning. As they spoke, they voiced palpable enthusiasm about what seemed to them to be a strong connection, even synergy, between their own pedagogical orientation—rooted in a particular reading of critical theorist Paulo Freire's notions of "dialogical" teaching—and what the new standards were call-ing them to do. One 4th-grade teacher, Paco[3], described this perceived resonance during a conversation with his grade-level teammates in the following way:

> I'm really excited. . . . Through the Common Core, we've kind of been able to
> fit in all our dialogue, and all we're doing is like opinion, argument, evidence,
> explain, Freire . . . push your thinking, reflect. . . . It's all integral to the Com-
> mon Core. . . . I'm like . . . this is what we were trying to do last year and now
> it's like the right thing to do (all laughing). I really feel like it's an exciting time.

Despite this perceived synergy between teachers' pedagogical stances and the CCSS, we were somewhat taken aback by teachers' excitement. In particular, we wondered how this group of committed, passionate, and well-prepared bilin-gual teachers could gravitate so strongly toward a set of standards that "have re-mained silent regarding bilingualism and bilingual education" (Flores & García, 2015, p. 16).

Indeed, for this reason and others, numerous scholars have raised concerns about using the CCSS with EBs (e.g., García & Flores, 2013; Menken, 2015; Solór-zano, 2015). Wiley (2015), for example, has argued that the CCSS's "failure to take the ethnolinguistic needs and resources of all students into consideration can re-sult in an implicit monolingual-monocultural bias against them," specifically by catering exclusively to students from the dominant group while creating a "false image of deficiency for language minority students" (p. 11). Menken (2015) has similarly problematized the CCSS as a de facto monolingualism/monoliteracy policy, underscoring the risks imposed by aligned high-stakes monolingual, standardized tests that rely on accommodations already shown to be both "ineffective" and "detrimental" for EBs (Menken, 2008, 2010), and that threaten programs designed for EBs' benefit.

In light of the contradictions between these potential shortcomings on one hand and these teachers' perspectives on the other, we were interested in learning more about the sense these teachers were making of the CCSS and about the CCSS implementation process they were undertaking. Thus, we asked if we could join them on their journey.

This book reports on 2 years of ethnographic research that grew out of that initial visit to the school—referred to throughout the book as "Playa"—and that explored the perspectives and experiences of 10 of its teachers, as well as the implications of standards-based reform for their own and their students' learning, mainly in the area of language arts/literacy. We focus on language arts/literacy for various reasons: because Playa self-identifies as a literacy-focused school; because language arts standards are particularly consequential for bilingual programs that aim—as Playa's program does—to cultivate learning and literacy in two languages; because English language arts (ELA) remains one of the most regulated and tested subject areas; because ELA frequently plays an academic gatekeeping role for students from nondominant cultural and linguistic communities; and because the CCSS emphasize the idea that every teacher is a "literacy teacher," in that disciplinary literacy should be at the heart of teaching practice and student learning within and across subject areas such as mathematics, social studies, and science.

In contrast to the relief-tinged, optimistic, organic commentary among the teachers referenced above, much of related public discourse about the CCSS has been and continues to be wrought with frustration and dissent. In addition to concerns about the new standards' potentially negative impact on EBs specifically, one can find evidence of broader debates about the CCSS splashed across popular media outlets and the Internet. Yet, standards have been a key feature of mainstream education reform since the 1990s, when, heeding the call of the 1983 publication of *A Nation at Risk,* policymakers and educators began turning to standards-based reforms based on the assumption that standards would help increase academic expectations for all students and especially those, like EBs, whom schools have long underserved (Hirsch, 1987; Ravitch, 1990a). Still today, those in favor of standards-based reform argue, for example, that by articulating "essential" knowledge and skills, standards establish baselines for learning and a "coherent" foundation around which to organize accountability mechanisms that can trigger school improvement (National Education Association, 2010; Porter, 2005).

Others, however, question the efficacy of reforms that hold schools and students accountable for implementing and mastering standards without also ensuring sufficient resources and opportunities for teachers to teach and students to learn what the standards specify (Darling-Hammond, 2001; Oakes, 2004). Some question the very investment in "improved" standards-based reforms, given the track record of their prior iterations. Still others worry that standards, especially common national standards, will serve to suppress, de-emphasize, and/or delegitimize knowledge considered relevant to local communities (e.g., Sleeter, 2005) and will contribute to the narrowing of instruction in ways that undermine learning, especially among EBs and other minoritized[4] students (e.g., Gutiérrez, Asato, Santos, & Gotanda, 2002; Gutstein, 2010; National Black Education Agenda, 2012).

Despite these misgivings, optimism about standards-based reform endures among proponents and has found ample encouragement in federal education initiatives. For example, Race to the Top—a federal grant program awarding states "points" for compliance with particular educational policies—incentivized CCSS adoption by offering CCSS-adopting states a "competitive advantage" in the grant application process. As of early 2017, 42 states and the District of Columbia had adopted the CCSS, and for most, implementation was under way. As these efforts proceed public unrest about the CCSS continues to bubble up, simmer, and at times boil over in states nationwide. Indeed, with the outcome of the November 2016 election, new questions have emerged about the degree to which the federal government will continue to endorse the CCSS moving forward.

Without question, this book—given the research on which it reports— speaks directly to popular debates about the new national standards, as well as to longer-standing debates about standards-based reform more generally. In this sense, it adds to an already significant body of literature.

At the same time, the book breaks from many research-based accounts of standards-based reform, which tend to focus on whether, to what degree of fidelity, and/or how teachers implement new policies as intended. As we describe in Chapter 2, this book does not focus on the fidelity of teachers' implementation because significant questions remain regarding the soundness of the CCSS, and, thus, the degree to which they ought to be implemented with fidelity, particularly when teaching minoritized youth. Taking the CCSS's contested nature into consideration, this book instead considers standards-based reform through the lens of teacher learning—that is, as a complex, social, multifaceted, and agentive process. In doing so, it takes as its central subject the tensions that arise for teachers at the crossroads of standards-based reform, high-stakes accountability, and equity-minded teaching.

In this, the book's introduction, we try to contextualize for the reader the research on which the book reports. We explain in basic terms what the CCSS are, what scholars and members of the public have said about them, and why it is important to study how teachers understand and use them, particularly in relation to minoritized youth. We also explain in broad strokes some of what makes Playa an especially powerful space within which to situate such a study, and what makes our participants an especially powerful population with whom to explore these crucial dynamics.

STANDARDS-BASED REFORM 2.0

Although the CCSS were officially released in June 2010, their development can be traced to 2007, when multiple stakeholders began discussing the prospect of national curriculum standards. As noted in the CCSS Introduction, these early discussions included key members of the organizations that would eventually lead the CCSS development process: the Council of Chief State School Officers (CCSSO) and the National Governors Association (NGA). The CCSS Introduction's claim that the standards respond to the "charge issued by the states to create the next generation of K–12 standards" likely reflects the CCSSO and NGA's central role and their respective members (i.e., representatives from individual states) (Common Core State Standards Initiative, English/Language Arts, 2010a, p. 64). Though not explicitly mentioned in the standards, additional organizations (e.g., the College Board, the Fordham Institute, etc.), foundations (e.g., the Bill and Melinda Gates Foundation, the Walton Family Foundation, etc.), and corporations (e.g., Pearson Education, inBloom, etc.) have also been and continue to be centrally involved with the CCSS and its rollout. This involvement ranges from the development of aligned materials, including assessments, to CCSS funding and dissemination.

It is not surprising, given the numerous players involved in their development and implementation, that the CCSS have been touted as capable of meeting a wide range of goals. These goals include raising academic expectations (e.g., Duncan, 2013), increasing coherence across states and school systems (e.g., Reville, 2014), enhancing the nation's competitiveness in the global market (e.g., National Governors Association, Council of Chief State School Officers, & Achieve, 2008), and strengthening national security (e.g., Council on Foreign Relations, 2012).

Of these goals, raising academic expectations has received the most attention, at least rhetorically. In particular, "raising the bar" has become a rallying cry surrounding the CCSS, as has the claim that the standards will cultivate in students "college and career readiness," which CCSS authors argue prior standards have failed to do. Indeed, the failure of standards-based reform to generate improved academic outcomes has mostly been framed by CCSS proponents and policymakers as a failure in the quality of prior standards, rather than a sign that standards-based reform—which lacks an empirical base to support claims of its effectiveness—may itself not be an appropriate solution to educational inequity (Sleeter, 2005).

In keeping with this framing, the first stage of CCSS development involved the creation of new standards for college and career readiness. These "define general, cross-disciplinary literacy expectations that must be met for students to be prepared [upon high school graduation] to enter college and workforce training programs ready to succeed" (Common Core State Standards Initiative, English/Language Arts, 2010a, p. 4). Released in 2009 as a standalone document, these 10 intentionally broad "anchor" standards hold steady across grade levels and serve as the "backbone" for grade-specific ELA/literacy standards.

The two sections (K–5 and 6–12) of the K–12 ELA standards that are designed for use by teachers like those in our study—multiple-subject teachers and secondary ELA teachers—are organized around four central strands: reading, writing, speaking and listening, and language. From kindergarten through 8th grade, these standards specify the skills and competencies students are expected to master within these four strands by the end of each academic year; they are the standards to which our participating K–8 teachers' practices were tethered. Further up the gradespan, teachers engage with standards that are classified somewhat differently; one band of standards applies for grades 9 and 10, while another applies for grades 11 and 12.

As suggested previously, one aspect of the CCSS that distinguishes them from prior ELA/literacy standards is their explicit reach into the disciplines. Accordingly, the CCSS's third section, also for grades 6–12, delineates standards for literacy in history/social studies, science, and technical subjects. Like instruction in other disciplines, these subject areas present students with discipline- and task-specific literacy and language demands. The CCSS take the position that (1) content-area teachers are best positioned to address these demands, given literacy's essential role in students learning content, and (2) language and literacy are best taught in context, including within the context of the disciplines.

Across the complete Standards document (Common Core State Standards Initiative, 2010a) several literacy competencies receive considerable emphasis. These include

- increasing students' competence in reading and producing informational texts (in part by decreasing the amount of instruction focused on literary texts);
- increasing students' competence in reading "complex" texts;
- increasing students' comprehension capacities through "close" readings of texts, including complex informational texts;
- increasing the frequency and quality of students' participation in oral academic discussion; and
- increasing students' comfort in consuming and producing arguments, with an emphasis on using textual evidence as support.

These and other competencies receive more detailed attention in subsequent chapters, where we report on our study's findings and the role therein of CCSS components and emphases.

Notably, the CCSS authors are clear in their intention for standards to define "end goals," rather than the content or curriculum. Aiming to provide teachers some discretion over standards-based instruction—or *how* standards are taught—the CCSS offer explicit content and curriculum recommendations only through exemplars found within the Standards' Appendix B. Social studies and science teachers, meanwhile, are expected to use the disciplinary literacy standards in conjunction with state content standards and/or the Next Generation Science Standards.

CCSS-ELA: A CONTESTED CORE

As mentioned above, perspectives on the CCSS vary. Some such variation can be attributed to state-by-state differences. In some states, for example, the CCSS's emphases on critical thinking and authentic language use may be deemed, as by our participants, a welcome improvement over prior standards' emphases on more skill-based, rote approaches. In others, the CCSS's structure may be critiqued as unwieldy, and its emphases as troubling departures from research-based practice.

Scholars' perspectives vary, too, particularly concerning the CCSS's potential impact on students from nondominant cultural and linguistic communities. Some have noted that features of the ELA standards may increase students' access to the kind of instruction—emphasizing higher-order thinking, academic language and peer-to-peer talk, and meaning over "basics"—that research indicates as essential to their literacy learning and overall academic success (Bunch, Kibler, & Pimentel, 2012; Quinn, Lee, & Valdés, 2012; van Lier & Walquí, 2012; Wong Fillmore & Fillmore, 2012).

Some of these same scholars are also among those who have raised concerns, including about some of the very same features that have generated praise. For example, whereas an emphasis on text complexity may increase access for EBs and other minoritized students (Wong Fillmore & Fillmore, 2012), questions remain about the CCSS's definition of text complexity vis-à-vis established, well-researched approaches for characterizing texts (e.g., Goldman & Lee, 2014; Hiebert & Mesmer, 2013; Mesmer, Cunningham, & Hiebert, 2012); the likelihood that CCSS text selection guidelines will lead teachers to rely on overly narrow measures of complexity (e.g., Fitzgerald et al., 2015; Valencia, Wixson, & Pearson, 2014); and the corresponding need for significant professional development in order to reduce the risk of disadvantaging EBs, especially (Bunch, Kibler, & Pimentel, 2012; Valdés, Kibler, & Walqui, 2014; Walqui, 2015).

Language-specific concerns like these often layer over more fundamental ones, such as previously mentioned concerns about the CCSS's overwhelmingly monolingual bent (Wiley, 2015) and insensitivity to young learners' developmental needs (Alliance for Childhood, 2010; Miller & Carlsson-Paige, 2013). Perhaps most fundamental, numerous scholars have questioned the capacity of any standards to "raise the bar" and increase "college and career readiness" given unaddressed but impactful out-of-school factors, such as wide income disparities and high rates of child poverty in the United States vis-à-vis other developed nations (Berliner, 2013).

IMPLEMENTATION UNDER PRESSURE

Despite dissent among researchers and educators, policies have historically pressed teachers toward implementing standards in less than optimal ways. In particular, the increased emphasis on (high-stakes) standardized tests since the

2001 passage of No Child Left Behind has contributed to schools using standards and aligned assessments in ways that (1) narrow the curriculum to focus on test content (e.g., Au, 2007; Crocco & Costigan, 2007) and (2) privilege instructional approaches that allegedly generate higher test scores at the expense of authentic learning (Hamilton et al., 2007; Nelson, 2013). In ELA especially, high-stakes standardized tests, together with mandated, test-driven ELA curricula, can lead teachers to interpret and deliver standards reductively—to emphasize, for example, decontextualized skill instruction while minimizing instruction that builds students' meaning-making competencies and writing capacities (Pacheco, 2010). Sadly, this tends to be the case even when the standards' authors indicate the importance of teachers using standards in locally sensitive, student-centered ways, and even if experienced, principled teachers "know better" than to teach to the test or otherwise succumb to policy pressure (Valli & Chambliss, 2007).

Not surprisingly, pressure to use standards in these aforementioned ways is most pronounced in poverty-impacted schools serving minoritized students. There, teachers are more likely to labor under "low-performing" labels and, therefore, tighter instructional monitoring and pressure to use standards in test-driven ways (Gutiérrez, 2006). Although a test-driven approach to language arts instruction can be harmful to all students, it is especially disadvantageous for minoritized students, for whom research suggests culturally and linguistically responsive, student-centered instructional approaches are most critical (e.g., Pease-Alvarez & Samway, 2012; Solórzano, 2008).

Despite these now well-documented patterns in standards implementation, there is still much we don't know about the role of high-stakes accountability policies in CCSS implementation, specifically. Currently, two testing consortia—the Partnership for Assessment of Readiness for College and Careers and the Smarter Balanced Assessment Consortium—are administering English-only standardized tests in states nationwide. Though dependent on state and district policies, such tests are too often tied to various high-stakes consequences, including grade promotion and school funding determinations, as well as teacher pay and tenure. Thus, while there is much to learn about teachers' interpretations and enactments of the CCSS, we can be relatively sure that as long as mandated CCSS-aligned assessments remain in place, they will have a profound impact on both, particularly in schools with linguistically diverse students.

EQUITY-MINDED TEACHERS AT THE FOREFRONT

Being mindful of the contexts surrounding standards-based reforms is key to understanding how and why standards get taken up as they do. Just as important, however, is an awareness of the role teachers play as "engaged mediators" between policy and practice, particularly in relation to standards-based reforms (Cohen & Hill, 2001; Spillane, 2002). Numerous studies have illustrated how the support surrounding teachers' work with standards, and teachers' varied interpretations of standards, can lead to considerable variations in classroom instruction (Coburn, 2004; Dutro, Fisk, Koch, Roop, & Wixon, 2002; Spillane, 2004).

Beyond this typical variation in implementation, or what some might call policy "slippage," are variations that result from teachers' critical engagement with policy. Such variations often manifest in the classrooms of teachers who hold explicitly equity-oriented visions for teaching, and who encounter tensions between their commitments to and knowledge of equity-oriented, student-centered instruction, and the often teacher-centered instruction that policies, including standards, may advance.

In recent years, especially, scholars have written about teachers' more critical policy work. Some have described how teachers actively resist policies they view as harmful to students (Achinstein & Ogawa, 2006). Others have offered examples of how equity-minded teachers strategically adapt standards and accountability-driven policies to better serve students from nondominant communities (e.g., Pease-Alvarez, Samway, & Cifka-Herrera, 2010; Sleeter & Stillman, 2007; Stillman, 2009). In these cases, teachers' policy enactments might best be described as appropriation rather than implementation, since the work may involve teachers drawing on their own values and expertise to make policies their own (García & Menken, 2010; Stillman & Anderson, 2015).

Not surprisingly, most of these studies, among some others (e.g., Santoro, 2011), illustrate the negative impact on equity-minded teachers of having to engage in this challenging policy-generated work. We, too, have witnessed the labor-intensive, demoralizing, even dehumanizing (for teachers and students), effects that high-stakes accountability reforms can have. That said, we've also recognized times when tensions between policy and practice have generated meaningful learning opportunities for teachers, particularly when otherwise supportive conditions were in place (Anderson & Stillman, 2013; Stillman, 2011).

ABOUT THIS BOOK

This book addresses substantively and empirically a topic—the implications of the CCSS for classroom practice—that has received a good deal of sensational, superficial, or speculative coverage in popular media. And it extends the related research base in a few ways.

First, it focuses on specific teachers: those who espouse commitments to multilingual, multicultural education, as well as to critical pedagogy, and yet who also work efficaciously, even enthusiastically, with standards, including the CCSS. Second, it focuses on a unique setting: a bilingual school with a demonstrated record of success in generating high outcomes among students, such as EBs, who have been underserved by standards-based reforms and standardized (English-only) assessments. Whereas much of the literature focuses on standards-based reforms in contexts marked by persistent *under*achievement among low-income students, students of color, and/or EBs, the school in question—which serves a population of students of whom 96% are Latinx (mostly of Mexican heritage), 58% are Spanish dominant, and over 60% are eligible for free/reduced lunch—is among the highest achieving in the state compared to other schools with similar demographics. Third, it draws on social learning theory to offer one of the first up-close ethnographic examinations of how equity-minded teachers work with the most recent wave of standards, the CCSS, which are now under implementation in most states nationwide.

By focusing in this way, we are able to explore the relationship among standards-based policy, local school conditions, and teachers' instructional practices across multiple classrooms, grades, and disciplines. Doing so illuminates crucial aspects of a controversial policy and a complex implementation process—aspects that are uniquely visible because of the school's high-functioning culture and "high-performing" status and the teachers' pedagogical orientation; commitment to bilingual, multicultural, and critical education; and exemplary work ethic.

In this sense, our study offers a glimpse into a kind of counternarrative to the often grim predictions about standards-based reform, teacher practice, and academic achievement among minoritized students. At the same time, we argue that when pressured, or just strongly compelled, to implement accountability policies, including the CCSS, even well-informed, dedicated educators run the risk of attending to policy-related demands in ways that undercut, rather than enhance, instructional quality, particularly for minoritized students.

Nonetheless, this book is not fatalistic about those dynamics and how they might play out across contexts. Rather, we argue that significant learning and instructional improvement can emerge when teachers bring their equity-oriented, specialized expertise, in this case about language acquisition and bilingual education, into "productive tension" with standards-based reforms, in this case the CCSS-ELA standards specifically. The inquiry at hand is, in part, instructive because it illuminates how local conditions conspired to press teachers away from holding in (potentially productive) tension their established practices on one hand and new policies on the other—instead increasing emphasis on the latter while diminishing attention to the former. With this book, we aim to make those local conditions—those particularities—visible to a wider audience. To do so, we've structured the text such that subsequent chapters stand on their own, while contributing to a broader narrative about what it means to teach for equity in these complex times.

Chapter 1, "The 'Dream' School as a 'Dream' Site," paints a portrait of Playa as a rich context for research, given the functional learning community it represents. Here we attempt to capture the school's essence by describing its mission; people, the 10 focal teachers especially; culture; emphasis on and allocation of certain resources; and connections to the surrounding community and partner institutions.

Chapter 2, "A Framework for Focusing on Policy Enactment," introduces our theoretical framework, cultural-historical activity theory, and its underlying assumptions, particularly about the role of culture and context in learning. The chapter incorporates examples to illustrate the framework's utility for exploring how policy tools, local norms, community members, and other factors mediate teachers' policy engagement.

Chapter 3, "Complexities of Context and the Consequences of a 'No Failing' Climate," delves into Playa's history and positionality. It situates Playa at the crossroads of four key shifts—concerning demographics, the passage of "backlash" policies, the proliferation of charter schools, and the rise of standards-based reforms linked to high-stakes accountability. Altogether, the chapter provides a deeper sense of the space where participants work and learn.

Chapter 4, "When Stance and Standards Intersect," homes in on foundational elements of what we call the "Playa Way." In particular, the chapter explains how Playa's teachers came to perceive the CCSS as resonant with their anti-deficit stance toward EBs. It then shows how that resonance eased teachers' normalization of struggle and prioritization of dialogue as key preconditions for learning.

Chapter 5, "'Raising the Bar' and Responsive Teaching, in Tension," explores teachers' efforts to actualize anti-deficit, CCSS-aligned instruction. The chapter addresses the pedagogical coherence that teachers marshaled, as well as the tensions that arose between "bar-raising" and the kind of responsive teaching that teachers espoused.

Chapter 6, "'Close Reading' of 'Complex Text' in Middle Grades," and Chapter 7, "The Common Core State Standards and Compromised Practice in the Early Grades," examine the differential impact of two CCSS intertwined emphases—"close reading" and "text complexity"—on classroom practice across the gradespan. Chapter 7 also addresses an intervention that helped create space for teachers to identify and reflect generatively on instructional tensions.

Finally, Chapter 8, "Teaching for Equity in Complex Times," synthesizes the study's most valuable takeaways. It discusses the "major mediators" of teachers' policy enactments and their consequences for learning. The chapter, and thus the book, closes with ruminations about and recommendations for advancing equitable teaching and learning, especially for teachers and students like those at the heart of our inquiry.

CHAPTER 1

The "Dream" School
as a "Dream" Site

Before it had a name, they called it "the dream school." And indeed, for those who huddled together over the kitchen tables where Playa was dreamed up, who opened its doors in the late 1990s, and who have watched it grow and change—flounder and find firm footing—over the past almost 2 decades, Playa has been a dream come true. In 2012, amid endless reform jargon and still-unmet educational promises, it was clear to us from our first visit that Playa was so much more than a few buildings on an otherwise ordinary neighborhood street; it was a beating heart and source of pride in its community.

As opposed to the mistrust and dysfunction that too often characterize schools, a sense of optimism, mutual care, and calm pervaded the start of each school day at Playa. As morning dropoffs unfolded around us, parents slicked back cowlicks and put final touches on already-perfect ponytails. Older siblings held the hands of younger ones. There were nods of recognition, greetings, and hugs, but no tears, no observable feelings of trepidation.

Family members milled about the yard and, if they chose, stayed and participated in outdoor opening routines until it was time for students to head into classrooms. Even still, at any hour, one might find in the library elders gathered around tables, telling stories in Spanish, sometimes crocheting. And at the day's end, it came full circle; teachers took to the sidewalks of the parking lot for dismissal, standing with students until caregivers arrived for gentle handoffs. In these ordinary moments, there were so many small, humanizing exchanges. The last time we visited, a few teachers peeked out at one another from under the broad brims of matching straw hats. Patiently fielding compliments and questions from the youth standing around them, they caught one another's gaze and giggled; a touch of pleasure, humor, and intimacy—the kind of thing that was both notable and utterly normal at Playa.

To be clear, we don't mean to suggest that Playa was a perfect place—no place is, certainly no school. But during the 2 years we spent there, it was evident that Playa *was* a profoundly functional and healthy learning community. Indeed, this was precisely why it presented such a rich context for learning in general and for research about learning among teachers and students in particular.

As Anne Brown (1992) once wrote, a context "must function smoothly as a learning environment before we can study anything other than the myriad possible ways that things can go wrong" (p. 141). In the 25 years since that writing, educational research has produced narrative after narrative detailing things "gone wrong," particularly concerning the educational experiences and trajectories of minoritized students. The field is so overpopulated by such narratives that many have called for the collection of counterstories and for the suspension of damage-focused research, which has served academics often at the expense of those who they study and who are far more than any "damage" done to them (Solórzano & Yosso, 2002; Tuck, 2009).

Keeping this in mind, we begin in this chapter with a portrait that characterizes Playa affirmatively—that captures and communicates, rather than glossing over, the school's overwhelmingly positive essence.

A DREAM TEAM

Certainly, Playa's scrappy, underdog ethos, hard-earned sterling reputation, and savvy self-presentation—all discussed in future chapters—were part of what had made this K–8 charter school what it was by the time we began our visits: an outlier among its peers, an esteemed elder among community-based charter schools, the school of choice for more families than it can accommodate, and proof positive for its founders of dreaming big. But ask anyone at Playa and they would say, first and foremost, that what initially made—and arguably still makes—Playa a "dream school" is its "dream team" of educators. And indeed, the 10 teachers across five grade levels who were the central participants in our study were among the most hardworking, thoughtful, intellectual, and passionate we have ever encountered, and they were just some among a larger staff.

Because we embed more detailed accounts of individual teachers in chapters where we feature their classrooms, here we provide just a taste in terms of insight into their backgrounds, commitments, and guiding principles. To start, Table 1.1 presents some key characteristics one might see reported in any research study—pseudonyms, races and ethnicities, years teaching, grade-level assignments, subject-area specializations, and so on. From just a glance, it is evident that Playa's teaching staff bucked national trends in terms of composition. While the nation's teachers are more than 80% White, female, middle class, and monolingual, more than 75% of Playa teachers at the time of our study were Chicanx/Latinx (as was reflected in our sample). Among our sample, six grew up in bilingual families in the community surrounding Playa and had since chosen to live there or near there still; two others were bilingual in Spanish and English as well; and three male teachers were among those enthusiastically staffing the early grades. These demographics were similarly reflected in Playa's administrative team: Playa's principal and the elementary, middle school, and high school co-principals, respectively. Three of these four administrators, for example, were Latinx, and all were fluently bilingual and former bilingual teachers. Not surprisingly, recent research suggests that bilingual educators like these—although a minority among teachers of EBs—represent crucial resources for EBs' learning (Hopkins, 2013).

Table 1.1. Teacher Assignments and Characteristics

Teacher Names	Year 1 Grade/ Subjects	Year 2 Grade/ Subjects	Language of Instruction	Bilingual	Race/ Ethnicity	Years Teaching
Ana	1st/LA/ Math/ Science	1st/LA/ Math/ Science	English	✔	Latinx	4–5
Sofia	1st/LA/ Social Studies	1st/LA/ Social Studies	Spanish	✔	Latinx	1–2
Ramón	1st/LA/ Social Studies	1st/LA/ Social Studies	Spanish	✔	Latinx	2–3
Rocio	1st/LA/ Math/ Sci	1st/LA/ Math/ Sci	English	✔	Latinx	1–2
Paco	4th/LA/ Social Studies	N/A	Spanish	✔	Latinx	5–6
Justin	4th/LA	4th/LA	English	✔	White	2–3
Julie	4th Math/ Sci	K–6 Math Coach	English		White	6–7
Sonya	8th/LA	7th/LA	English	✔	Latinx	5–6
Miriam	7th/LA Social Studies	6th/LA/ Social Studies	Spanish	✔	Latinx	9–10
Lynette	7th/LA	6th/LA	English		White	13–14

It may come as a surprise to some that Playa, a "high-performing" school, em-ployed a fair number of teachers who were relatively new to the profession, with only 1–3 years of experience in full-time teaching. But in contrast to the tendency for such teachers to flounder in their early years on the job, at Playa they mostly seemed to thrive. Elsewhere, newbies might be left to sink or swim, and veterans might keep to themselves or even resent newer colleagues (Kardos & Johnson, 2007). At Playa, however, new teachers were folded into a well-organized network that promotes cooperation and collaboration, and they were engaged as equal participants. Often they had been hired only after spending significant time at Playa in some capacity (like student teaching), and if not, they were substantially vetted through hiring procedures intended to gauge their "fit" with the school's mission, culture, and community. Consequently, distinctions between newer and more experienced educators were often blurred in terms of teaching practices and leadership roles, professional relationships and social circles.

Playa's teachers also shared numerous personal and professional attributes that can't be captured in a table. Some are even hard to convey in words, because they're so much about the palpable spirit with which people work and live. Some such attributes were evident during our earliest visits to Playa, because of how teachers talked with us, and one another, about their potential participation in the study. Most connected their desire to participate with their sincere love of their craft, one another, their students, and the community, and with their commitment to reflect on and improve their practice through any available opportunity. Over time, we came to understand this will to reflect and drive to improve not only as a sign of teachers' individual identities and strong work ethics, but also as their shared sense of what it meant to teach at Playa, and what the teaching profession should be and should be for.

The teachers' sense of themselves as diligent laborers, deep learners, advocates for bilingual education, and principled instructional leaders came through repeatedly in individual and focus group interviews, during which they talked at length about their desire to bring passion and authenticity to their practice and to always get better and even become "the best." Although such comments reflected a degree of competitiveness—in fact, some teachers even mentioned feeling like they had to "up their game" upon seeing colleagues plan a stellar lesson or create a beautiful classroom environment—teachers' respectful and admiration-rich regard for one another and for students always took precedence over any concern for personal recognition. For example, individual 1st- and 4th-grade teachers regularly attributed their own successes or growth to grade-level colleagues, without whom, they claimed, they couldn't have developed a unit of study, come up with such good ideas, recognized a shortcoming in their practice, or figured out how to support a struggling student. As 1st-grade teacher Ramón once said, "I'd be nothing without my team." Meanwhile, teachers who had comparatively less opportunity to collaborate (e.g., at the middle school level) also spoke highly of colleagues and often speculated that they would be better teachers with more input from peers.

Just as the teachers regularly recast individual accomplishments as collective ones, they also often deflected compliments about their work by emphasizing what we later learned to be a school- and even districtwide ethos of putting students first—what the school principal and superintendent talked about as "basing decisions on student needs, not adult ones." To say that the teachers took the notion to heart feels akin to understatement. Indeed, it was a core principle undergirding their understanding of the school's mission and shaping, fundamentally, the work they did individually and together.

A MISSION THAT MATTERS

There's a difference between merely having a mission and actually being mission driven. Being mission driven means that the espoused mission matters. And it did at Playa. The mission statement during the time of our study indicated that Playa's aim was to improve student achievement through its "core" ideals, which included commitments to critical pedagogy, dual language education, standards-based instruction, and linking students' academic work to their "real life" experiences. The statement additionally committed to valuing family and community participation and to Playa serving as a local, national, and global "model" of education.

On a daily basis, adults and children at the school put this mission into practice in big and small ways, which we discuss throughout this book. Being mission driven also implies movement in a particular direction, toward something—what we might think of as a shared goal or horizon. People at Playa, for example, worked concertedly together to foster students' language learning and consciousness raising through a dual-immersion program grounded in a particular interpretation of critical pedagogy. At the same time, they worked to foster greater accountability—to ensure that students were prepared, in their words, "for the future." Ask pretty much anyone at the school what Playa was about, and you'd hear some version of the same.

This mission was noticeably reflected in the action unfolding within individual classrooms and across the entire school; teachers and administrators "practiced" the mission daily, passing their shared commitments on to students. Perhaps most obviously, Playa's dedication to the "dual language education" component of its mission was evident in the school's 50/50 dual-immersion model. Standing in stark contrast to bilingual programs that draw on students' home language(s) with the ultimate goal of developing students' English monolingualism, Playa aimed to facilitate bilingualism and biliteracy among all students. All students (pre-K–12) received half of their daily instruction in English and the other half in Spanish. Although the program employed a language separation model, teachers held relatively holistic views of language and language learning. Thus, while a class might be designated as an exclusively English or Spanish instructional space, students could often be seen and heard using both languages, moving with ease between the two as they developed a new skill or made meaning of a new concept. Whereas many dual-immersion programs would react adversely to students' language "hybridity" out of fear that it might undermine students' development of either language, teachers accepted, even encouraged, students to draw on their full linguistic repertoire across classrooms, what García and Wei (2014) call *translanguaging*. This belief that students' bilingualism develops simultaneously within a holistic linguistic system rather than as a reflection of the sum of individual language strands as an expression of teachers' depth of commitment to, and sophisticated understandings about, bilingualism and biliteracy.

As indicated above, all of the administrators and the majority of Playa's teachers, including 8 out of the 10 in our study, were fully bilingual. For many, Spanish was their first language; however, regardless of teachers' own bilingualism, all professed a deep regard for bilingualism/biliteracy and an unwavering commitment to the 50/50 model and to bilingual education in general. For example, Sofia recounted searching around for programs such as Playa's that support even young students, like her 1st-graders, to develop "a strong base" in both languages; this search was guided by her belief "as a mom and as a teacher too" that children should learn about different peoples "from the inside . . . understand the language and understand the authors and understand the culture. . . . " Sixth-grade teacher Miriam talked similarly about bilingualism's central place in her conceptions of effective teaching and described how working at Playa allowed her to honor this conviction. Recollecting her reaction when she first learned about Playa, she commented,

> I was like, ". . . this is heaven!" And then 50/50, and like the idea that everybody would be bilingual/biliterate by the time they leave, so I said, "This is the place . . . this is where I need to be."

This kind of commitment to bilingualism and biliteracy extended beyond Playa's formal structures and staffing. It was embodied in the myriad informal interactions that occurred throughout the school—in the main office, the leadership suite, the teachers' lounge, or the playground—and that were just as likely to unfold in Spanish as in English. Both languages were viewed and utilized as academic, intellectual, social, emotional, and cultural means of communication. Both were treated with equally high regard.

A CULTURE OF CARE

A culture of care also pervaded Playa's open-air hallways and classrooms. In conversation, administrators and teachers alike talked about the "love" they had for one another and for students. This love was palpable and observable. It sounds simple, but we noticed immediately, for instance, how frequently adults at Playa hugged one another and the tenderness of touch among community members.

As seasoned K–12 employees and school-based researchers, we often spent time together in debriefing sessions talking about the strikingly respectful—indeed, loving—ways that teachers engaged with one another, and how that seemed to set the tone for interactions with and among students. For example, in the lounge at lunchtime, we literally never heard teachers speak about students or families in disparaging ways—a practice that too often plagues faculty lunchrooms in schools serving minoritized youth. Instead, we frequently heard teachers sharing stories of specific students' successes. At times, they would also discuss organically their lessons or the problems of practice they were wrestling with; often they would seek advice, which their colleagues seemed happy and unsurprised to provide.

The respect and care among colleagues was mirrored in teachers' interactions with students, which often reflected the kind of culturally responsive, authentic care that is shown to play a crucial role in the educational experiences of minoritized youth, particularly Latinx students (Valenzuela, 1999). It was common to see teachers, especially those with local roots, treat students with the kind of love they might show their own children, during both social and academic exchanges. More than once, for example, we observed 7th/8th-grade teacher Sonya engage in nurturing conversations with students before and after class and solicit from students during class knowledge garnered from their own families about a particular topic. We observed her sharing with students lessons she learned about community, fairness, privilege, and responsibility while growing up just miles from Playa. And we experienced how, in conversations with us, she connected those life lessons to the decisions she and her husband—also a teacher—made to work and raise their own family in the community, too. Teachers of younger students, meanwhile, often spoke of blurred lines between home and school; many recounted attending weekend events honoring students, in addition to spending time with their own families. Ramón, for example, balanced weekly dinners at his parents' home with regular attendance at students' birthday parties and first communions.

In so many ways, teachers' ethics of care were rooted in their own backgrounds, both familial and educational: their life stories; their pathways through school; and their intergenerationally learned appreciations for home, hard work, humility, and radical love. Seventh-grade teacher Miriam, for example, shared how her commitment to students and families linked back to her upbringing in a house, not far from Playa, where her extended family hosted meetings for community activists. Rocio, meanwhile, explained how her experiences coming to the United States from Mexico as a monolingual Spanish speaker helped her connect authentically with students and families. And when asked about parents' contributions to the school, 4th-grade teacher Paco emphasized, "they're already doing so much"; he and others consistently spoke like this—in ways that reflected recognition of and appreciation for kin and caregivers.

However, this regard for students and families was not contingent on having grown up nearby, being a Spanish speaker, or being an insider to Mexican and Mexican American culture. For example, critical of the simplistic historical narratives and "inauthentic" learning experiences that characterized his own suburban schooling, Justin asserted that all students, most especially his own, deserved and would thrive under a more meaningful and critical education. He and other White teachers—like Lynette, who grew up "where everybody's White, and . . . I never heard Spanish really"—were unflagging in their affirmation of students' cultural wealth and boundless capacities to learn.

As Valenzuela's (1999) research might predict, we consistently observed teachers' expressions of care reciprocated by students, as illustrated by their evident affection for, trust in, and willingness to work hard on behalf of one another and their teachers. On so many occasions, we watched as students of all ages invested themselves so fully in working together that they completely tuned us out. They oriented toward one another with care, collaborated to solve difficult problems, and supported those around them—for example, those working in their less-developed language or struggling with tasks or concepts. In addition to offering one another academic support and cooperating better than most adults we know, children at Playa simply treated one another kindly almost all the time. Typical squabbles that, in our experiences elsewhere, tend to occur among middle schoolers—think cliques and gossip—or 1st-graders learning to share space, materials, and adult attention weren't present during our time at Playa.

A STALWART AND SOMEWHAT DISTRIBUTED LEADERSHIP APPROACH

Playa's strong school culture also stemmed, in no small part, from the stability and leadership of the administrative team, and the longstanding, impassioned, and charismatic principal in particular, Dr. Ruiz, who had led Playa since the school's inception. Teachers revered him for his educational vision and commitment to Playa even when they admitted some disgruntlements. Teachers respected his tenacity in staying true to his school vision, even during the early years—discussed more in Chapter 3—when Playa was threatened with closure. They also loved him for supporting them through hard times, for celebrating their successes, for challenging them to see leadership potential in themselves, and even for pushing them to work harder than they thought possible, which often left them feeling deeply rewarded.

Whereas administrative turnover is common among many urban schools, Playa's other administrators had also been present for many years. At the time of our study, Mr. Pacheco, the elementary school co-principal, had been at Playa for over 10 years. Ms. Cook, the middle school co-principal, had been there for over 5. Individual teachers also served as leaders. And not only those who—like Lynette and Sonya—had taught at Playa for over a decade and who "lived through" trying times (e.g., when it was labeled a "failing" school), but also those who were newer to the profession, like Ramón, Sofia, Rocio, and Justin. At Playa, teachers reported a sense of shared leadership, particularly via their presence on the instructional leadership team, comprised of one representative teacher from each grade level. At these bimonthly after-school meetings, run by Dr. Ruiz, teachers and administrators often discussed schoolwide practices as a way to promote consistency across grade levels. For example, in one instructional leadership team meeting, the group talked at length—philosophically and practically—about annotations. As they talked, teachers worked to identify how they might teach students at each grade level to mark up texts in order to enhance comprehension, critical analysis, and meaning-making during "close reading," a CCSS-driven instructional emphasis we discuss in more detail in upcoming chapters.

A SCHEDULE AND SOCIAL NETWORK
IN SUPPORT OF (AMBITIOUS) TEACHING

Developing standards-based curriculum, a stated emphasis in the school's mission, is one of the practices for which Playa was known and admired throughout its district. Administrators expected teachers to construct curriculum—four units per year—starting from the standards. Playa's teachers worked hard to do this each year.

While we caught wind of teachers' collaborative efforts outside the school day—late-night email exchanges, weekends spent talking about curriculum units, and long phone calls over future lessons—their impressive work ethic around curriculum development was most transparent to us during designated common planning time. Each week, while students attended enrichment classes, grade-level teams met for 2 hours during the school day to make sense of the CCSS, reflect on lessons, analyze student work, and plan instruction. This time involved serious intellectual labor on the part of teachers as they worked to design meaningful standards-aligned thematic units and to ensure that lessons reflected the school's high expectations. To this time, which was prioritized and protected in Playa's schedule, teachers brought intellectual curiosity, vigor, and perseverance.

In addition to weekly common planning time, Playa dismissed early every Friday, so the entire staff could engage together in mostly on-site, school-led professional development. Administrators expected that the topics addressed during these sessions—whether by themselves, teacher leaders, or university professors—would be enacted in classrooms the following week. This expectation often meant that teachers spent considerable time after school on Fridays and over weekends reworking lesson plans in order to incorporate new emphases and strategies.

The push to routinely incorporate new ideas and strategies into teaching practice reflected a shared expectation and sense of self—namely, that working at Playa required engaging as teacher-scholars. The high-level intellectual and scholarly demands were exemplified by the kind of professional development initiatives in which the faculty engaged over the summers. One year, for example, they read and dissected sections of critical educator Paulo Freire's classic work, *Pedagogy of the Oppressed*. From their sharing with us, it was clear that they focused on two related Freirean concepts in particular: banking and dialogue.

Freire's notion of banking draws on the metaphor of a bank, to suggest the traditional mode of teaching in which teachers deposit knowledge into students' heads while students passively accept this knowledge rather than being encouraged to question or being positioned as knowledge generators themselves. Playa's teachers considered this concept the antithesis of their aim as teachers. As discussed in future chapters, they often spoke candidly about their commitment to "not banking" as a way to avoid being complicit with "institutionalizing" students through the machinery of school. The primary way teachers avoided "banking" was via incorporating dialogue, especially student-to-student dialogue, as a cornerstone of their shared practice. Indeed, teachers were constantly working to incorporate more dialogue into their lessons, encouraging students to ask questions, to "push one another's thinking," and to construct knowledge together. This emphasis could be seen throughout the school. The word *dialogue* was sprinkled across bulletin boards, lesson plans, and casual conversations among teachers and students, as were phrases that spoke to the ideals underlying this emphasis, like those featured in handmade signs on Justin's classroom walls: "dialogue changes thought" and "learning is a process fueled by curiosity and asking meaningful questions," among others.

Whether on Fridays or over summers, professors from the local university, with whom Playa has longstanding partnerships, often participated in or co-led these schoolwide professional development experiences. In addition to drawing on the local university for support, Dr. Ruiz taught there as an adjunct professor, and in that role, brought many teachers to Playa from its bilingual credentialing program. In fact, Dr. Ruiz actively recruited particular university students to student teach at Playa and then hired from among them those who he felt really "fit" with Playa's culture. Eight out of the 10 teachers in our study earned their bilingual credentials from this university, and 8 out of the 10 started at Playa as student teachers and/or paraprofessionals and were subsequently hired as full-time faculty. This multitiered school–university partnership generated benefit in both directions, with the university providing Playa with many of its excellent teachers and at least some of its professional development, and with Playa providing the university with a "model" bilingual school wherein its future teachers could see and "put into practice" the university's teachings.

Investing in this partnership not only reflected Dr. Ruiz's pragmatic and strategic savvy, but also his visionary nature. Just as he envisioned Playa before it existed, he also envisioned the kind of people who could bring it to life and sustain it. The right teachers, Dr. Ruiz asserted, were the essential ingredient in Playa's success. Dr. Ruiz understood the importance of having professionalism, passion, and authentic care permeate how teachers planned, practiced, and engaged with one another, paraprofessionals, office and custodial staff, visitors, volunteers, and even us researchers. He understood that their presence would have to bookend and bolster students' school days in ways that were quotidian and extraordinary all at once.

As mentioned, many of Playa's teachers—including most of those in our study—completed the same teacher preparation program, and thus likely entered the profession with similar knowledge, skills, and goals. Yet there were things about them that ran deeper and extended beyond what any formal training could claim. Thus, we weren't surprised when Dr. Ruiz brushed aside a question concerning criteria used for hiring new staff. Rather than listing characteristics, qualifications, skills, or dispositions, he conceded that he "just knows" when he's found someone Playa should hire. In his words, "it's just a feeling"—one that we won't deign to name but felt ourselves.

A JOYFUL GRIND

As the anecdotes above suggest, Playa's culture was shaped just as strongly by hard work and perseverance as it was by love and respect, stability and structure. Adults and children at Playa worked incredibly hard at their respective "jobs"—whether developing curriculum and lessons or learning new concepts and skills. The diligence with which both teachers and students approached their work emanated from and reflected Playa's mission "to enhance student achievement" at seemingly any cost. Even without administrators' presence, teachers held themselves to an exceptionally high standard, often pushing one another to "perfect" their work.

Students, too, worked assiduously and in two languages to meet the demands of a challenging standards-based curriculum. As we discuss throughout the book, we observed lessons in which, for example, 1st-graders curled little fingers tautly around pencils and leaned over teeny desks to write lengthy essays about deforestation and child labor and 8th-graders engaged in heated, substance-rich, decorous debates about segregation. Across the gradespan, we saw students completing rigorous tasks in English and Spanish, as expected, and responding with hard work to the significant press by their teachers to achieve at always-higher levels in both languages. Certainly, it bears mentioning here again that, in addition to engaging in these challenging classroom tasks, Playa students have persevered to perform well on annual standardized exams, too. With nearly 70% of students scoring "proficient" or above on the most recent ELA and math state standardized exams, Playa routinely outperformed most California schools with similar demographic profiles.

On many occasions, teachers were candid about challenges associated with working at Playa: long hours; intellectual, interpersonal, and emotional labor involved in, for example, creating curriculum from scratch; and pressure, self-imposed and otherwise, to always improve, change, and "perform" to the highest level possible. But, even these kinds of comments were typically followed by expressions of pride, intrinsic reward, and joy that accompanied teaching at Playa —what Miriam summed up as, "working here is like a breath of fresh air." The collaborative artwork included in Figure 1.1 below, created by one team of teachers during a year-opening retreat activity, captures this complex dynamic well.

With strength beyond their size, akin to the legendary ant, Playa's teachers shouldered a sometimes impossibly-heavy-seeming load; propelled by passion, they faced work-related anxieties, obstacles, and fears, but they also experienced deep dedication, familiarity, and fulfillment.

A SENSE OF SELF-DETERMINATION AND ACCOMPLISHMENT

Beyond pride, intrinsic reward, and joy, a unique rhetoric of control—indicative of an underlying sense of agency and hard-fought self-determination—permeated the discourse among Playa's staff. Teachers thought of themselves and Playa as proactive, rather than reactive, when it came to responding to outside pressures and mandates such as those imposed by new policies. The school's approach—early and agentive—to CCSS implementation is a prime example of this tendency. Instead of waiting for the CCSS to be thrust upon the school by external entities, Playa's administrators and teachers began working with the CCSS before they were required, reflecting a kind of shared mantra, as stated by one teacher, that "things aren't done to us; we handle things." This sense of ownership over policy changes and self-determination in the face of changing political terrain stemmed in part from Playa's history as a charter school that overcame an earlier "failing" designation and prided itself on never again being in the position of having to implement a particular curriculum or set of instructional strategies simply because those

Figure 1.1. Collaborative Artwork Created by a Team of Playa Teachers

beyond the school required it of them. Because of its particular history, further discussed in Chapter 3, Playa's people were buoyantly committed to staying "ahead of the curve."

Playa's demonstrated record of exemplary student achievement in the years since being labeled "low-performing" was a pillar of pride supporting its strong school culture. It was also, along with the school's noteworthy dual language model, among the reasons the school was able to fulfill the part of its mission dedicated to serving as a model for others locally, nationally, and beyond. During the 2 years we spent at Playa, we observed numerous people—everyone from district leaders to university professors to educators from Sweden—conducting school "walk-throughs." For those who frequent urban schools, these were not the surveillance-tinged, superficial, compliance-oriented "walk-throughs" that so many teachers dread. These were tours for visitors who had come from near and far to see academic excellence, highly regarded programming, and accomplished bilingual teaching in action. Dr. Ruiz, along with other administrators and teachers, took great pride in the fact that educators from around the world viewed Playa as a place from which they could learn about exemplary instructional practice, particularly for emergent bilingual youth.

To be sure, at the time of our study, Playa was serving explicitly as a leader and a leading-learner within and beyond its own district. For instance, several district schools had started a professional development group that supported teachers and encouraged them to discuss their experiences with the CCSS. To the monthly meetings, Playa teachers brought their own challenges and questions in order to assist with problem posing and problem solving. They also shared struggles and discussed ideas for improving practice. Though Playa's teachers viewed these meetings as learning opportunities, it was also clear from being there that they were seen by others as leaders among the group, in part because they began working with the CCSS earlier than others and in part because of their many successes and noted "best practices." This leading-learner role was one that was recognized by teachers from the other participating schools and considered by Playa's teachers to be another representation of doing things the "Playa Way."

A RECORD OF UNDENIABLE OUTCOMES

As impressive and inspiring as the above description is, any portrait of Playa feels incomplete without acknowledging the work that students—shepherded by their incredible teachers—regularly produced. Because we spent time in classrooms at various grade levels, we find it apt to feature examples of student work that bookend the gradespan. Our goal is not to showcase Playa's most exceptional student work, but rather to showcase the kind of work we routinely encountered at Playa and that profoundly reflected the following features: teachers' high expectations and ambitious instruction; students' overall work ethic and effort, including their willingness to work hard in response to teachers' expectations; and students' ever-blossoming biliteracy, which was evident throughout their schooling at Playa.

These first samples of student work (Figures 1.2 and 1.3) offer a glimpse into Playa 1st-graders' writing. As a research team, we still laugh when recollecting the first time we walked through Ramón's classroom door, and, upon noticing the student writing—in this case, lengthy essays about child labor—hanging on the walls, we wondered confusedly to ourselves, "Wait, isn't this supposed to be 1st grade?" Like the writing samples we saw that first day, those featured here reflect the social justice themes that many Playa teachers take up, even with young children. For example, in the English writing sample (Figure 1.2), a 1st-grader has used language one might expect from an older student—for example, *inhumane, separate,* and *announced*—to write persuasively and with passion about the Lemon Grove Incident, the United States' first successful desegregation case (i.e., *Roberto Alvarez v. the Board of Trustees of the Lemon Grove School District*), which was argued and won in California and on behalf of students who resemble those filling Playa's classrooms today. The Spanish writing sample (Figure 1.3), drawn from a unit on human rights, is similarly substantive. In this case, a student has defined deforestation and described its many impacts, including those on animals, the climate, and humans. Notably, in the student's plea to end deforestation—developed out of his responses to a set of teacher-provided questions—we see emerging understandings of what it takes to craft a convincing argument.

Across these writing samples, students used sophisticated language with deftness, and often in ways that underscored the power of their multilingualism, specifically their capacity to draw dynamically from across multiple languages,

Figure 1.2. A 1st-Grader's Writing About School Segregation

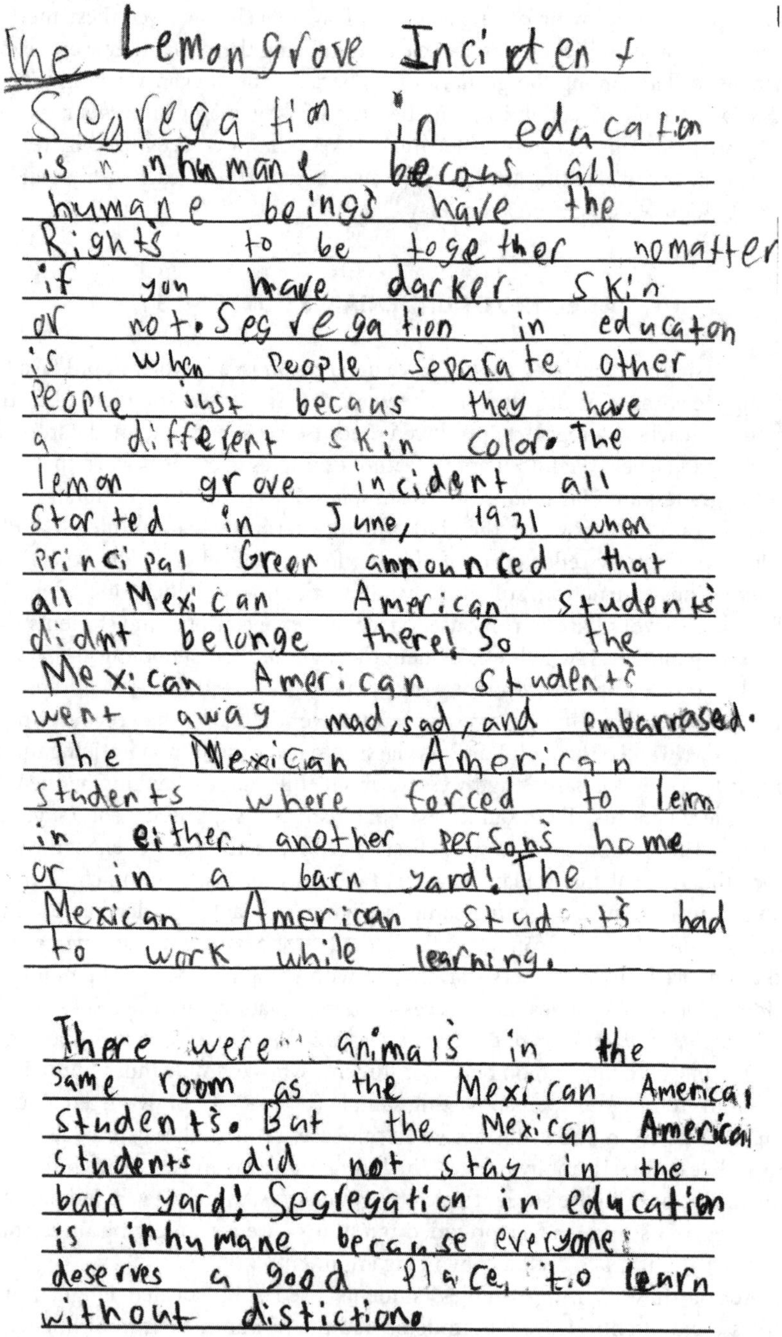

The Lemon grove Incident

Segregation in education is n inhumane becous all humane beings have the Rights to be togethr nomatter if you have darker Skin or not. Segregation in education is when people separate other people just becaus they have a different Skin Color. The lemon grove incident all Started in June, 1931 when Princi pal Green announced that all Mexican American students didnt belonge there! So the Mexican American studentds went away mad, sad, and embarrased. The Mexican American Students where forced to lern in either another persons home or in a barn yard! The Mexican American studtnts had to work while learning.

There were animals in the same room as the Mexican American studentds. But the Mexican American students did not stay in the barn yard! Segregation in education is inhumane because everyones deserves a good place to learn without distiction.

Figure 1.3. A 1st-Grader's Argument Against Deforestation

La deforestación es cuando cortamos arboles. En mi opinión, la deforestación es mala porque cuando cortan arboles los animales pueden morir. También la deforestación es cuando cambia el clima de las bosques o de los lugares. La deforestación es cuando los bosques no pueden eliminar el dioxido carbono. La deforestación es un proceso de la desaparición de los bosques causada algunas veces por el hombre y otras por la naturaleza. Por las razones mencionadas yo creo que la deforestación es mala porque la selva puede desaparecer en 100 años.

exemplified, for example, in the closing comment in Figure 1.2. There the writer—likely drawing on her knowledge of Spanish—has argued that, "everyone deserves a good place to learn without distinction," a claim that echoes the common phrasing *sin distinción*, meaning to do something irrespective of differences or without discrimination (for example, as in *Todas las personas tienen el derecho de aprender sin distinción de raza, edad, ni sexo*). Both examples also illustrate young students' skillful handling of academic language across disciplines (social studies and science). They additionally demonstrate students' comfort using conventions—such as varied sentence constructions, capitalization to start sentences and proper nouns, commas for multiple purposes, and so on—which, while perhaps introduced in 1st-grade classrooms elsewhere, are often not taken up with such facility.

Writing at this level in one language is quite an accomplishment for a 1st-grader. Writing at this level in two languages embodies what Playa was all about: going "higher" and "beyond what's expected," taking it "to the next level," being "the best." The writing rubric below (Figure 1.4), created by teachers to evaluate students' writing, and used in this case to assess the writing captured in Figure 1.3, corroborates this very point: Even work this stellar often wasn't treated as exceptional at Playa; rather, there was always room, indeed a press, for students to improve.

As the other examples illustrate (Figures 1.5 and 1.6), middle schoolers—some having benefited from as many as 9 years of bilingual/biliteracy education at Playa —produced equally impressive work. Like their counterparts in other grades, Playa's middle school teachers often anchored their literacy instruction with social justice themes. In Sonya's case—which we explore in depth in Chapter 6—this involved taking students on a several-months-long journey guided by a thematic focus on "racial, cultural, and socioeconomic differences" and their connections to "misunderstandings, prejudice, and violence." As key projects for this unit of study, students produced written analyses of various narrative and informational texts. Figure 1.5, for example, features an 8th-grader's analysis of Bob Dylan's "The Ballad of Emmett Till," a song she selected from a menu of thematically linked choices. In her essay, the student has dug confidently into figurative language—asserting, for example, that the lines "if you can't speak against [injustice] . . . your eyes are filled with deadman's dirt, your mind filled with dust" mean that you are "worthless" and "might as well be dead" if you aren't capable of "voicing your opinion" and "making a difference." She also has demonstrated throughout, in her own bracing and at

Figure 1.4. Informational Writing Rubric

Level	Organization and Content
Advanced 4	• Includes all the characteristics of Proficient work • Includes descriptive language to describe the historical event • Uses advanced academic vocabulary • No grammar, spelling, or punctuation errors • Expresses a unique tone
Proficient 3	• Clearly responds to the prompt • Includes an introduction, historical event, and conclusion • Writes complete and coherent sentences • Makes a few grammar, spelling, or punctuation errors • Writes legibly and with capitalization where needed
Developing 2	• Attempts to respond to the prompt • Includes an introduction, historical event, and conclusion • Writes complete and coherent sentences • Makes various grammar, spelling, or punctuation errors • Writes legibly and with capitalization where needed
Beginning 1	• Does not respond adequately to the prompt • Introduction is not evident • Writes in a disorganized way • Vocabulary is limited • Writes illegibly in a manner that distracts the reader • Writes with numerous grammar, punctuation, and attempts to respond to the prompt • Includes an introduction, historical event, and conclusion • Writes complete and coherent sentences • Makes various grammar, spelling, capitalization and punctuation errors

times colloquial prose, astute understandings of the lyrics, and their connections to the themes at the heart of the broader unit of study. In doing so, the student has drawn from an impressive arsenal of vocabulary, appropriately deploying words such as *somber* and *allusion* and sophisticated turns of phrase (e.g., *he was disgusted with humanity*) that convey her intellectual and visceral understanding of the text. Worth noting, too, is the care and criticality with which the student unpacked several lines of lyrics, demonstrating her capacity to ground her ideas with textual evidence, itself a skill emphasized by the CCSS.

Social studies and Spanish teacher Miriam had a similar instructional vision for her 6th-graders who, during the time of our study, were well into a unit study of world religions. Like Sonya's students, Miriam's were offered creative and relevant ways to engage with curriculum that—given its subject matter—students might view as boring and/or disconnected from their lives. In Figure 1.6 one student has taken the opportunity to engage social studies content creatively and in a way that made sense to her, by creating a graphic novel/comic strip depicting an encounter between Jesus and the Prophet Mohammed (which, though not featured here, accompanied a series of world maps and a comprehensive timeline that this same student crafted to depict the spread of the world's major religions). While the comic, by virtue of its format, might at first glance seem simplistic or juvenile, closer examination reveals its creator's nuanced subject-matter understandings about the core principles of Christianity and Islam. Indeed, the student

Figure 1.5. An 8th-Grader's Introduction to Her Analysis of "The Ballad of Emmett Till"

The Ballad of Emmett Till by Bob Dylan, was written to raise awareness of the unjust murder of a young black boy, Emmett Till. The tone of The Ballad of Emmett Till is somber and ashamed. What I think Bob Dylan was trying to say with this Ballad is that the murder of Emmett Till was wrong; that it is a disgrace that no one did anything about it. He states that it was a shame to humanity, "for you let this human race fall down so God-awful low." He says that if you can't speak out against this kind of thing... your eyes are filled with deadmen's dirt, your mind filled with dust..." Meaning that if you aren't capable of speaking out and voicing your opinon; making a difference, you are worthless. You might as well be dead. To me, Bob Dylan seems to be disgusted with humanity; ashamed that these things go on and no one stops them. His attitude carries over to the tone; somber and ashamed. However disappointed he is, in the end Bob Dylan writes that if we stand together, unite, we could make a change, a difference.

Figure 1.6. An Excerpt of a 6th-Grader's Comic Strip about the Core Principles of Islam and Christianity

has incorporated them into a playful dialogue that even an uninformed/younger reader could enjoy and learn from. Though not included in Figure 1.6, the student strutted her writing savvy from the outset by setting a casual tone when she had Jesus and Mohammed ask, upon bumping into one another, "*¿Cómo te va con tu religión?*" (How's it going with your religion?) A lighthearted, information-rich exchange in which Mohammed and Jesus demonstrate their mutual respect for one another follows (part of which is featured in Figure 1.6), for example, when Jesus suggests that "*los principios de cristianismo están basados en mis enseñanzas, tal como islamismo se basa en las tuyas*" (Christianity's principles are based on my teachings just as Islam is based on yours), and then Mohammed claims to have forgotten about Christianity's underlying principles and history, which leads Jesus to provide a lengthy explanation, after which Mohammed returns the gesture. Through these writing moves, the student has created an opportunity to share substantive knowledge about the topic, including a description of "*los cinco pilares de islam*" (the five pillars of Islam), as well as a reference to the alleged miracles and supernatural powers that led many to embrace Christianity (e.g., "*la popularidad del cristianismo incrementó cuando corrieron noticias de los milagros y poderes sobrenaturales . . .*"). Like the English writing sample above, this example illustrates the student's solid grasp of academic vocabulary.

ON PLUMBING THE "PLAYA WAY"

It is important to us to be clear here. Our subsequent chapters are in no way a challenge to this chapter's portrait, to these truths about Playa as deeply functional in so many ways. To our view, it was this very functionality that made it easier to see, and with depth and nuance, the complexities—indeed, the contradictions and tensions—that arise as teachers navigate policy in their daily practice. What the remainder of the book does do is add dimension to and complicate this overwhelmingly positive portrait, both by offering more detail and by shedding light on what we find in the shadows of that positivity. Doing so, we draw explicitly on our study's theoretical framework, described in Chapter 2, to situate Playa historically, to flesh out the contradictions and tensions that are endemic to teaching and to the work of the 10 teachers on whom we focus, and to address the implications of those contradictions and tensions for teachers' and students' learning.

CHAPTER 2

A Framework for Focusing
on Policy Enactment

As the prior chapter describes, in the 2 years we spent visiting Playa, we were struck by the high level at which the school and its teachers functioned. In addition to inspiring us, spending time in a school like Playa made us acutely aware of its value as a uniquely generative site for learning about the complexities surrounding teachers' work with policy in general and with new standards specifically, in this case the Common Core State Standards (CCSS). In particular, it was evident that such a site would enable us to develop understandings about how teachers make meaning of and use the CCSS, and how their work with the new standards interacts with a range of in- and out-of-school factors. We knew that certain nuances and complexities might not be as visible in schools where high-stakes accountability pressures and other reforms have engendered challenging, even disabling working conditions, such as isolation and low morale (Nichols & Berliner, 2007)—conditions that, by "fogging our lenses," might limit our abilities to see and understand how and why teachers were taking up the standards as they were.

While at Playa, we were fortunate and grateful to experience an open-door policy: We had access to formal gatherings such as grade-level meetings, leadership team meetings, districtwide professional development sessions, student award ceremonies, and meetings with school visitors. This open-door policy also allowed for extensive hangout time on the playground and in Playa's dropoff/pickup area, central courtyard, staff lunchroom, teacher workroom, and school library. In these spaces, we engaged with a variety of school staff and community members. We also just sat back and observed how things worked at Playa.

Our site visits generated a hefty amount of data, the collection of which we organized around three core questions:

- What meaning do teachers make of the CCSS, particularly in language arts/literacy? What does that meaning-making entail?
- How do teachers use the CCSS in their language arts/literacy teaching practice? How does their meaning-making shape their instruction and vice versa?
- What role does context play in teachers' responses to the CCSS? Which mediating factors matter most, and with what implications for students' opportunities to learn?

Although pursuing these questions and collecting a rich composite of data represented a gratifying (and even at times exhilarating) enterprise, sifting and sorting through extensive fieldnotes is never a small or simple undertaking.

To address challenges inherent to the work, our team relied on theory as both an anchor, in the sense of fixing our focus, and a rudder, in the sense of directing our forward motion. As we describe in more detail below, we used theory—specifically cultural-historical activity theory, or CHAT—in numerous ways. For example, using theory helped us to frame the problem we were trying to understand and the questions we were seeking to answer; informed the study's design, including decisions about which kinds of data to collect and which methods to use; helped us organize and analyze a complex corpus of data; and supported us to clarify and communicate findings.

POLICY IMPLEMENTATION RESEARCH: A PRIMER

As with our own, any inquiry reflects decisions about which topics to explore and which details to home in on or leave unexamined. Though varied in terms of the specific decisions they reflect, traditional policy implementation studies often rest on certain assumptions about policy itself—for example, that a given policy's underlying values are publicly accepted and acceptable, and that fidelity to policy as intended by policymakers should be the primary goal of implementation (O'Donnell, 2008). Relatedly, many reflect a relatively narrow focus on implementation fidelity and its connection to student outcomes and/or to teachers' participation in fidelity-focused professional development (Cohen & Hill, 2001; Darling-Hammond, 1998). Despite variation among such studies, we group them under the heuristic heading of traditional—by which we mean both *typical* in the sense of being well represented, and *technical* in the sense of being fidelity focused.

As other scholars have illustrated (Cohen & Hill, 2001; Darling-Hammond, 1998; Spillane, 2004), traditional implementation studies also tend to assume a behaviorist stance, positioning teachers as passive recipients of policy-related knowledge, generally acquired through externally provided professional development. This stance promotes a view of teachers as technicians who are expected to accept a shared, as-intended vision of policy and a standardized approach to enacting policy in practice.

Notably, numerous empirical investigations challenge this framing by providing evidence of teachers actively making meaning of policy alone and together (Allen & Penuel, 2015; Coburn, 2001). Of particular relevance to this book, research has shown that teachers negotiate their own values and commitments and the potentially opposing values of policies, and in doing so they shape their own enactment of and professional growth around the very mandates meant to structure and condition their craft (Sleeter, 2005; Stillman, 2011; Stillman & Anderson, 2015).

For these reasons, among others, we did not approach this study with the goal of understanding the degree to which teachers' instruction reflects with fidelity policymakers' ideas. As noted in the Introduction, while certain features of the

CCSS may merit cautious optimism, others have underscored the standards' potential to diminish language-minoritized students' opportunities to learn. In addition, because we ground our understandings of teachers' policy work in research that demonstrates teachers' role as engaged mediators in relation to policy, we are less interested in exploring whether teachers implement standards as intended by others, and more interested in how teachers interpret and use standards, how overlapping contexts interact with their efforts, and how opportunities for teacher and student learning shift as a result.

Indeed, we view teachers' encounters with the CCSS as fundamentally a matter of learning. And, we take an explicitly social and situated perspective on learning in order to generate dynamic, contextually sensitive, and agentive—or what Penuel and colleagues (2014) call "actor-oriented"—understandings of teachers' policy-related work. In framing teachers' engagement with the CCSS in this way, we aim to offer insights for practitioners, researchers, and policymakers about whether and how standards can be taken up without doing harm. We also aim to explore whether and how, when coupled with other efforts, standards might even engender transformative learning, particularly for minoritized youth and their teachers.

POLICY ENACTMENT FROM A CHAT PERSPECTIVE

The theoretical perspective that guides our inquiry into teachers' CCSS engagement is cultural-historical activity theory, or CHAT. CHAT, which aims to better elucidate the social and cultural dimensions of individual and organizational transformation, is a strand of learning theory rooted in classical German philosophy, materialist conceptions of history, and the works of Soviet psychologists Lev Vygotsky, Alexander Luria, and A. N. Leontiev (Engeström, 1999b). CHAT provides a cohesive framework that binds together insights from time spent at Playa, while also offering a compelling alternative to the limitations of traditional policy implementation research. In what follows, we explain CHAT's central tenets and its affordances in supporting researchers to understand with more nuance teachers' policy-related work and learning.

Policy Enactment as Situated, Dialectical, and Mediated Activity

As mentioned, a CHAT perspective primes us to look at teachers' work with policy as situated activity—as nested within a complex, collective, and dynamic system, wherein multiple elements interact, contribute to development, and undergo change themselves as a result (Engeström, 1999b, 1999c). This premise is reflected in our use of the phrase *policy enactment,* instead of *policy implementation,* to describe the focus of our study. To us, this is a substantive (rather than semantic) distinction, one reflecting our shift away from *implementation's* more technical and behaviorist connotations and toward *enactment's* social and cultural complexity, as embodied action shaped by the *enactor's* identity, values, knowledge, and expertise.

From a CHAT perspective, in the context of activity, individuals (known as *subjects*) act on and through their environment, as well as on and through physical and conceptual artifacts (or *tools*), in collective work undertaken by various *community members*, governed by explicit and tacit *norms and rules*, as well as a particular *division of labor*, and oriented toward some fundamental human or institutional need (or *object*) (Engeström, 1999c; Roth & Tobin, 2005). For example, in the activity at the heart of this book (i.e., Playa's teachers' work with policy), teachers engage with various tools (e.g., standards, instructional materials, lesson plans, pedagogical strategies, etc.), community members (e.g., colleagues, administrators, students, and parents), norms and rules (e.g., expected behaviors and comportment as determined by the profession, state, district, and school), and divisions of labor (e.g., specific teaching assignments and distinctions among roles), and they do so with particular goals or objects in mind (e.g., teaching in both equity-oriented and standards-aligned ways) (Engeström, 2009). Figure 2.1's graphical representation helps us to visualize such a system and its constituent elements.

Unlike studies that assume a linear policy implementation process, inquiries guided by CHAT assume a degree of dialecticism and mediation, which are captured in the graphic's many bidirectional arrows. Dialecticism refers to a kind of mutuality, whereby all elements of an activity system are seen as simultaneously shaping and impacting one another (Davydov, 1999; Roth & Lee, 2007). For example, policy tools like the CCSS impact teachers and the object toward which their actions are oriented; at the same time, teachers interpret, shape, and enact policy tools like the CCSS in their own ways.

Mediation, meanwhile, refers to a dynamic whereby an activity system's elements work through one another. For example, individuals act through the mediation of others, the environment, and the artifacts and materials they use in their work (Engeström, 1999b). Thus, rather than focusing on direct, causal relationships—for example, that x (e.g., policy implementation fidelity) leads to y (e.g., a particular student outcome)—inquiries like our own explore how an activity's constituent elements mediate or shape one another, collectively construct and carry out the object, and bring about certain outcomes.

By framing policy enactment as situated, dialectical, mediated action, CHAT provides a powerful framework for exploring how, why, and to what ends teachers work with the CCSS, and it affords our research several advantages vis-à-vis more traditional policy implementation studies. First and foremost, this framing emphasizes that learning, including teachers' learning through policy engagement, is necessarily social—that it does not simply occur inside a teacher's head, but requires "additional cognitive resources that are to be found in the sociocultural milieu" (Cole & Engeström, 1997, p. 3). Simply put: Where and with whom teachers work matters profoundly to their learning. This, in turn, suggests that teachers' professional knowledge construction, both in general and in relation to the CCSS specifically, is a "community-based, collective enterprise" (Ellis, 2014, p. 217).

Second, and relatedly, just because activity is collective and community based does not mean that it is uniform and internally coherent. Rather, CHAT presses us to seek out and render a multivoiced—or heteroglossic (Bakhtin, 1981)—portrait

Figure 2.1. Activity System (Engeström, 1987)

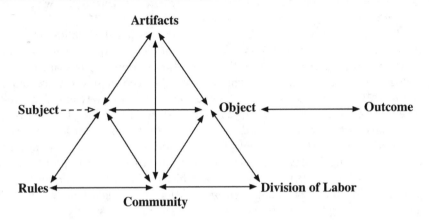

of policy engagement that considers the range of actors (e.g., students, teachers, administrators, professional development providers, district leaders, policymakers, etc.) and entities (e.g., individual schools, school districts, test development organizations, the state, etc.) involved, as well as the power dynamics, resonances, and disjunctures among and between them (Engeström, 1999a).

Third, by treating activity holistically and as the unit of analysis, CHAT rejects an artificial separation between subjects and their environments—in this case, teachers and their classrooms, schools and communities—and instead provides a means by which to better understand their interconnected and interdependent nature (Roth & Tobin, 2005). CHAT helped us, specifically, to recognize teachers as thoughtful agents who continuously shape and are shaped by the school community and the broader social context and to recognize the environment as influential, but not as overly deterministic in its conditioning of teachers' work (Roth, Tobin, & Zimmermann, 2002). Such framing is particularly important in a study like our own, wherein the school as a context for learning was as much a source of interest as the study participants, and where understanding the interplay between that environment and those teaching and learning within it stood to shed light on how policies like the CCSS are interpreted and used.

Policy Enactment as Historically and Socioculturally Mediated

An activity system—like the one we studied at Playa—develops out of specific sociocultural and historical contexts, with which the system dialectically interacts. This very quality is, according to Engeström (1999a), part and parcel of what makes the activity system an especially useful unit of analysis. In addition to its aforementioned strength in treating activity holistically, CHAT also attends concertedly to activity's sociocultural and historical dimensions. "If the unit is the individual or the individually constructed situation," Engeström explains, "history is reduced to ontogeny or biography." Likewise, "if the unit is the culture or the society," he continues, "history becomes very general or endlessly complex." Conversely, "if a collective activity system is taken as the unit," he argues, "history may become manageable," while also moving "beyond the confines of individual biography" (p. 26).

Understanding teachers' policy-related work "beyond the confines of individual biography" not only requires an analysis of the immediate context within which their work occurs (i.e., the school), but also some probing of that context's ecological historicity—what we might think of as Playa's own lifestory. According to Ellis (2011), such an examination should happen on two levels: at the "microgenetic" level, where attention is given to the history and culture of a particular classroom or school, as well as its development over time; and at the level of "evolutionary" streams, where one looks to the broader societal culture and history for understanding the environmental conditions that gave rise to and continue to influence a school (p. 191). Attention to this historical dimension is represented in Figure 2.2 by the line running horizontally below the triangle, looped as it is to interrupt what might be interpreted otherwise as a purely linear concept of time.

Whereas our love of teaching might have trained our focus on the dynamics of classroom practice and school culture (by default) and the role of the CCSS therein (by design), CHAT directed our attention toward those dynamics and reminded us to keep ourselves open to broader (and evolving) mediating influences of federal initiatives, local and state-level debates and policies, education reform trends within and beyond California, and so on. Put another way, CHAT supported us as we strove to do justice to teaching not only as an art and a science (our bias as teacher educators and former teachers) but also as a historically contingent and state-mediated profession. By this, we mean a profession in which

> An agency, usually a state organization, acts as a mediator between the profession (*i.e., teaching*) and its clientele (*i.e., students*) in deciding the profession's client population (*i.e., which students, specifically*) and in broad terms what should be provided for its clientele through a legal framework (*i.e., education policies generally and the CCSS specifically*) and the overall allocation of resources. (Ellis, 2014, p. 218, quoting White, 2006, p. 207; emphasis added)

We also mean a profession that is common, and yet contested and changing as it endures. Indeed, teaching—especially in public schools—has always been a "pluralistic" profession and thus subject to the "persistent internal tensions" that arise from having diverse stakeholders "project different identities and purposes" on teachers; at the same time, the specifics of those "persistent" tensions shift consequentially over time (Kraatz, 2009, p. 71). Thinking about teaching in these ways made it crucial for us to attend to how Playa's teachers' meaning-making and practice, including as it related to the CCSS, was supported or constrained by the state's accumulated and evolving role in regulating their activity.

Equally important was an understanding of learning that recognizes learners—whether teachers or students—as complex cultural beings, whose meaning-making and development are mediated powerfully by their preexisting knowledge, lived experiences, and interests, and who both shape and are shaped by the social and

Figure 2.2. Activity as a System Among Systems

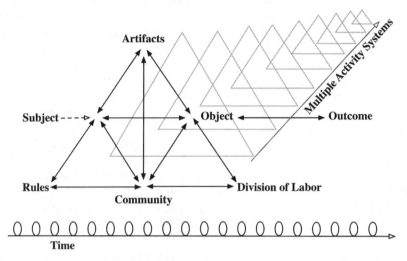

cultural contexts in which they are situated (Gonzalez, Moll, & Amanti, 2005; Gutiérrez & Rogoff, 2003). Indeed, CHAT compelled us to view Playa's community members—and particularly those at the heart of our inquiry—as products and producers of the various cultural contexts they traverse, and as important contributors to and participants within the culture of Playa itself. It also pressed us to consider how standards-based instruction at Playa appeared to acknowledge and leverage teachers' and students' cultural resources—including their linguistic resources—for deep and meaningful learning. Such consideration is critical given our focus on how teachers facilitate learning among students who are members of nondominant communities—communities that have historically been framed and treated as deficient by schools, rather than as replete with resources and assets for learning. It is also critical in light of our study's focus on literacy instruction and the CCSS-ELA standards, especially given the role of literacy and language as the key symbol systems through which thinking is mediated (Vygotsky, 1978).

These historical and sociocultural considerations are at the heart of Chapter 3, where we situate Playa's collective identity and the work of its teachers at the crossroads of multiple shifts—concerning demographics; discourses around diversity, citizenship, and democracy; the rise of neoliberalism and market-based reforms in education; and a policy climate anchored by standardization and high-stakes accountability—all of which mediate how educators understand and take up the CCSS in practice.

Policy Enactment as Occurring Within a System Among Systems

CHAT also pushes us to consider how other systems adjacent to, proximal with, or imbricated by Playa's might impact the school and its educators' CCSS enactments. As Figure 2.2 suggests, an activity system never exists in isolation.

CHAT suggests that when activity systems pursue similar or interconnected objects, they may share permeable boundaries across which tools can pass (Engeström, 1999a). In Playa's case, because the state, district, and school adopted the CCSS—an instructional policy developed by a consortium of educators, business leaders, and policymakers—the CCSS can be understood productively as a kind of "boundary artifact" that spans several interrelated activity systems (Akkerman & Bakker, 2011). For example, consider how an artifact like the standards-aligned Smarter Balanced Assessment mediates activity in different systems—whether oriented toward the writing of policy, the crafting of actual assessment tools, the assessment-related decision-making of local districts, and teachers' day-to-day practice.

In accordance with the principles of dialecticism, however, boundary artifacts do not travel into other activity systems in pure or unchanged forms. Rather, they are negotiated and reworked by adopting systems, which in turn are changed by the introduction and adoption of those boundary artifacts. This perspective thus directs us to look for the varied and generative ways that policy ideas and materials become meaningful and manifest in and through the complex interactions of the many mediators described earlier.

Additionally, because boundary artifacts are imbued with goals that are often foreign or disparate to those of the activity systems that adopt them, it follows somewhat logically that tensions and contradictions often result, as when a school enacts a reform or implements a tool that conflicts with its espoused mission, the goals of some among its teachers, and/or the needs and desires of students and their families. Thus, when we investigated Playa teachers' adoption of the CCSS, we attended both to how policy was taken up by participants and to how the activity system itself changed and with what implications for learning.

MAPPING MEDIATORS

To help make our use of this theoretical perspective more transparent, we mapped against the generic graphical representation of (some of) the many mediators at play in Playa teachers' work (Figure 2.3). Especially important for our study, this mapping reminds us that people, like artifacts/tools, have meditational power. In its graphical simplicity, it helps us identify and name the various community members who participate in some way in the activity system, which in turn encourages us to consider how various relationships—among and between teachers, students, administrators, families, district personnel, and so on—mediate teachers' policy engagement.

Mapping the focal activity system in this way also helps us clarify how community members' interactions connect to established rules, norms, and divisions of labor. The map we offer is imperfect and incomplete, but it is comprehensive enough, we hope, to convey how complex teachers' work with policy actually is. In providing the overarching graphic here, we especially want to make visible a central aspect of our analysis—namely, that the activity of our core participants,

Figure 2.3. Playa Through An Activity System Lens

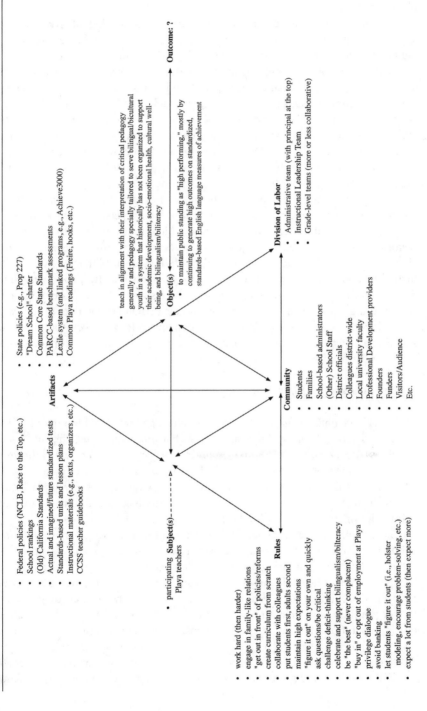

- Federal policies (NCLB, Race to the Top, etc.)
- School rankings
- (Old) California Standards
- Actual and imagined/future standardized tests
- Standards-based units and lesson plans
- Instructional materials (e.g., texts, organizers, etc.)
- CCSS teacher guidebooks

- State policies (e.g., Prop 227)
- "Dream School" charter
- Common Core State Standards
- PARCC-based benchmark assessments
- Lexile system (and linked programs, e.g., Achieve3000)
- Common Playa readings (Freire, hooks, etc.)

Artifacts

- teach in alignment with their interpretation of critical pedagogy generally and pedagogy specially tailored to serve bilingual/bicultural youth in a system that historically has not been organized to support their academic development, socio-emotional health, cultural well-being, and bilingualism/biliteracy

- to maintain public standing as "high performing," mostly by continuing to generate high outcomes on standardized, standards-based English language measures of achievement

Object(s)

Outcome: ?

participating **Subject(s)**—
Playa teachers

Community

- Students
- Families
- School-based administrators
- (Other) School Staff
- District officials
- Colleagues district-wide
- Local university faculty
- Professional Development providers
- Founders
- Funders
- Visitors/Audience
- Etc.

Division of Labor

- Administrative team (with principal at the top)
- Instructional Leadership Team
- Grade-level teams (more or less collaborative)

Rules

- work hard (then harder)
- engage in family-like relations
- "get out in front" of policies/reforms
- create curriculum from scratch
- collaborate with colleagues
- put students first, adults second
- maintain high expectations
- "figure it out" on your own and quickly
- ask questions/be critical
- challenge deficit-thinking
- celebrate and support bilingualism/biliteracy
- be "the best" (never complacent)
- "buy in" or opt out of employment at Playa
- privilege dialogue
- avoid banking
- let students "figure it out" (i.e., holster modeling, encourage problem-solving, etc.)
- expect a lot from students (then expect more)

Playa's 10 participating teachers, tended to orient simultaneously toward multiple objects, or motives.

Of course, within any community, different members bring different motives, some of which may resonate or conflict, and not all of which will be equally pertinent to the activity at hand. For example, while families who choose Playa might advocate for an especially strong emphasis on heritage language because of a desire to see their children become biliterate in Spanish and English, administrators with similarly strong commitments to biliteracy might—compelled by pressure to "perform" —privilege English outcomes because of the capital those outcomes represent in the current accountability system. At Playa, a wide range of motives were always in play. Of special interest to us were those multiple—and at times seemingly competing— motives held concurrently by the study's core participants. As Figure 2.3 depicts, two particular motives, or objects, were especially prominent.

One prominent motive involved the quest to employ the CCSS in ways that aligned with Playa's interpretations of critical pedagogy generally and with pedagogy specifically tailored to serve bilingual and bicultural Latinx youth in a system historically not organized to support such students' academic development, socioemotional health, cultural well-being, and bilingualism/biliteracy. Even on its own, this motive is layered and complex; though it was not always understood in precisely the same way by different participants, a strong, shared sense of its general meaning emerged across their reports and enactments. The other motive was to employ the CCSS in ways that would help maintain Playa's much-touted public standing as "high-performing," mostly as determined by outcomes on standardized, standards-based, English-language assessments.

A Closer Look at Multiple Motives

Playa teachers' policy engagement was powerfully animated by both of the aforementioned motives, the specifics and somewhat inherently conflicted nature of which we address in the subsequent chapter. What matters most here is the very idea of multiple motives coexisting at all times for teachers—as they do for almost all people within any activity system, albeit to varying degrees. We unpack this idea with an example from outside of education—to make the idea more tangible, and to illuminate its potential applicability.

Let's begin by imagining an adult—in this case, a working parent of young children—who names cooking as a favorite pastime. As this person considers the activity of preparing dinner—particularly when schedules are busy and consistent bedtimes a must—he or she may be motivated primarily by the family's collective need for the children to receive nourishment in a timely manner. By choosing to foreground this motive, the outcome of activity seems quite predictable: the quick preparation of a simple, nutritious meal. On other occasions—perhaps on a weekend or in advance of a special event—this same person may be driven by a different motive such as, for example, joyfully preparing something elaborate and delicious for loved ones. Privileging this motive, the preparatory and cooking process might be more complex and time consuming, and the product might be quite different from a simple worknight supper.

In this scenario, we can see how, even though the activity of preparing food for others may by driven by multiple motives, it makes sense to privilege one over another, depending upon the activity's specific context and goals. We can also see how privileging one motive mediates the nature of the activity, as well as its outcome. Indeed, privileging one motive over another might also mediate a tool or artifact—say, a recipe—and how the parent-cook uses it, as a loose guide in one situation or doctrine in another.

Various theorists working within the CHAT tradition have suggested the need to think about multiple motives, or objects—like those driving the parent-cook's activity from meal to meal—as operating within a particular order of sorts, what Leontiev (1978) has called a "hierarchy of motives" (Kaptelinin, 2005). With this framing, we are reminded that motives rarely exist or operate on a level plane: One almost always holds more power in a particular activity and/or moment, and in relation to various and dynamic (contextual) factors.

Importantly, privileging one motive does not mean that others disappear; instead, motives tend to move into the foreground or background in situation-specific ways, while still mediating—if relatively less powerfully and/or consequentially—the processes, tools, and outcomes of activity. Given the dynamism and complexity with which motives factored into Playa's educators' work, we came to understand this foregrounding and backgrounding not so much as linearly ordered, as the term *hierarchy* would suggest. Rather, we came to understand them more as parallel streams—at times swelling and receding, exerting more or less power, crossing and intertwining, but always coexisting, often mediating one another.

Applied to the cooking scenario, this conceptualization suggests that the parent-cook's delight in the creative process and desire to make something special might encroach on daily cooking—for example, the parent-cook might not settle for preparing something bland for dinner—even if this motive for preparing food is (appropriately) backgrounded by more pressing needs and goals—for example, the rumbling bellies of hungry children and approaching bedtimes. Meanwhile, when this parent-cook engages in a more involved, creative, less-hurried project, the efficiency that drives routine cooking may very well shape special occasion cooking, too, even if to a lesser degree.

As this example hopefully conveys, motives/objects can also be more or less aligned or at odds with one another. In this mostly "at-odds" scenario, for example, we can imagine what might ensue if cooking's "creative" and "special" motive overtakes the "efficiency" motive during daily dinner preparation. While the resulting meal might be tastier than typical, it might also bring some less desirable consequences—such as cranky kids and delayed bedtimes that complicate the next morning. Meanwhile, if cooking's "efficiency" motive overtakes the "creative" and "delicious" motive, we can imagine that a dish might fail to meet the parent-cook's standards or those of a special occasion.

In this scenario, it is quite evident that the parent-cook recognizes different motives/objects for cooking. And this awareness likely supports the parent-cook in privileging motives/objects that best serve the activity's context, purpose, and goals, and considering the possible consequences of one motive/object being privileged over another.

But, awareness alone cannot protect entirely against the privileging of a potentially "compromising" motive/object—and importantly, "compromising" here might mean varied, shifting things. Indeed, various mediating factors can be counted on to complicate matters. For example, a hard day at work might lead the parent-cook to view dinner preparation as a welcome opportunity to decompress, thereby encouraging the privileging of creativity and enjoyment over efficiency, quite possibly with some unintended consequences.

It is also possible for motives/objects to appear on their surface to be quite similar, despite less visible contradictions. When this is the case, actors may struggle to prioritize the motives/objects that are best suited to the activity and/or to notice when potentially compromising motives/objects have moved to the foreground.

Although this parent-cook example may conjure images of an active or even messy kitchen (especially for those who experience cooking as stressful or a chore), it is certainly "neater" than the activity of Playa's teachers—namely, navigating new national standards and maintaining high English-language standardized test scores in a bilingual school. In the cooking scenario, the activity at hand is relatively concrete, the stakes relatively low, and the motives/objects uncomplicated by power, politics, or competing ideologies; of course, they could be if we wrote it differently—for example, incorporating tensions around who cooks vis-à-vis who is cooked for, or who decides, and how, what is to be eaten. Nevertheless, the scenario is useful for illustrating how the idea of a "hierarchy"—or perhaps more appropriately, separate "streams"—of motives/objects might help us understand human activity and, in this case, Playa teachers' engagement with the CCSS.

Specifically, this framing helps us to recognize and unpack those aforementioned two core motives/objects that animated Playa teachers' work: practicing critical and culturally responsive pedagogy tailored to the needs of bilingual and bicultural Latinx youth, and maintaining Playa's "high-performing" status, as determined by high scores on standardized tests. In light of the two motives' potentially contradictory nature—which teachers themselves acknowledged—one might assume that teachers would privilege the first motive over all others. This was certainly the case at times; in such instances, the "outcome" of activity often involved standards-based instruction infused with teachers' values, knowledge, and expertise. However, applying a CHAT lens also helped reveal how Playa's complex context, including the fraught histories influencing its formation and evolution over time, significantly mediated the ordering of teachers' motives and their policy engagement. This mediation, as we detail in Chapter 3, left teachers susceptible to patterns of thinking and practice that had important and not always positive implications for their CCSS enactments with EB youth.

POLICY NAVIGATION AS PROFESSIONAL LEARNING

Our theoretical grounding challenges the behaviorist leanings of research that treats teachers' policy-related learning as the acquisition of as-intended-by-policymakers knowledge, the product of traditional professional development experiences, and the means to ensure implementation fidelity—which in today's policy climate is often monitored, measured, and met with consequences (e.g., merit pay, tenure decisions, probation status, school closure designations). Instead, we take the view that policy enactment entails and potentially engenders significant learning, wherein teachers negotiate multiple and at times competing motives, or objects; identify collective problems concerning policy; propose, contest, negotiate, and actualize solutions; and, in so doing, reaffirm and/or reconstitute their professional identities and practices. This view is rooted in three CHAT-related assertions about the nature of deep learning.

Learning as Appropriation

The first assertion—that deep learning is fundamentally ontological and oftentimes involves *appropriation*—provides a helpful lens for understanding why and how activity systems like Playa's both reproduce and develop new social practices. For example, when teachers begin participating in the practices of a particular school community, that community quickly teaches them (implicitly and/or explicitly) how classroom instruction "is" and "should be" in that context. This occurs through an apprenticeship-like process of *internalization* (Davydov, 1999; Engeström, 1999b), whereby novices replace or join in alongside more experienced "others" (Vygotsky, 1978) and acclimate to established norms.

In this way, activities unfolding within the school—including ways of practicing that have been carried over from the past—are carried forward into the future. At the same time, novices make meaning of such practices for themselves; their own prior knowledge and past experiences mediate that process, as do the particularities of their respective classroom contexts. In other words, novices appropriate collective practice by making it their own in small and significant, simple and sophisticated ways (Lektorsky, 2009). Inherent to this process are changes in the way participants view themselves and their own practice (Lave & Wenger, 1991; Lektorsky, 2009).

The concept of appropriation offers special purchase in analyzing teachers' policy engagement and the personal and pedagogical shifts such engagement catalyzes (Stillman & Anderson, 2015). Our prior research suggests that when teachers engage with new policy tools, like the CCSS, they are not merely learning *about* policy and/or changing their practices in relation to it, as might be a common focus in policy implementation studies. Rather, they are engaging in a continuous learning *project* that has consequences for how they come to see themselves, or as Edwards and Kinti (2010) put it, for their learning about how "to be" as educators and people (p. 129). Thus, our efforts to understand how Playa teachers interpreted and used the CCSS involved attending to shifts in their practices and their ways of viewing and presenting themselves, too.

Reflecting CHAT's dialecticism, teachers' emotions and visions of who they are and who they "*want* to be" (Lampert, 1985, p. 184) can support them not to consume policies, but to act, in essence, as policy coauthors (Stillman & Anderson, 2015). As in our prior research, we suspected this angle might be analytically generative here too, particularly given the 10 teachers' clear and coherent educational vision and sense of authentic purpose—co-constructed through substantial personal and professional interaction—and the likelihood that their established *intersubjectivity*, or shared sense of subjective experience, would shape their policy-related meaning-making and enactment. Thus, rather than focusing on the degree to which Playa teachers mastered policy—in the sense of learning to use the CCSS as intended by others—we paid attention to how teachers took ownership of policy tools as they engaged with them. Put another way, we sought to understand how teachers reauthored tools like the CCSS by "moving" them from the realm of ". . . other people's mouths, . . . other people's contexts, serving other people's intentions" and making them "one's own" (Wertsch, 1991, quoting Bakhtin, 1981, pp. 293–294).

To be clear, this process of making policy tools "one's own" was nuanced and contingent, not neat or complete; to our view, this is what makes our analysis most interesting. Understanding teachers' work as mediated in multiple ways, we were drawn to those instances in which teachers seemed reluctant to adapt or coauthor the standards, reticent to make them "their own." In particular, we were interested in what those instances could teach us about how broader social and cultural factors were influencing teachers' individual and collective work and learning, as well as their sense of agency in relation to both.

Importantly, enacting one's own appropriated versions of a given policy—or what CHAT theorists call *externalization*—leads to variation. As newcomers are apprenticed into the profession and their respective schools, for example, their teaching practices inevitably depart (typically by degree) from those of other teachers (Engeström, 1999b). Over time, small departures can develop into more substantial differences, which can become sources of tension within an activity system. Such tensions exist alongside those generated by other elements of the system, including, for example, aforementioned boundary artifacts and the presence of multiple and sometimes "at-odds" motives/objects. When conflicts or tensions such as these arise, participants (or subjects) tend to react to one another by shifting how they operate somehow—whether through resistance, synthesis, cooperation, innovation, and so on—and in turn changing and developing (incrementally) the shared activity. CHAT theorists identify this change and development as a foundational source of learning, given its "expansion of a subject's action possibilities in the pursuit of meaningful objects in activity" (Roth & Lee, 2007, p. 198).

Learning as Expansion

The idea that tensions are endemic to activity and that their reconciliation can lead to the expansion of consciousness represents what Engeström refers to as *expansive learning* or *learning by expansion*. The idea that learning grows out of attempts to collectively "resolve the uncertainties that arise from the discoordinations that are a necessary part of all human experiences" suggests that Playa teachers can learn from efforts to resolve, for example, discontinuities between their established understandings and practices and what the CCSS seem to be asking of them (Cole & Levitin, 2000, p. 79). Indeed, our own prior research illustrates that tensions between teachers' existing knowledge and literacy instruction on the one hand, and literacy standards and prepackaged standards-based curricula on the other, can be productive for teachers, particularly when conditions enable them to apply to their instruction the learning that results from their problem-solving efforts (Stillman, 2011).

Today, there is relatively widespread agreement that transforming instruction and/or student outcomes will require providing teachers with opportunities to work together on problems of practice. While we agree that transformation requires collaboration, we also consider it crucial to acknowledge Engeström's (1991) contention that collaborative work must be *critical* in order for it to engender deep learning. That is, collaboration or "abundant horizontal interaction" among teachers has been linked, for example, to healthier school cultures (Hargreaves, 1992) and to more deliberate instructional planning (Vescio, Ross, & Adams, 2008), Engeström contends that transformations in consciousness result only when these interactions are mediated "by stories of problematic situations and their solutions" (p. 252). It is through participation in *contexts of criticism* that subjects are supported to "analyze critically and systematically their current activity and its inner contradictions" and experience the growth and change that this analysis brings about, both for them and, in turn, their environments as well (p. 254).

Given the key role of tensions and contradictions in triggering learning and transformation, and the centrality of tensions and contradictions in learning to teach writ large (Britzman, 2003), we made every effort in data collection and analysis to identify tensions and contradictions that arose as Playa's teachers worked with the CCSS. In some cases, this involved identifying tensions and contradictions; in other cases, it involved noting when teachers themselves identified tensions and contradictions within their own work. In all cases, we sought to uncover how and why the 10 teachers learned and experienced growth (or didn't) in their practice and their professional identities. Across cases, we explored the different types of tension and contradiction with which particular teachers identified and grappled, and the degree to which and how their grappling with tension and contradiction seemed to generate learning, instructional change, or alternative outcomes.

Tensions, their complexities, and their potential for generativity became so central to our understanding of teachers' work with the CCSS and thus feature prominently in subsequent chapters where we home in on areas of teaching practice within which such tensions emerged most acutely. By structuring readers' experience in this way, we aim to offer insights into the different dimensions of teachers' learning that occurred in and through their CCSS engagement, as well as insights into the implications of their learning for them and for their students. Our ultimate aim, then, is to be, like CHAT itself—both practice-based and future-oriented (Sannino, Daniels, & Gutiérrez, 2009)—in the service of equity-oriented teaching and learning.

CHAPTER 3

Complexities of Context and Consequences of a "No Failing" Climate

In order to understand Playa as a place of work for the 10 educators whose labor is at the center of our study, and for the handful of administrators we also interviewed and observed, it helps to put Playa as a context *in context*—socially, culturally, and historically. Thus, this chapter addresses Playa's position and positionality at the intersection of four crucial and consequential shifts that have resonance at the national level, and that have been acutely felt in California specifically: the changing demographics of the population and of schoolchildren in particular, the rash of "backlash" policies and pedagogies that have cropped up alongside and in response, the proliferation of charter schools as one indicator of market logics' incursion into public education, and the spread of standards-based reforms linked to high-stakes accountability structures.

Look up the word *positionality* in the dictionary and one might find a simple definition like "the quality of being positional." We use the term *positionality* here, as others have before us (e.g., Alcoff, 1988), to suggest how something is situated or positioned in a given field, particularly in relation to other features and players and social categories (including race, class, gender, and language, among others) and to raise questions about connections among one's position, power, and perspectives on knowledge. Positionality, in this sense, is less about essential or objective qualities or labels, and more about how one—person, entity, or group— is *positioned* or *fits* in relation to the structures of society and the cultural practices of communities, and what identities, knowledges, and ways of being are assumed and constructed as a result.

After attending to some core conditions that gave rise to Playa's particular position in the field, in this chapter we trace Playa's past and present (at the time of our study) while also positioning it vis-à-vis prevailing political and policy discourses.

DIVERSITY AND THE DEMOGRAPHIC IMPERATIVE

The first shift, concerning demographics, is arguably the most obvious, even if only witnessing greetings and goodbyes exchanged among Playa's parents and children, teachers and students, colleagues and community members.

California, a demographic bellwether, is one among the first four so-called "majority-minority" states, including Hawaii, New Mexico, and Texas. Such states are projected to proliferate in the coming years—by the year 2060 totaling 22 states that together will account for about two-thirds of the country's population (Texeira, Frey, & Griffin, 2015). Not surprisingly, three of the current four states—and one of those soonest to turn—are, like California, situated along the U.S.–Mexico border.

Given that California leads the nation demographically, and that schools are often sites where demographic shifts emerge early and evidently, it makes sense that more than half of the state's K–12 students were Latinx in 2014 and almost a quarter were classified as English learners (ELs), of whom more than 80% were Spanish speakers (California Department of Education, 2015). Educators across so many of the state's schools, whether in urban areas or rural farming communities, whether serving K–12 students or state college enrollees, enter classrooms each day that give credence to the claim that "brown is beautiful," and bountiful.

While demographic shifts are undeniable, they have never been without their discontents. Despite the accelerating rhetoric of postracial America during the Obama presidency, especially ample research—and the rhetoric and result of the 2016 presidential election—confirms that racism remains an entrenched reality, that political power continues to tip disproportionately in favor of the White and wealthy, and that fear among White Americans about becoming a racial minority may ultimately lead them to respond in ways that shift their politics further to the right (Craig & Richeson, 2015). The very phrase *majority-minority*—oxymoronic as it is—speaks to the resiliency of Whiteness as the mainstream default frame of reference.

Even in California, where diversity is an element of everyday experience for most people statewide, equity and inclusion remain elusive. Known widely for its ethnic and cultural pluralism, its left-leaning politics, and the liberal lifestyles of, say, Berkeley and Venice Beach, California has also been a site of significant discrimination. Those who the "border crossed" and who came to the Golden State from elsewhere were often—and in many cases still are—subject to oppression.

As in most places, schools have been a heated front for battles over citizenship and civil rights. Landmark desegregation cases played out and were won in California. *Mendez v. Westminster*, for example, successfully challenged segregation in the state's schools, thereby affirming in the late 1940s the right to an equal education for so many students like those now attending Playa. Yet California's schools overall, like public schools nationwide, remain far from an integrated ideal (Orfield & Ee, 2014), in part because of the dynamics of residential segregation (Lichter, Parisi, & Taquino, 2015), including outflight among Whites and more affluent residents in diversifying communities (Semuels, 2015).

In this context—indeed, on the ground in communities like the one surrounding Playa—the term *diversity imperative* takes on multiple meanings. It signals, as the *Encyclopedia of Public Health* suggests, both demographic changes themselves and the "corresponding pressure" those changes place on the public sector. In education, where the term has featured in debates around affirmative action especially, it also signals the educational, economic, civic, and national security rationales—indeed imperatives—for promoting diversity in learning environments (College Board Access and Diversity Collaborative, 2009). And in K–12 schools, it takes on more specific meaning, too. As Delia Pompa, former bilingual educator and now senior vice president of the National Council of La Raza, puts it: The nature of demographic change in California and countrywide means, inevitably, that, "to improve achievement overall, we've got to improve achievement for Latino students" (Maxwell, 2012).

In our view, and in the view of our study's participants, these imperatives are not just instrumental in nature; diversity of the kind reflected in California's K–12 public schools—schools like Playa—also confers moral imperatives upon the education system and education professions, both of which have a responsibility to serve their diverse public well. This means not only creating and sustaining environments that make learning possible for all students, including Latinx students and/or those who may not yet speak English fluently, but also educating all students in ways that honor their full humanity.

XENOPHOBIA, BACKLASH PEDAGOGIES, AND BILINGUAL EDUCATION

A second, related shift is the strong resistance to the "browning of America" (e.g., Frey, 2014) and immigration's role in "driving our demographic makeover" (e.g., Taylor, 2014). Indeed, it was amid heated public discourse about immigration's impact on the state's economy and the purported strain on public services by migrants from Mexico and Central America, especially, that California's Propositions 187, 209, and 227 emerged. All three represent what some have come to call "backlash" policies, because they target Spanish-speaking, Latinx immigrants, specifically.

For example, Prop 187—the Save Our State ballot initiative of 1994—sought to establish a screening system for the purpose of denying undocumented immigrants access to basic public services, including nonemergency health care and education. Among its specifics were requirements that K–12 schools confirm students' citizenship status and deny admission to those who could not prove it. Responses from civil rights organizations were swift and successful; Prop 187 was ultimately declared unconstitutional. Nevertheless, its passage revealed substantial political rifts along racial and ethnic lines.

California's Proposition 209, meanwhile, passed in 1996, effectively eradicating affirmative action programs from public schools, colleges, and universities, as well as other state agencies and state-sponsored organizations. Proposition 227, the English for the Children Act, emerged a few years later, fueled by the finances and activism of outspoken conservative Ron Unz. The proposition outlawed bilingual education under all but a few conditions.

Despite a now strong evidence base in favor of bilingual education (e.g., August, Goldenberg, & Rueda, 2011; Brisk, 2005; Thomas, Collier, & Collier, 2011), Unz and others argued that such programs were a costly and ineffective experiment that privileged multiculturalism over assimilation and rapid acquisition of English, the "language of economic opportunity" (California Ballot Measure, 1998). Unz's claim was that because bilingual programs delivered instruction in two languages, thus diminishing English instructional time, they ultimately disadvantaged those they purported to serve. Such arguments compelled many voters and forged common political ground with more xenophobic strands of public discourse, which together colluded in helping to pass the initiative.

Not surprisingly, Proposition 227 had a devastating impact on bilingual programs, teachers, and students statewide. Its passage meant having to "transition" nonnative speakers into English as "rapidly and effectively as possible." It meant transforming bilingual and multilingual classrooms into "English only" settings, where Structured English Immersion (SEI) and Specially Designed Academic Instruction in English (SDAIE)—or "sheltered"—approaches were put into place, officially relegating primary languages other than English to subordinate status.[1] It also required that "English learners" (ELs)[2] take English-language standardized tests once they completed just a single year of schooling in the United States. Under 227, bilingual education remained an option, but a scarcer one that parents had to opt into via in-person written consent and become aware of virtually on their own, because the law prohibited schools from circulating pertinent information. Despite vociferous opposition from education researchers and bilingual educators statewide—including some who ultimately went on to found Playa—Proposition 227 lent popular legitimacy to spurious claims about bilingual education's evidence base, created conditions that were denigrating of native language, and required of teachers various things, such as withholding native language instruction and assigning greater status to English than to Spanish, that contradicted their professional expertise and ethical commitment to emergent bilingual students.

With the benefits of bilingualism touted widely today (Bhattacharjee, 2012; King, 2013) and bilingual programs emerging as an increasingly popular choice among savvy, native-English-speaking families (Anderson, 2015; Watanabe, 2011), it might seem on the surface that bilingual education is on the rebound. In fact, in 2016, more than 70% of California voters passed Proposition 58, which essentially turned over Proposition 227 by again allowing "non-English languages" in public school classrooms. This rebounding isn't necessarily untrue and, at the same time, it also doesn't mean that those who stand to benefit most from high-quality bilingual programs have access to them or that once they are enrolled in bilingual programs, they receive equitable treatment. For many advocates in the Southwest, bilingual education remains a labor of love in the context of budget austerity and still-strong anti-immigrant backlash.

CHARTERED TERRITORY

The influence of Unz—a single, wealthy, White individual without K–12 experience—over the educational options available to kids of color speaks to trends that have emerged and accelerated over the past few decades. Of course, public education in the United States has always been inextricably tied to the political economy and shaped by the interests of elites. Public schools have been seen as a means to secure and advance democracy, deculturize and Americanize indigenous and immigrant youth, produce an efficient workforce with "necessary" distinctions between laborers and leaders, and solve social problems like poverty and racism (Oakes, Lipton, Anderson, & Stillman, 2013).

Recently, public education has also become a popular field of play for business elites, philanthropists, and so-called "edupreneuers" who see it as a potential engine for generating profit (Kumashiro, 2012; Peterson, 2014). In essence, as the wealth gap has expanded and privatization has penetrated previously public sectors (e.g., health care, prisons, the military), the moneyed have garnered what many argue amounts to outsize influence in education policy and, specifically, in the creation, transformation, and closure of public schools that serve "other people's children."

The charter school movement represents a core manifestation of this trend. Charter schools were initially conceived of as laboratories for reform, meant to infuse the public system with choice and competition (Budde, 1988; Chubb & Moe, 1990). Their roots are often traced to Milton Friedman's mid-1950s arguments (e.g., 1955) in favor of enabling informed families to "vote with your feet" from among schools competing for enrollment; this, Friedman believed, would promote quality (Friedman & Friedman, 1980, p. 28). Alongside political conservatives, those in the private sector embraced these ideas, laying the groundwork for substantial investment from venture capitalists and philanthropists in recent years.

To be clear, conservatives were not charter schools' only initial supporters. They were also touted early on by union leaders such as Al Shanker, primarily as a means for empowering teachers to draw on their expertise to improve their own working conditions and innovate in their students' interests. Of course, for various reasons, teachers' unions have since become some of the charter movement's most vocal critics.

The Golden State opened its first charter school just 10 years after the 1983 publication of *A Nation at Risk*, which presented a scathing critique of education in the United States vis-à-vis other countries and attributed much of our so-called underachievement to a lack of academic rigor. Since then, California's charter segment has grown to include more than 1,200 schools—the most in any one state and more than a sixth of those nationwide. This growth has been enabled by subsequent legislation and other homestate advantages: supports like the Charter Schools Development Center at CSU Sacramento; well-heeled advocacy organizations like the California Charter School Association and New Schools Venture Fund; and deep-pocketed philanthropists (e.g., Bill Gates and Eli Broad), as well as business leaders (e.g., members of the Walton clan) and lesser-known technology and entertainment elites (e.g., Reed Hastings of Netflix), with interest in making educational investments close to home.

Charter schools now serve a sizable-and-growing minority of California's, and the country's, students. While varied, these schools share common features. Their charters, or agreements, are typically approved by districts and/or states for a period of 5 years and specify operating procedures, goals, and targets. They most often begin by petition, initiated by parents, teachers, community members, and/or charter operating entities. Charter schools are freed from most of the regulations to which traditional public schools are subject. Their students are not assigned to them but choose to attend and/or are selected by lottery, with funding generally following students and often supplemented by private donations and grants. Competition with traditional public schools ensues and, in some cases, generates tension and even hostility. While charters can be closed if they fail to meet agreed-upon outcomes—based on the same tests taken by public school students—relatively few have been; the number of closures has grown, however, in recent years as school closure has become a more common consequence under federal policies such as No Child Left Behind and initiatives like Race to the Top. Charter schools are usually able to hire their own teachers and staff without having to abide by union contracts; whereas 68% of traditional public school teachers are unionized, only 7% of charter school teachers are, and mostly because their states' laws, unlike California's, stipulate that charter schools follow district's collective bargaining agreements (Cohen, 2015).

Despite these commonalities, charter schools vary. Most are new "start-ups" as Playa was but some are conversions, constructed by transitioning regular public schools to charter status. Charter schools can be progressive or traditional in pedagogical orientation; thematic or vocational in focus; brick-and-mortar, virtual, or hybrid in terms of delivery. They can be stand-alone schools, members of small regional or boutique networks, or part of larger franchise, like charter management "chains." While many are created and managed by those who identify with the underlying market logics that support charters' existence, progressives, alongside conservatives, have seized upon charter mechanisms to establish schools that are organized around particular conceptions of teaching and learning. Perhaps not surprisingly, Playa was one such school, because charter-enabling laws provided a rare, if not singular, mechanism for ensuring bilingual education's survival following the passage of Proposition 227.

The expansion of charters over the past 2-plus decades has complicated the already complex ideological terrain of public education. Consider, for example, schools described by Antonia Darder (2015) as having been "developed by critical educators, parents and communities of color themselves, who infuse their educational programs and curriculum with deeply emancipatory values and culturally democratic pedagogical practices"; certainly these schools, like Playa, are rooted in reasoning beyond market logics and the press to privatize. In fact, in some cases, such schools have emerged in response to public systems that have been unable or unwilling to offer humanizing educational experiences for minoritized youth. Consider also that today's traditional public schools often reflect corporate incursion and institutional racism, both of which cast a pall over the meaning of *public* in practice. And certainly for some teachers of color—whether a minority among coworkers, pushed out of their positions, or struggling against standardization and scripting—charters may offer improved working conditions, in the rare instance that they reflect less authoritarian tendencies and honor teachers' cultures and languages alongside those of their students.

These realities, Darder explains, raise important questions, such as the following: "How can we structure our political arguments in ways that do not demonize teachers working in charter schools, yet still pose important and necessary critiques? How do we respect and engage charter school teachers in solidarity as cultural workers, who are also struggling in whatever ways that are open to them to serve our communities?" These are questions, certainly, that resonate with us, given the amazing teachers who participated in our research and the way we experienced Playa ourselves.

STANDARDS AND STAKES

A fourth and interrelated shift involves the turn toward standards-based reform tied to high-stakes accountability. *A Nation at Risk* is often considered a starting point for the standards movement nationwide, because it framed U.S. schools as failing writ large and argued that regaining prominence in the global economy and ensuring national security depended upon significant reform. Certainly, this opened the door for conservative thinkers—those who are well known, like Diane Ravitch, assistant secretary of education in the early 1990s, and less known, like Ron Unz—to publicly criticize multicultural and/or bilingual education as socially divisive, lacking in academic rigor, and focused on developing minoritized students' self-esteem rather than intellect (Ravitch, 1990b; Schlesinger, 1992).

In response, many states—including California—began looking to standards as tools for increasing educational quality (Berliner & Biddle, 1995). This was encouraged by scholars (O'Day & Smith, 1993; Smith & O'Day, 1991) and accelerated by 1994's Improving America's Schools Act, which made the development of standards a precondition for states to receive federal funds, in much the same way that Race to the Top incentivized states' adoption of the CCSS.

In the early 1990s, also akin to more recent rhetoric, proponents of standards-based reforms argued that "clear" and "challenging" standards would provide teachers with much-needed guidelines, would ensure that all students develop "deep understanding of academic content, complex thinking and problem-solving" regardless of race or residence, and would offer a means by which to hold schools accountable for student learning as measured on standards-aligned tests (e.g., O'Day & Smith, 1993, p. 264). Even those who might be otherwise inclined to caution against the danger of standards concurred that they stood to play an important role in interrupting the systematically subpar education, rooted in deficit thinking and low expectations, that poor children, children of color, and "ELs" often received.

By the mid- to late 1990s, most states had standards in place and were developing and/or implementing assessments to measure students' knowledge of them. The tendency early on was to be as prescriptive and systematic as possible; hence,

California's lengthy and detailed standards documents in reading/language arts, mathematics, natural science, history/social science, and visual/performing arts. Over subsequent years, these documents worked their way into administrators' "standards talk," teachers' daily planning and practice, and even the work of California teacher educators, who in 2001 were required under the law to align courses in credential programs with the K–12 standards.

In California, as in many places, standards-based reforms of the 1990s did not fulfill their stated promise for minoritized students, their teachers, or their schools. The anti-multicultural and anti-bilingual discourses, and the market logics, of the prior decade carried forward into new initiatives and wreaked havoc once hitched to high-stakes accountability. For various reasons, adverse impacts were especially acute in K–12 language arts.

First, California's English language arts (ELA) documents themselves were cumbersome, with more moving parts and pieces than other content areas. Second, the documents were deeply imbricated with a political and normative discourse that devalued native languages other than English as well as students' native languages competencies, while framing monolingual English speakers as the model against which to measure language development among "ELs" (Sleeter & Stillman, 2005).

Third, the reforms did nothing to address well-documented structural barriers—inequitable funding, inadequate textbooks and teachers, placement in low-track classes, disproportionate representation in special education, and so on—facing students of color, low-income students, and "ELs." Fourth, the standards advanced a restrictive and reductive definition of literacy; the guidelines for literacy instruction were comprehensive in scope and sequence, but they reflected internal contradictions and conflicted with many teachers' professional expertise concerning how to meet the needs of culturally and linguistically diverse students (Sleeter & Stillman, 2005). For example, although documents referenced "scaffolding" as a necessary component of effective teaching for EB students, they featured the least dynamic forms (e.g., providing "simplified texts and "immersion" in English). More globally, the standards emphasized skills-based, phonics-first (through grade 12), direct instruction, and thus pressed teachers to focus on discrete skills in decontextualized, highly sequential ways. These approaches worked against the interests of "ELs" especially, who were expected to develop higher-order skills and knowledge only after having mastered lower-level skills that are hardest to learn when extracted from meaningful content and social interaction around that content (Matas & Rodriguez, 2014).

Fifth, prompted by accountability policies, many districts across the state adopted scripted ELA programs that further constrained teachers' latitude to tailor instruction according to their professional expertise and knowledge of students. Sixth, reflecting nationwide trends, the California tests themselves were ill-suited to gauging what students, particularly culturally and linguistically diverse students, actually knew and were able to do (Solano-Flores, 2008); as a result, they sapped instructional time and student engagement, while offering teachers little useful information to guide future instruction.

All the above were exacerbated by federal mandates requiring that states hold students, teachers, and schools accountable by tying standardized test scores to symbolic and financial carrots and sticks. In California, this meant testing at every grade from 2 to 11, calculating and publicizing every school's Academic Performance Index (API)—a rating that characterizes a school according to its achievement growth overall and in relation to similar schools—and placing schools that did not make "adequate yearly progress" on probation. Schools labeled "low performing" under this system were among the most likely to adopt scripted programs, given requirements and inducements under federal programs such as Reading First.

Clearly, high-stakes accountability placed pressure on public school educators. The pressure on those working with minoritized youth in urban schools was particularly onerous, or "tight" (Gutiérrez, Asato, Zavala, Pacheco, & Olson, 2003); indeed, their schools were most likely to be labeled "low performing," and thus, most likely to receive the "tightest" surveillance of teaching and the most acute pressure to elevate test scores. As a result, they especially were pressed to adopt reductive notions of reading (Pacheco, 2010), privilege mandated, test-aligned programs over locally responsive curricula (MacGillivray, Ardell, Curwen, & Palma, 2004); focus on the most-tested subjects (Crosland & Gutiérrez, 2003); and teach toward tests in order to avoid public humiliation, financial penalty, or state takeover, and averse "gatekeeping" effects that low scores can have for language minoritized students (Gándara & Hopkins, 2011). All of the above made for "at-risk environments" that significantly endangered learning for "ELs" (Ruiz, 1996).

That said, teachers also exercised agency within constraint, developed reservoirs of adaptive expertise, and found ways to draw on their professional knowledges and identities to interrupt pressure to standardize instruction and assessment. In essence, they took up and expanded upon what Coburn (2004) calls the "bounded autonomy" afforded to them. Those possessing specialized preparation, credentials, and professional development that was focused on meeting the needs of "ELs" were among the most likely to face stringent directives about how to teach and to experience deep conflicts between their personal–professional knowledge and policy mandates; they were also among those best equipped to teach "against the grain" (Cochran-Smith, 1991) and "take back the standards" in the service of "ELs" (Pease-Alvarez & Samway, 2012; Sleeter & Stillman, 2007; Stillman, 2009, 2011; Stillman & Anderson, 2015. In California then, the most besieged and the most agentive teachers were often one and the same—those who were bilingual themselves, who held special authorization to teach "ELs,"[3] and who worked with the state's Latinx students in low-income urban and rural communities where schools often carried "low-performing" labels. These are the very kind of teachers who banded together to create Playa later that decade.

Standards and Stakes, 2.0

More than 15 years ago, Sergiovanni (2000) used the term *standards stampede* to capture the careening-forward cultural "common sense" that standards had come to represent as "the one best way" to improve schools at the turn of the 21st century (p. 76). Today, the term *stampede* would resonate for many in terms of capturing the energy and force of CCSS implementation. In California, however, the CCSS—adopted in 2010 and slated for full implementation soon after—take on a particular character in light of prior ELA standards, which proved to be cumbersome and conflict-inducing for many educators.

The CCSS-ELA standards are inarguably leaner and in many ways assume of teachers and students a higher degree of intellectual engagement. Or, as one Playa administrator put it, whereas California's standards were "more literal," the CCSS are "more analytical." In that sense, they are closer to the kind of standards for which the initial architects of standards-based education advocated—namely, standards that "allow for maximum flexibility and creativity at the local level," while still providing teachers with clear direction (Smith & O'Day, 1991, p. 248). Thus, it is perhaps understandable if concerns about the CCSS—the interests they reflect and the kinds of instructional rigor they encourage—are somewhat less acute among California educators because of the relative "flexibility and creativity," that they might seem to represent.

Even if the state's educators are inclined to see the new standards through the lens of their problematic predecessors, the CCSS remain controversial in California as they do elsewhere. Unsurprisingly, such a large state contains within its borders those who take issue with the reach of the federal government and the perceived erosion of states' rights, those who harbor concern about national standards privileging dominant perspectives at the expense of local funds of knowledge and community-based needs, those who philosophically oppose the underlying market logics and substantial involvement from private interests and elites outside education, and so on.

We would contend that controversy around the CCSS is not just to be expected, but it is to be desired, given what is known (and remains unknown) about the impact of standards-based reform on California's youth. The mainstream narrative around national standards—as with state standards 2 decades ago—relies on the rhetoric of "scientific evidence" (e.g., test scores as "objective" measures of learning) and righteous "coherence" (e.g., among standards, assessments, materials, etc.). Together, both contribute to a sense of neutrality, efficiency, and universality concerning standards and the instructional and assessment practices they encourage. Yet, as California's recent history indicates, standards-based reforms run the risk of affecting students of color and students considered "ELs" more severely than their White, native-English-speaking peers, particularly under conditions of high-stakes accountability (Gutiérrez, 2006; Gutiérrez, Baquedano-López, & Asato, 2000). In light of this, it remains crucial to question the presumed innocence of standards like those at the heart of our research. After all, even the most avowedly equity-minded policies can function as "backlash pedagogies" (Gutiérrez et al., 2002) if they disproportionately disadvantage language-minoritized students or render their needs somehow less visible or less met.

PLACING AND PARSING PLAYA

We recognize Playa as being situated, consequentially, at the intersection of the prior four shifts. The community into which it was—and still is—woven reflects the demographic shifts of the past few decades and portends the projected shifts mentioned above. Not far from the U.S.–Mexico border, Playa sits on a two-lane street, off a main boulevard, in a neighborhood that has a small-town feel but is part of a midsize and growing city in one of the state's major metropolitan areas. While the city is roughly 60% Latinx, the area surrounding Playa, like many places in the region, is closer to 75% Latinx overall, with a diverse mix—Asian, Black, multiracial, and non-Latinx White families—also calling it home.

Like many modern cities, Playa's is bifurcated by a freeway that marks socio-economic and racial distinctions. To one side, the population is wealthier, with nearly two times the median income and higher proportions of White and Asian residents; to the other side, where Playa sits, the population is lower income and more Latinx. In 2014, Playa itself served a student body that was 95% Latinx and, by design as a Spanish–English dual language program, just over 50% heritage Spanish-speaking.

For those living nearby in modest bungalows and squat few-story apartment buildings, the median family income hovered in the low to mid-$40,000s, which qualified most families of four to six for free or reduced-price lunches. The percentage of families receiving free and reduced lunch at Playa, on the rise in recent years, crept up to nearly 66% from just under 50% in 2006.

A multicultural hub and economic engine, the adjacent boulevard is peppered with regional and national franchises, Southeast Asian small businesses, and stretches of Spanish-speaking establishments, including eateries with *nopales* and *tacos de tripa, lengua, o cabeza* on the menu. Signs of environmental and economic struggle, familiar markers in immigrant communities of the Southwest—asthma clinics, unemployment agencies, people seeking day labor, and well-worn jalopies—are all around; so, too, are markers of pride, like neatly trimmed rose bushes edging otherwise drought-scorched yards. Not surprisingly, markers of encroaching gentrification appear as well—a Starbucks here, a billboard for loft-style apartments there.

Playa's region remains an emblematic swath of country. At points a boomtown, it has expanded and contracted alongside upsizing and downsizing American institutions: certain kinds of agriculture, military investment, industrial growth and erosion. Like much of California and the country, midcentury investments in infrastructure were not sustained during subsequent periods of limited public spending. And in the intervening years, neighborhoods like Playa's—typically poorer and browner than those around them—suffered especially the ill effects of proximity to aging power plants, high-traffic corridors, and so on. Not long ago, Playa's zip code was among the top ranked in the state for pollution vulnerabilities, including groundwater contamination, diesel pollution, traffic density, and hazardous waste (Cal/EPA & OEHHA, 2013). And then of course, there is the nearby U.S.–Mexico border, a physical and political boundary over which traffic flows with regularity and with complex consequences for community demographics and economics.

In recent years, the larger city of which Playa and its immediate neighborhood are part has been lauded for its livability, its environmental initiatives, its investments in rehabilitating certain areas and in reinvigorating the pro-business climate, and its educational options and outcomes. Since the mid-1990s, these options have included charter schools, which have enjoyed support from local business leaders who viewed them as a means to relieve overcrowding born of immigration and population growth, cater to diverse interest groups, and prepare young people for the new economy. When Playa opened its doors in the late 1990s, it was one of about 175 charter schools in California—a number that doubled over the subsequent few years under legislation that lifted 100-schools-statewide and 10-schools-districtwide caps. In that context, Playa quickly became one among a rapidly growing number supported by the business community in its own and nearby districts.

Almost 15 years later, when our study began, Playa occupied a unique spot, geographically and politically. A "high-performing" bilingual school in a predominantly working-class Latinx neighborhood, it was part of what its city boasted about when narrating its ascendency and marketing itself to the developers and moneyed classes that the city hoped would bring added resources to within its boundaries—a campaign so successful that new residents at times outnumbered seats in the schools that arguably helped attract them. At the same time, as a successful school in a regressive funding state (i.e., one that typically spends less on low-income than high-income districts) subject to significant immigration flow, Playa was also pointed to as an exemplar of just how much can be accomplished by hard work in the face of humble conditions.

Among charter schools, meanwhile, Playa was regarded as a respected and composed elder with deep roots in the dry Southwestern ground and branches of influence that stretched city- and nationwide. People from all over the world came to visit, interested in the school's longevity and now shining example. A dual-immersion school, it had been forged out of necessity—a response on the part of its dedicated educators to aforementioned anti-bilingual education policies and concerns about U.S. schools' capacity to educate Latinx youth fairly, both of which gained momentum in the 1990s. It had cut its teeth in California's choppy post-227 political waters and survived the tumult of first-generation high-stakes accountability, and now it was thriving. Given Playa's success at the time of our study, it is tempting to gloss over the journey it endured from its founding, to floundering, to failing, and then fêted. Doing so, however, would mean missing out on much of what made Playa the place it was during our 2 years there—namely, those formative experiences that unfolded and those sensibilities that developed vis-à-vis shifts addressed above. Indeed, both continued to shape its culture so powerfully.

Language, Love, and *Familia*

Like many charter schools, Playa got off the ground initially only because of financial resources put up by politically conservative, pro-charter forces. Interestingly, however, Playa's often-repeated creation story almost always omitted that detail. Seemingly unintentional, the omission was still telling. For Playa's founders, administrators, and teachers, being a charter school was more instrumental than political. The educators in our study never identified in any overt way as being part of a broader charter school movement or even being pro-charter in a global sense. What they were, however, was explicitly pro-bilingual education and *anti-"institutionalism"*—a term that some used to describe the role of schools in socializing students (and teachers) to "patterned ways of thinking" in keeping with the status quo.

It wasn't until well into the study that we learned from a district-level administrator how exactly preexisting, positive relationships between local business leaders and district leaders yielded Playa's start-up capital. As Playa's own staff had done, this district-level administrator recounted how the seeds of "a dream school" were sown by a small group of bilingual educators gathered around a kitchen table and talking about what it might look like to create a school that would really prepare students like theirs for the 21st century. The group's idea for a locally responsive school with a global focus and a dual-immersion program stretching beyond 5th grade, he explained, was "loved" by a local business leader, who made Playa one of "his pet projects" and fronted "several million dollars" to purchase land and fund construction, provided that the school would serve the community's "neediest students." Playing down politics and playing up pragmatism, the district official explained the dynamic simply: "Every dream needs to have someone to, you know, fertilize, sunlight to grow, and he was part of it." That Playa—a school espousing a commitment to critical pedagogy—was made possible by the private wealth of a pro-capitalism conservative is precisely the kind of "pesky complexity" that Antonia Darder (2015) refers to when cautioning the "left" against painting charter schools and their teachers with too broad a brush.

To be clear, dreaming up a new dual-immersion school in the late 1990s was dreaming in defiance of the nightmare that Prop 227 represented for bilingual educators statewide. It was also dreaming marked by some desperation. Seizing upon emergent charter mechanisms to create havens for endangered teaching and learning, and finding ways to hitch the radical roots of bilingual education to the mainstream/Whitestream discourse of "free market reform" for "21st-century" education represent what some might call "visionary pragmatism" in practice (Collins, 1998; Sleeter, 2005), a capacity to pursue lofty goals while adapting responsively to real-world exigencies. This kind of pragmatism, we argue, is deeply embedded, arguably by necessity, in Playa's collective consciousness, which collected (so to speak) and crystalized over time as the "dream school" drew likeminded folks through its doors, including some staff who were still on board when we were there.

One of the first of these staff members was the current principal, an administrator at a nearby school when openings at Playa were announced; having been among those who dreamed together at that kitchen table, the opportunity "called" and he applied. It was a chance, he believed, to be part of a school that would defy the achievement gap, disrupt "self-fulfilling prophecies that were being instilled in kids [elsewhere] . . . the whole notion of Latino kids and African American kids don't learn," and nurture students' cultural and linguistic competencies. Others who joined came for similar reasons, often as pulled to Playa as they were propelled from schools that were evolving in painful ways after the passage of Prop 227. These dynamics had a profound impact on the norms that were woven into Playa's foundation, developed further over time, and mediating all activity.

Still full of emotion nearly 15 years later, one staff member recounted what it was like to experience his first major "clash with the system" upon seeing the language and culture he loved, and the principles he held dear, so violated:

> I was really proud of my language, I was really proud of helping students acquiring their first language. . . . I still remember my principal coming in and [saying,] "You know what, Julio . . . to be honest with you we really don't care about what you're doing with Spanish. I just want you to give me 10 names out of your list because we're gonna transition them to the English-only classrooms, and we need to look good on paper that we are transitioning students to English." This is what she bluntly told me. I remember that day I said, "You know what, I can give you the list . . . but I'm gonna also give you my resignation by the end of this year. I'll tell you right now . . . I don't agree with what you're doing so I cannot continue working for you. I'm not gonna abandon the kids right now, but I'm just gonna let you know that this is my last year here. I know there's a school out there that is gonna value what we do for students to keep their language and here I go."

Similar sentiments echoed in the accounts of others, like Miriam, a middle school Spanish language arts and social studies teacher, for whom conflicts between "politics" on the one hand, and her background, personal commitments, and "philosophy" on the other pressed her out of one school and toward Playa:

> I was having issues . . . the district was starting to transition the kids [to English] too soon in my eyes. It's like 3rd grade [and] already some kids were already starting to transition; they were losing their language, the Spanish, and to me, I mean, bilingualism was the thing I wanted for all children. . . . That's when I started talking to people and I found out about Playa. . . .

Although not everyone came having faced wrenching post–Prop 227 personal–professional conflict elsewhere, everyone came wanting very much to be at Playa, in particular. This was often connected to a sense of place, both geographical and cultural. Sonya, for example, opted away from a position in a higher-income neighborhood in order to be in a familiar "environment" and among those who felt akin to the family she cherished. At Playa, her culture had currency for connecting authentically with her students and teaching her content complexly, and this made a difference in how she felt about herself and her work:

> I'm proud of my roots. . . . I'm teaching here as close to that that I could get. . . . The kids, the students that I teach, come from the same background as I did, so I make a lot of connections with them when it comes to their struggles and their home life, and things like that. For example . . . I was doing a lesson on credible sources. . . . That's one of the Common Core standards—finding credible sources. . . . I said, "Well, do you think your mom is a credible source?" And they're like, "Well, no," you know. "Okay, well, pretend you're 5. Is your mom a credible source? If she tells you the moon is made out of cheese, are you gonna believe it?" "Well, yeah. . . . " And then I try to make connections. . . . "Okay, well, growing up, my mom told me that if I took a shower and went outside with my hair wet, I was gonna get sick." And then all the kids are like, "My mom tells me that all the time!" (laughter) "Well, is it true?" . . . and they were like, "Well, no, 'cause I went outside and it was cold and I didn't get sick." "Well, then, what's the science behind it? So is your mom a credible source? . . . My mom, well, yeah . . . she is a very credible source, on parenting and things like that, but when it comes to illnesses and your immune system, I don't know . . . " (laughter). Having those connections like, "Hey, when you have the hiccups you get a red string and put it on your forehead with saliva. That gets rid of the hiccups." And just making those cultural connections, the kids are like, "Oh, my mom does that, too." I'm like, "Did it work? What if the string was blue? Would it work?" (laughter). And they're like, "No, it's kind of crazy. We do all those things because our moms tell us to." "Exactly, so Wikipedia is like your mom, not always a credible source. So when you go to do your research, don't rely on Wikipedia." So . . . stretching that connection between the culture and all that. Now, working here at this school, it's like an extended family.

We heard the word *family* repeatedly, but just as often the word *familia*, too, which in basic translation might mean the same thing, but it also carries deeper cultural resonance, signaling "family values" of interdependence, respect for tradition, loyalty, and impassioned hard work on one another's behalf. As 1st-grade teacher Ramón put it, "Coming from the Mexican culture, family, *familia*, that's everything." Personally for Ramón, whose own mother had insisted that Spanish be spoken at home, *familia* was the reason he couldn't imagine conversing voluntarily in English with his siblings or moving too far away, despite family members' encouragement to go and see more of the world if he wanted; interacting with them "on a daily basis, or at least a weekly basis" outweighed any temptation.

Professionally for Ramón, it meant that teaching—in Spanish, especially—was "a lifestyle" more than a job: "You're part of the family . . . the students' family; they see you probably more than they see their parents during the week . . . and you're a mentor to them, so . . . you have a great responsibility."

According to Playa's principal, this way of thinking—"this strong connection to heritage"—was foundational to the school's culture by design: "So that people feel strongly connected to the system that we've created and they're a part of. It's *that* identity. It's *their* identity. . . . It's tied to *familia*." Under these terms, then, the "stakes" involved in teaching are more than high; they are deep—connected to personhood and cultural preservation—in ways that differ from the "high stakes" of today's accountability systems.

Failing *La Familia*

The sense of "great responsibility" Ramón spoke about was something all Playa's educators shared, which was precisely why it was so painful to feel at any time that one was or could be "failing." If teaching wasn't just a job but "a lifestyle," and if colleagues and students weren't just fellow employees and recipients of services but kin, then floundering at work was akin to failing *la familia*. For those who lived through the school's early struggles, this feeling of failure was not an abstraction; it was sense memory.

Six years after its founding, Playa fell short of the state-mandated levels of achievement on standardized test scores and faced the two-pronged "stick" of state accountability under No Child Left Behind: It received a low-performing label and was put on watch for closure as a "program improvement" school, which it was particularly vulnerable to given its charter status. Suddenly, this school, born in part to buffer against "backlash pedagogies," was accused publicly of not providing for its EB students. Suddenly, this school that had kept bilingual education alive in an inhospitable policy climate faced the threat of extinction.

None of this was for lack of effort; as Dr. Ruiz explained, "We were doing really, really, really a lot of work . . . working really hard, but there was something missing. . . ." By all accounts, it was a heartbreaking and harrowing time. "It's difficult to relay the feeling that we had at that moment," explained Mr. Pacheco. "The feeling . . . was full of failing, the feeling *of* failure because we *were* failing. We were failing our students."

The school responded in multiple ways. They revisited their bilingual program and shifted from a 90/10 to a 50/50 model. They focused on coherence and consistency within and across grade levels. They homed in on academically challenging and linguistically responsive teaching practices—the "type of instruction," they explained, "we know that traditionally Latino kids do not get." They established multiple methods for tracking student outcomes. And they also worked on "getting the wrong people off the bus," whether letting teachers go or encouraging them to leave, and rebuilding a staff, all of whom were "on board" with the school's vision, mission, and expectation "to see the results . . . to see our kids being prepared for the future."

The school saw almost immediate dividends. Fewer than 5 years after being placed in "program improvement," Playa reached the second-highest level of ranking for schools in the state regardless of demographics. Along with these achievement gains came the "carrots" of accountability reform: The school received coveted "distinguished school" status, accolades from various entities, and recognition from district and state leaders.

Phoenix Rising

These experiences with accountability's sticks and carrots mediated the school's culture in four central ways. First, Playa's transformation forged a "phoenix" identity among staff, who looked at their remarkable journey as proof that they together, their *familia*, could overcome something as serious as "program improvement" and could emerge from struggle even stronger. As Sonya put it, "We rose from the ashes. I mean, we were getting ready to be closed down, to what we are now—a distinguished school! And doing it teaching two languages, that's the big part."

This narrative of ascendency contributed to a sense of confidence in the school's capacity to adapt in the face of adversity, to survive, and to thrive as a leader and innovator in doing so. It also made a kind of gospel out of working with, rather than resisting, whatever was handed down. Sure, there were times when some recognition was given to policies as constraining; for example, Dr. Ruiz admitted to some frustration with a system that places schools "into a box" based on assessment outcomes alone. But even those comments were coupled with the can-do, must-do, and will-do attitude, evident in Dr. Ruiz's summation: "That's just the way it is . . . so you need to work within that structure."

The "Playa Way" of working was particular; it involved a refusal to view oneself as subject or subordinate to "that structure," and an unflagging confidence in one's capacity to triumph. Dr. Ruiz described the mindset: "We're in the driver's seat. We're moving things. We're gonna continue to move regardless of the obstacles."

Although it might seem like naive narration to some, it was a principled professional stance at Playa. It reflected a deeply held belief, shared by Playa's administrators, all of whom had many years of classroom experience, and well voiced by the middle school co-principal, Ms. Cook—namely, that "the best teachers are the ones who know how to adapt," who take policy and content and instructional strategies and "make it their own." It was also a belief embraced by teachers, who understood, like Miriam, "that here at Playa the philosophy is, you're presented with something new, you take it, and you make it your own, and you make it Playa's."

Not surprisingly, then, this stance powerfully mediated administrators' and teachers' response to the arrival of the CCSS. To them, it was both unremarkable, in that it was just another aspect of the "structure" to which they would "adapt," and central, in that it had implications for daily practice. Though Playa's educators made sense of the CCSS and adapted to it in particular ways, which we detail further in subsequent chapters, the fact that they would adapt to it—that they would "make it their own . . . make it Playa's"—was never up for debate.

Second, teachers and administrators who had experienced the school's early struggles underscored how the threat of closure bred unity by necessity. As Sonya put it, the feeling at the time was, "Hey, we're gonna be taken over by the state if we don't get our test scores up. You know, nobody believes in us, we're a dual-language school. . . . We don't have anybody to back us up." Their response was to batten down the hatches: "Okay, then we're gonna do it, we're a team, a lot of support, a lot of motivation." Ultimately, this served to deepen Playa's preexisting "we're all in this together" atmosphere.

It also birthed some arguably family-like, but not necessarily positive, dynamics. One was a kind of generational divide between those who were present during "program improvement" and still felt the memory of failure in their bones, and those who came after and for whom "failing" was an abstraction (albeit an anxiety-provoking one). This was not a rift so much as a disconnect—one that led Sonya and Lynette to describe the staff as "family" in the present, and yet "not as connected as we were before" and "not as family as we used to be." The disconnect, at its roots, was in the degree of urgency felt by veterans, who had seen "failure" up close and now recognized it as always possible, and "new staff," who simply saw the school and its students as secure in their success:

> New staff members . . . they get the fruits of what we did. And I don't mean that in a negative way. . . . They feel that [students here are already] performing. "They know what to do . . . I don't have to push. . . ." This moment, right now, is the time where we *do* need to continue [to push] because this is a reflection of us . . . and it's interesting that new members don't see that . . . they haven't had the history.

This quote, from elementary co-principal Mr. Pacheco, suggests that it was as if the accountability climate had inflicted a kind of post-traumatic stress on Playa's veteran educators, a condition that they carried with them and that newer teachers, by their own admission, sensed and respected, but could not fully feel or understand as their more experienced colleagues did. And while we make that comparison with some reservation, given the gravity of post-traumatic stress suffered by combat veterans, we are struck by the similarities in how, as a condition, its impact nevertheless has implications for entire family systems, not just those who suffered most directly.

Facing and then overcoming the public shame and threat to existence imposed by "program improvement" also seemed to inscribe or amplify patriarchal dynamics common to both schools and families/*familias*. Across the board, staff expressed deep respect for the school's administrators, particularly its "visionary" founding principal, who led through tough times, refused to compromise on matters of principle, and exerted a herculean effort (along with others) to ensure that Playa overcame its "low-performing" status. Even with a team of four administrators, three of whom were men, Dr. Ruiz was a kind of singular father figure for the school and its staff. It wasn't uncommon to hear teachers say things like, "Dr. Ruiz is the reason I'm here" or "If he leaves, I don't know what will happen. . . . " And, as Dr. Ruiz described, it was his own father who served as his most essential "role model" in cultivating a school culture marked by "a sense of belongingness, a sense of identity, a sense of who you are, and because you know that, you're excited to be a part of it"—those essential elements Dr. Ruiz pulled from across practical texts by Richard and Rebecca DuFour, theoretical pieces by Paulo Freire, Ira Shor and Henry Giroux, and research articles on school change:

> My father . . . talked about this whole sense of *being*. . . . I saw it in him, and I'm thinking, "I wonder if it can be done in a school? I wonder if we can create that feeling, the respect, the honor, the integrity within the system. . . ." It's hard to explain, but . . . we've created this culture where people feel connected to one another. . . . And they don't want to let people down because they have this respect for one another. And if they don't have the respect with one another, they will tell them why they don't, and it's working. . . .

In the same way Dr. Ruiz revered his own father for creating the conditions for interaction characterized by authentic respect, many staff revered him, too; this cut both ways, as we'll discuss later on, when it came to engagement around policy and practice, specifically.

Whatever the downsides of that reverence, daily life at Playa did evidence a kind of "radical love" that wasn't contingent on superficial niceties, but rather was grounded in deeper commitments to collective, courageous, and critical engagement (Freire, 1970, 2005; Kincheloe, 2008). Consider, for example, the ease with which Lynette, one of a few monolingual English-speaking staff members, joked about being "the first White, non-Spanish-speaking teacher . . . the token . . . the original," but then quickly shifted to note the significance of co-presenting with a respected colleague and together providing a "model" that also happens to be multiracial—where, for example, "she's the Mexican, and I'm the White, and we were the perfect partnership, what we have. . . . "

Importantly, by "perfect partnership," Lynette and others didn't mean "without conflict" or necessarily "with conviviality." Rather, Lynette explained that even if she didn't "socialize" with a colleague outside school, "when I'm here [at Playa] we're a family." And by family, Lynette meant that she could expect more than polite praise: If she went to her grade-level partner saying, "This is what I'm thinking for this standard," she could count on an honest reply from her—for example, "No, this needs to change . . ."—despite Lynette having 7 years more experience. While the dynamics were different, Julie described a similar kind of trust among her grade-level team, whose members sometimes debated heatedly. As Julie put it, "We have that love for one another," so much so that when there is conflict, "there's still the love;" moreover, she explained, "The love gets built through the conflict"—a crucial, productive dialectic in emancipatory education (McLaren, 2000).

This is not to say that all was lovey-dovey at Playa. Acts of radical love coexisted alongside practices and interactions that sometimes felt hierarchical in a general sense and patriarchal in particular, despite distributed leadership structures and rhetoric. Fellow administrators admitted feeling frustrated, for example, when faced with an "I'm the boss, and this is my way" approach and having to "sometimes . . . buckle down and just say okay, I'll do it your way." Instructional leadership team representatives at times recounted functioning more as conduits of information than participants in shared decisionmaking. Teachers, meanwhile, expressed being pushed beyond what they sometimes felt ready for (e.g., "I would have never seen myself as a leader at a grade level if he hadn't said, you're gonna be the leader for that team"); and though they stated that it was "always a learning experience" and that they could often recognize their growth, they confessed to feeling some discomfort, stress, and diminished agency. Saying "no" did not always seem like a real option or it risked leaving them out of favor—a precarious place to be vis-à-vis *la familia*'s father figure, someone regarded with great fondness and slight fear, as one administrator described it, like "the good guy . . . like dad."[4]

Admittedly, Dr. Ruiz's leadership style was direct, disciplined, and rooted in what he described as a sense of urgency and a respect for what he knew teachers and students could accomplish. As he explained,

> No beating around the bush. No trying to make someone feel good because this and this and they may need this in their life or whatever. No, this is what it is [pounding sound]! And having that approach of you know boom, boom, boom [three clapping sounds] and really kind of, "Okay, there's no hidden agendas. This is it. This is the expectation. Yeah, there's gonna be times to celebrate, you know, but when we celebrate is when we all—all—within the system collectively feel that we've done something to change something."

The borders between this brand of *directness* and *being directive* were often blurry. But whereas such blurriness might have proven quite conflict inducing elsewhere, here Playa's history, the high degree of intersubjectivity among its staff, and deep and diffuse respect for its principal did much to defray dissent.

The third way that Playa's experience in the accountability climate seemed to mediate its culture was by catalyzing and/or accelerating a kind of internal drama. We use the term *drama* not in a negative sense per se, but rather to signify how the spectacle that the accountability climate made of "underperformance," including at Playa previously, informed an almost insatiable drive for instructional improvement on the part of administrators, a commitment to constant change schoolwide, and concomitant concerns among teachers not to be seen as lazy or "less than" and to become "the best."

Insofar as an ethos of insatiable improvement was concerned, it was as if no learning outcome or teaching approach would ever be "good enough." As Mr. Pacheco put it:

> If we don't push the students to the next level, it's because we're not doing our jobs. And back then [when Playa was "low performing"], we were not doing

our job. So this is a never-ending story. . . . And that's kind of like the premise . . . at our school, and I do hear teachers talking about that—that we will always be pushing . . . that the expectation is always something else, something more; what else can you do?

Here, we see how any relenting around the "push" for higher academic achievement gets tethered back to earlier failures and read implicitly through the lens of complicity with the very "institutionalism" and "self-fulfilling prophecies" about underachievement that Playa's founders sought to defy. On a classroom level, as we discuss in Chapters 6 and 7, this incessant push led to almost religious fervor around selecting "more complex" texts, for example, as evidenced when an administrator took issue with 4th-graders reading *The Circuit,* a beloved book designated as having a reading level of grade 5.5, an interest level of grades 6–8, and a Lexile measure of 880L, on the grounds that "it wasn't complex enough" and that the teacher could have used "higher-level and more complex text to take the students to another level."

This ethos of insatiable improvement was then connected by administrators and teachers to a corollary "never-ending" pursuit of professional challenge and constant innovation that became Playa's "new normal" post-program improvement:

We're probably gonna have new theorists next year and we're probably gonna have different training next year on different pieces that [the principal] has found. . . . That's been something that has become "just get used to it, just know that we're not gonna stay in one place; we're gonna keep moving, keep changing."

To our eyes and ears, teachers had mostly become "used to" precisely what one administrator described above. As Lynette put it:

The philosophy is never to be comfortable, you know, things are always changing . . . seeing what are they doing in those [other] schools that's working and bringing it back here . . . in order to make us better. Here at Playa, I can never open a plan book and say, "I did this last year at this time, I'm gonna do it now," because it doesn't fit the goal or the philosophy . . . the direction that we're heading. So, the philosophy would, I guess, be: "Be ready for change and be ready for challenge."

This expectation for constant change, especially at a school where teachers create curriculum from scratch collectively, conferred significant labor. Consider Ramón's description of work life at Playa:

We come in on the weekends, we stay here on Friday afternoons 'til like 6 or 7 just prepping for the following week, we pretty much revise our lessons every single day, we stay here late. . . . Sometimes you miss birthday parties or just minor family celebrations. . . . At the beginning of the year you just get the packet of standards; and that's it. . . . You don't get a basal, you don't get something to guide you; it's like it all comes from you, so it's exhausting sometimes . . . but it's super rewarding. . . .

Across the board, we heard repeatedly that Playa was a place that expected longer work hours than other schools, and there were no complaints from teachers about that. We also saw, in equal measure, that exhaustion and that sense of reward, the latter of which appeared to salve the former, if not physically then spiritually; in other words, while teachers—especially newer ones—at times seemed to be running on fumes, peering out over dark under-eye circles as students completed graphic organizers that teachers had crafted with care in the wee hours, on all but a very few occasions they radiated joy and pride. Summing up the situation as follows, Sonya explained:

> This is our saying: "If you could survive here, you could survive anywhere, so if you could teach 1 year here and make it out alive, you can teach anywhere." . . . It's not structured to be a cakewalk. . . . Nobody's gonna hold your hand here.

Over and over again, we heard Playa's teachers proudly refer to themselves as "overachievers." Their inclination to put in extra effort and hours left them relatively unconcerned about being in what Lynette admitted was a "non-union school" with "no protection." It also left them relatively unflustered by administrators' expectations and corollary invitation to "get off the bus" with support in finding "somewhere else to go" if those expectations were too much.

We also heard repeated references to competitiveness among, but not necessarily between, Playa's teachers. These were complicated conversations in which teachers tended to admit competing with one another—as the prevailing policy discourse might embrace and encourage—but then they would back off those claims and into the language of "non-competitive," or they would contradict themselves somewhat in saying that they wanted to be "the best" or "not last," and at the same time saying that they weren't trying to "win" or "rank" over others. Regardless, they mostly described any competition as productive, in terms of building community among teachers and supporting student learning.

> *Miriam:* It's not like we're doing it to compete to see who's the best. . . . It's just the natural thing that we want to make [what we're doing] equally good, like, "Oh, I can't believe [so-and-so] is putting that activity together! Well, I need to, you know, step it up, step it up, you know." Like my rigor is not enough, my focus is not enough. . . . You now need to make sure that we're all . . . going like this (handed gesturing upwards). . . . Yeah, in a non-competitive way. . . . You don't want to be the last one, or the one where other people are like, "Um, ewww, what's up with your classroom?"

Ramón: I think that we all like to be challenged. . . . I think we all want to be the best, and I think a lot of the teachers here are super competitive . . . but I don't think in a negative way, where it's like they're competitive and they're gonna protect what they do. It's like they want to share what they do, and they want to allow everyone to come in and see what we're doing in the classroom so that other kids have that opportunity that they may not have.

Whatever contributors propelled them to work so hard and so much, it was something they reported loving about Playa and at the same time recognized as requiring "definitely hard work" (Ramón), above and beyond the work of teachers at other schools, and keeping "you on your toes . . . maybe a little bit too much sometimes" (Miriam).

Finally, the ethos of insatiable, constant improvement—of self and school—was encouraged and enforced through norms of accountability. These involved the kind one might associate with typical administrative quests for higher test scores (e.g., disaggregating assessment scores by grade level and class, and expecting teachers to take ownership of them), but also in the ways that were more diffuse and distributed—aspects of the culture itself. Sonya described it this way:

It's a very demanding school. Expectations are high coming from adminis-tration . . . accountability within your peers and your colleagues, and with parents and even with the students. So if you can't handle high levels of stress, then it's not the school for you.

As Sonya's comments suggest, it was a kind of common sense at Playa that to demonstrate one's Playa-ness, one must survive its rigors—make do, innovate, and rise stronger from whatever the ashes may be—much like the school itself did. In essence, it was the "Playa Way" or the highway.

COMPLEXITIES IN, AND OF, CONTEXT

In tracing Playa's journey from inception as a "dream school" to its early days of be-ing labeled "low performing" to its eventual, but tenuous, attainment of "high-per-forming" status, we see how shared commitments and resonant cultural frames give meaning to the work, well beyond its technical elements. In positioning Playa at the intersection of the aforementioned four shifts, we see how complicated mat-ters of context are regarding EBs' education. We also see how traumas inflicted by the political climate and policy context, even when triumphed over, are not entire-ly left behind. A source of ongoing stress, angst, urgency, and pride, they lingered at Playa—informing an achiever (no failing) and survivor (phoenix) identity and fueling an unrelenting press for more and more, higher and higher.

By treating policy as a site of struggle—discursive, as much as pedagogical—we hope to remind readers that even what may appear on its surface as compliance in a simple sense belies a more complicated and mediated process. To this very end, we return often ourselves to a quote from Deborah Britzman's (2003) seminal text on learning to teach; in it, she writes that "trying to learn how to educate others is far more complex, ambiguous, and paradoxical than supposed in the reigning binary split of success and failure and the rigid notions of authority and control that follow" (pp. 1–2). Learning is, as Britzman argues, "never so cut and dried," and most certainly not—as our analysis in subsequent chapters shows—when learning to teach in ways that are responsive to deeply held beliefs and to the demands of those structures that are not of one's making but nevertheless are where one's labor unfolds.

CHAPTER 4

When Stance and Standards Intersect

When [Playa] started, it did not follow the traditional model of education. . . . All students were given the same opportunities to succeed. The administration and teachers decided to take away labels of language, special needs, or economic status that were constantly placed on students. In its first year, 190 students were dispersed heterogeneously in classes throughout the day. . . . Our motto is "innovation for student success."

Narrated by a professional newscaster, these opening lines filled Dr. Ruiz's office, where our research team was being treated to a special screening of a new video describing Playa's educational vision and approach. Originally created in response to a district report that used standardized test scores to identify individual schools' progress and areas for growth, the video—the administrative team explained— would now be used for inspirational and promotional purposes, part of how Playa would share its story and successes with the world.

We begin this chapter with the quote above because it captures the centrality of Playa's teachers' and administrators' unwavering faith in all of their students' capacities to achieve at high levels. Just as importantly, it captures some of the ways in which teachers and administrators expressed and acted upon this faith—for example, by resisting certain aspects of "traditional" schooling and committing themselves to continual reform in pursuit of the "student success" that they believed to be so possible.

In this chapter, we explore Playa's school context by describing the particular brand of academic rigor that permeated the school and the perspectives on teaching, learning, schooling, and emergent bilingual (EB) students that undergirded it. We home in on related tensions that emerged, especially concerning how much struggle and scaffolding learners need to experience in order to learn well and deeply. Finally, we show how these dynamics characterized aspects of teachers' learning experiences, too, and in doing so amplified the idea that providing significant challenges and space for learners to "figure them out" represented the highest form of respect for learners' intellect. We conclude the chapter with a discussion of how these norms and dynamics complicated the terrain for Playa teachers, easing and at the same time also compromising their interactions with the Common Core State Standards (CCSS).

AN ANTI-DEFICIT STANCE TOWARD EMERGENT BILINGUAL STUDENTS

To anchor what follows, we go, via vignette, inside a Playa classroom to mark a shift in focus toward classroom life and the commitments and contextual factors that most shape what unfolds therein. We aim to emphasize the fundamental connection between the chapter's core content—teachers' shared ideas about teaching EBs—and teachers' practice, which becomes the central focus in subsequent chapters.

Although Playa considered itself a "literacy focused" school, the vignette below about 1st-graders' engagement during mathematics reminds us that while language arts policy and instruction were our study's focus, neither we nor Playa's teachers saw mathematics as somehow out of bounds. Over and over again, we heard Playa educators describe Playa as a school where all teachers viewed themselves as literacy teachers at all moments of the day. This was an aspect of Playa that predated, but was also amplified by, emphasis on disciplinary literacy embedded in the CCSS. At Playa, the belief was that students would not just be learning to read, write, speak, and listen in two languages, but also learning content—including mathematics—through reading, writing, speaking, and listening in two languages.

Anchoring Anti-Deficit Stance in the Classroom

Midmorning in early December, 22 students gathered on the rug as 1st-grade Spanish language arts and math teacher Rocio introduced the day's focus. The class had been using *greater than, less than,* and *equal* symbols to compare one- and two-digit numbers the prior day. Today's task—comparing number sentences —was more complex.

For 10 minutes, Rocio engaged students around a few phrases and examples written on chart paper. Before releasing students to their seats, Rocio reiterated directions: "You and your partner are going to *figure this out* using the base 10 blocks, using the number lines, and using the hundreds charts." All of these had featured in students' work while on the rug but, by design, not exactly as they were to be used in pairs. "Make sure that you communicate with your partner, that you talk to your partner. Don't separate the work. All of you, both of you, are doing each part together, so that you understand, okay?"

Just a few minutes later, students were at their desks, huddled over specially made, placemat-like worksheets. A quiet calm hung in the air, and at the same time there was an industrious hum—the accumulation of almost a dozen disciplined duos working at "figuring this out." Rocio, meanwhile, circulated, intervening here and there and noting patterns; these, she explained, would inform her decisions at the end of the session, when she would regather students on the rug to debrief.

Kelsey and Antonio started like most others by writing their names atop the worksheet built for two. They then elected to begin in its upper-right quadrant— with number lines—and agreed to each work on one of the two number sentences.

Antonio, methodical but less developed in his motor skills, finished a few seconds after Kelsey, at which point she exclaimed, "Mine is 15!" to which Antonio replied, "Mine is 14."

She continued: "Mine is greater than yours because I went all the way to the back [of the number line]. . . . And you went all the way to the 14. . . . " Antonio nodded and watched as Kelsey drew a greater-than sign between the number lines, oriented downward so its open end faced the sentence Kelsey had solved. "Let's write it," Antonio suggested, pointing to the blank space adjacent to where Kelsey had finished making her mark. "Over here, let's put 14 . . . is . . ."

Kelsey watched as Antonio wrote. "Yeah, 14 . . . is greater than 15 . . . is greater than . . . hmmm . . . no . . ." She realized she would have to read in the other direction, from right to left, to use *greater than* accurately, perhaps not realizing she could read from left to right using *less than* instead.

When Antonio finished, Kelsey exclaimed, reading from right to left, "Fifteen is greater than 14!" And then she added, sincerely, "You did it good, real good. . . ."

Antonio began reading aloud the directions for the next worksheet quadrant: "Compare the sentences with the base 10 blocks. . . ." Kelsey followed up: "I'll do the units! You do this one and I'll do this one. The one [number sentence] that we worked on already, we still work on that one."

As they drew ones and tens, they paused to watch one another, count together, and comment on each other's work. At one point they discovered a discrepancy between Kelsey's sum in the first quadrant and her drawing in the second. "Wait . . . " she said, and without further words exchanged, they re-counted—first together, then separately.

"It's different!" Kelsey stated as Antonio checked her work. Unsure, Antonio looked up at her and then down at the worksheet. "First we're going to do this part," he proposed, pointing to the third quadrant. "And let's discover if it's 15 [like the first quadrant] or 14 [like the second], okay?"

Kelsey nodded emphatically, as Antonio helped her determine where to start on the number line.

After just a few minutes, they realized and erased Kelsey's error, and Antonio watched closely as Kelsey redrew $8 + 7 = 15$. This time, the sums and the comparisons were in sync.

The last quadrant required a written explanation—not just the answer but also how they knew it was correct. Rocio passed by and Kelsey shared, "I'm trying to think of a sentence. . . . We're both thinking. . . ."

"Good," Rocio said, moving on to another pair.

Antonio began, "In the number line . . ." and Kelsey echoed him excitedly, "In the number line . . ." They repeated and extended it together: "In the number line . . . mine is 15 and yours is 14 and mine is greater than yours." Antonio offered an amendment: "But we could write it like, *In the number line 12 + 2 equals 14 . . .*" Kelsey smiled and nodded and they spoke the rest of the sentence in unison, "*and . . . and 8 + 7 equals 15.*" At that point, Antonio was holding his pencil, Kelsey at his side. "Write that!" she said, wriggling. "That's a good answer! Good! Good!"

Articulating Principles of Anti-Deficit Practice

What makes the vignette notable and representative of practice and policy engagement at Playa? To us, most fundamentally, it is Rocio's anti-deficit stance, which is evident and enabling throughout. Four pillars, or guiding principles, propped up this anti-deficit stance, which itself was shared by other Playa teachers as well.

Pillar I: Expectations, Held High and Deeply

During our earliest visits to Playa, we couldn't help but notice the consistency with which teachers like Rocio voiced and demonstrated conviction, not only about their students' capacities to learn, but also about their own responsibilities to cultivate among students high academic outcomes. Comments to that effect emerged across all initial interviews when we asked participants to describe their own as well as Playa's overarching "philosophy" of education. Eighth-grade teacher Sonya's response, for example, reflected what we heard from others: "You don't water down or dumb down your lesson because you don't think that they're gonna get it," she explained. "If you're gonna teach here, you can't think that. . . . " In keeping with this idea, one administrator explained that "the expectations set by the school" for teachers included to "never give up on [students]," no matter how challenging they might be and to always provide whatever "support mechanism that they need in order for them to be able to acquire the next level."

Fourth-grade teacher Paco spoke similarly, emphasizing that high expectations must apply for teachers, too:

> [Parents] are leaving their student with me and . . . the students' success has to do with my ability to listen to them and entertain their issues with seriousness and respect. . . . It goes hand in hand with the [school] philosophy.

Harkening back to notions of *familia* described in Chapter 3, Paco's comment speaks to how, at Playa, holding high expectations involved acknowledging the trust that parents placed in educators, dedicating oneself to fulfilling professional, as well as social and cultural, responsibilities, and challenging outright those who appear not to see Playa's students (or ones like them) as fully capable.

Although asset-oriented beliefs were cultivated through activities such as hiring interviews, administrator observations, and schoolwide professional development, an abiding faith in students' capacities had crystalized for some teachers prior to working at Playa. First-grade teacher Ramón, for example, suggested that for many colleagues, such beliefs were nurtured during preservice preparation.

> Going through [the university program from which 65% of Playa's teachers and 80% of study participants graduated] . . . we learned a certain philosophy where anyone can be successful in the classroom; it's just a matter of you, as a teacher, finding that way to make them successful, and to have them discover that they are able to be successful.

It was also clear that for many teachers asset-oriented beliefs about students and families were rooted fundamentally in their life experiences and had developed before they became teachers.

Reflecting on his upbringing as a way to underscore the cultural wealth (Yosso, 2005) that is present in neighborhoods that are often framed through a deficit lens, Ramón, mirroring the views of other teachers, explained, "People look at it as being a bad area of [this city]. But I grew up not knowing that; I always had everything I wanted . . . a really good experience." Sonya, too, echoed this inclination—shared by others, especially those who grew up nearby—to view Playa's surrounding community in a positive light. "I love it," she stated simply. "I wouldn't want to teach anywhere else."

This high and deeply felt regard for where students came from, and for what they were capable of, powerfully undergirded the "Playa Way." It was central to teachers' "affective labor," the kind of labor in which "teachers' power to act and their commitment to practice is governed by feeling, passion and the ethics of care rather than by the 'terrors of performativity' (Ball, 2003)" (Kostogritz, 2012, p. 399) and for which the primary aim is not a grade, score, or standard met but the "opening up [of] a social learning environment that triggers an affective response from students" (p. 402). It was part of what informed, for example, the decision-making of a teacher like Rocio, who expected so much—affectively and academically—of her young students.

And to be sure, 1st-graders are young—especially in early December—and typically energetic, egocentric, and prone to distraction after more than 10 minutes working together on a single worksheet. Indeed, it is no minor feat that Rocio's 1st-graders—some of whom were engaging in their less developed language—were willing and able to do as Kelsey and Antonio did. Yet, at Playa it was considered normal to see students—including such young ones—working together for extended periods, complimenting one another spontaneously when adults weren't looking, and resolving for themselves things that might elsewhere become reason to stop or request assistance.

Pillar II: Bilingualism as Beneficial and Beautiful

One of the most enduring expressions of an anti-deficit stance, and one of the central "sites" of affective labor at Playa, was the school's commitment to bilingualism and biliteracy. Not surprisingly then, its staff held additive or language-as-asset perspectives (Garcia, 2005; Ruiz, 1984); in other words, they viewed heritage language as an essential part of students' identities and an essential tool for making meaning of the world and acquiring a new language. For many, such perspectives profoundly shaped their professional trajectories; elementary co-principal Mr. Pacheco, for example, was propelled away from a previous post, where administrators undervalued bilingualism and Spanish in particular, and toward Playa instead.

For other participants too, commitments to bilingualism and biliteracy were foundational to their understandings of high-quality teaching in general and for

Latinx youth especially. Ramón, for example, suggested that bilingual education builds students' confidence in their own abilities:

> [Students] see themselves as being successful in at least one classroom, and they know that their learning here [in Spanish] is gonna transfer over into their English classroom. They might not be there 100%, but they see that they can get there by having that language support. Even with my Spanish learners, a lot of them are very strong in English, and when they come here [to Spanish] they're not as confident, but they're able to realize that . . . how they are in English eventually is gonna transfer to what they do in Spanish. . . . That's definitely our goal.

And in this case, the shared "goal" was linguistic in the most concrete sense, but also life-applicable in conveying that we all have strengths and areas for growth and that the former are among our most essential tools for addressing the latter.

Others similarly characterized students' bilingualism as a powerful resource for learning and pointed to its benefits beyond school, as well. Fourth-grade math and science teacher Julie, for example, viewed students' developing bilingualism/biliteracy as a "head start" that would enable "success" out in the world:

> I think, this kid is struggling so much, what is gonna happen in 10 years? . . . [But] this kid has a head start because he knows two languages. . . . They're gonna be successful because they have a strong cultural background, this strong foundation of two languages . . . an advantage compared to so many people.

In taking these perspectives, Mr. Pacheco, Ramón, Julie, and other Playa staff actively challenged dominant discourses about minoritized cultures and languages, which often frame native Spanish-speaking and/or immigrant students as somehow "less than" their English-dominant peers, and languages other than English as barriers to language and literacy development and academic achievement (Garcia, 2005). By valuing bilingualism over monolingualism, and embracing a dual-immersion approach versus a transitional one (that expects students eventually to relinquish native or heritage language in order to develop English proficiency), Playa staff challenged the ways that schools are traditionally organized to assimilate students into mainstream cultural practices, including English-only linguistic practices.

Implicit in this commitment to bilingualism is also the (necessary) accompanying belief that all students have the capacity to become fully bilingual and biliterate—a markedly higher expectation for learning than tends to be held by monolingual schools, even the most celebrated, highest-achieving ones. This belief was evident in Playa's very structure, too, which ensured all students' exposure every day to academic content and literacy instruction in Spanish and English. Such a structure on its own stands as a marked departure from the logic of Proposition 227, which privileged English over all else and advocated that students learn the language *as* content before learning content through the language and vice versa. Thus, while we see only English in the vignette above, we can be sure that Kelsey and Antonio experienced affirming and challenging instruction in Spanish that same day.

Pillar III: State Standards as Surmountable

Building on statements about students' inherent capacities, cultural and linguistic assets, and "competitive" advantages vis-à-vis non-EBs, Playa teachers and administrators also expressed a belief in all students' capacities for deep and critical thought. As Rocio put it about her 1st-graders, "Even though they're 6 years old, they have opinions, they have a voice, and they have ideas," which she and others believed should be honored, encouraged, and centered in the learning process.

According to 4th-grade teacher Justin, for instance, engaging together around scholarly readings led Playa's teachers to recognize their students' natural inclinations toward creativity and criticality, as well as to recognize how schooling tended to teach such inclinations out of students rather than to help them flourish. Justin explained:

> Another thing that we incorporated . . . was not fearing our own thinking mind, so starting with doubts and questions is perfectly normal, and that as you start school as a 4- or 5-year-old that you are super inquisitive and you are super excited to learn and you are always asking questions and you are a critical thinker and then for some sad reason, the educational system kind of squashes that and says well, no, the most important thing is that you stay in your seat and that you listen. . . .

Justin's teammate, Paco, concurred and characterized Playa's embrace of deep and against-the-grain thinking among students as evidence of the school's atypical and accelerated interpretation of academic rigor. "Once we established that in the classroom," Paco explained, "there's been a higher level of respect and a higher level of rigor because [students] feel like what they're doing is some type of resistance to the structure that they're in." In this case, by "structure" Paco meant both the institutional structure of schooling and the tendency for teachers to engage in what multiple participants described as "institutionalizing" practices that ultimately socialized students into the status quo.

Although new national standards are arguably tools of, not against, the "institution" of schooling, Playa staff consistently connected their own high expectations for students to their adoption of the CCSS, in part because they saw the CCSS as consonant with the "Playa Way." For example, 4th-grade teachers shared that, with the advent of the CCSS, policy "finally" concurred that they were practicing as they should—"doing what we were supposed to do." Illustrating this perceived connection between embracing the CCSS and upholding high expectations, Justin, echoing other Playa staff, said:

> I talk to [non-Playa] teachers . . . and they talk about the Common Core like it's this evil beast in the hills and they don't know how to tame it, like . . . what

are we gonna do? . . . I was even in a conversation with a woman . . . and she's like, man, it's just so crazy; the kids aren't ready for it. . . . I was like, really? I think the kids are begging for something. I think the teachers are the ones that are resisting the change. They might be a little scared to have to change *their* routine.

Referring to the CCSS emphasis on academic language, for example, Ramón argued affirmatively, "We can't water the curriculum down . . . they have to know the language, we can't be afraid to teach them the academic language."

Consider, for example, the CCSS's prominent place in the vignette—especially the 1st-grade mathematics standards, which have been subject to debate in the public forum (e.g., Burris & Murphy, 2013), but less so at Playa. Rocio's instruction addresses most evidently Number and Operations in Base Ten Standard B.3: "Compare two two-digit numbers based on meanings of the tens and ones digits, recording the results of comparisons with the symbols >, =, and <." It also addresses various CCSS-emphasized grade-level "mathematical practices," including "make sense of problems and persevere in solving them; use appropriate tools strategically; attend to precision," and so on (Common Core State Standards Initiative, 2010b).

Consider, too, how Rocio's instruction reflects high expectations that are general—for example, that 1st-graders engage in ambitious, sustained, joint productive activity—and that are also content-specific, in ways that arguably go beyond grade-level standards: for example, that student pairs apply to number sentences their still-developing understandings about how to compare numbers using symbols;[1] that they do so without much guided practice beyond a few whole-group collaboratively solved problems; and that they draw from across visual representations, constructed using different mathematical tools (e.g., a number line or a hundreds chart) to determine the relationship between number sentences and the accuracy of their work.

In essence, Playa's administrators and teachers were inclined to view the CCSS as a clearable hurdle, rather than an intimidatingly high bar. If anything, teachers seemed to harbor skepticism in the government's capacity to adequately challenge students, EBs especially, which partly explains teachers' tendencies to ask more of their students than the CCSS did and to orient themselves toward standards one or more grade levels beyond the one they currently taught. Ultimately, almost every comment offered by participants framed Playa's relative embrace of and extension beyond the CCSS as rooted in broader beliefs about students' inherent capacities to learn and their right to rigorous academics.

Pillar IV: Labels as Gateways to Low Expectations

As suggested by this chapter's opening quote, a key way that Playa staff expressed high expectations for all was in their explicit objection to labeling students. This was especially evident in our discussions with them about students' language proficiencies, which typical schools serving "ELs"/EBs (e.g., Haskins & Huber, 2015) use to sort students and often to rationalize high-stakes decisions such as ability grouping, class placement, and grade promotion. Such practices have been shown to adversely affect "ELs"/EBs (among others), including by over-assigning them to remedial courses and special education (Artiles, Kozleski, Trent, Osher, & Ortiz, 2010; Callahan, 2005; Gándara, Rumberger, Maxwell-Jolly, & Callahan, 2003; Samson & Lesaux, 2009).

Although Playa staff adhered to state laws stipulating the specific assessments that schools must administer to nonnative English speakers, they rejected outright using assessment results to label or rank students or to drive high-stakes decisions. Teachers often situated this rejection in broader beliefs about language as a holistic system—for example, that human experience necessarily involves deepening language learning over a lifetime and within and across various contexts.

Elaborating on this premise, Justin framed the learning of multiple languages as a unified process rather than multiple, distinct processes (Garcia & Wei, 2014):

> I'm learning Spanish still. I'm still learning English, you know. I don't like that whole idea English language learner. . . . I'm still an English language learner. It's my native language but I'm still learning English. You know there's words I learn every day and errors that I realize I've been making for 34 years and I'm like, oh wow, I need to fix that.

Teachers lamented other forms of ranking and labeling too, including those derived from district- or state-mandated ELA and mathematics assessments. Rocio, for example, believed that thinking about students in terms of their numerical scores risked obscuring their full dimensionality as learners: "Instead of saying, 'Oh, he's a 2, or he's a 1, or he's a 4 . . . .' But who are they? What do they like? . . . What is it that they are shy about or they are scared about?"

Articulating these concerns, Rocio captured the Playa-wide regard for students as whole people. She also acknowledged how current accountability demands and logics seemed to press teachers, even at a "high-performing" school like Playa, toward narrower ways of knowing, identifying, and classifying students, and away from knowing them more authentically and working to adapt instruction in nuanced, responsive ways.

That regard for students as whole people explains, in part, Rocio's multifaceted rationale for pairing Kelsey and Antonio:

> Kelsey . . . [is] very vocal, she's always trying to participate, and . . . she has her own mindset, and it sometimes is very difficult to change . . . not to change, but to think in a different way because she's so stuck onto her own way that she doesn't want to try anything else. And Antonio . . . he's a very [high-achieving] student, but . . . sometimes he needs more vocabulary to express his thinking. . . . I know that they will be learning a lot from one another, because Kelsey has a lot of vocabulary, and Antonio has a lot of intellect.

It is worth noting the asset-orientation woven almost invisibly throughout Rocio's comments. What she described as "very vocal" with a "mindset" often "difficult to change," others might describe differently—think: "handful" or "challenge" or "stubborn." Kelsey ambled, wriggled, and called out, often simultaneously, throughout the day. In fact, during the slice of classroom life captured in the vignette, Kelsey was talking, gesturing, and rocking her weight back and forth the entire time; of course, she was also engaged, on-task, and persistent, collaborating with Antonio for an uninterrupted 20-minute stretch—a testament to Rocio's stance and the related decisions she made to enable their partnership to unfold as it did.

Somewhat ironically, teachers' rejection of labeling also came through in comments about all Playa students' "giftedness." Many teachers proudly mentioned having become GATE—Gifted and Talented Education—certified through participation in required, on-site professional development sessions commissioned by Dr. Ruiz. Sonya, for example, shared that Playa maintained a relatively unified perspective on students' academic abilities and on correspondingly ambitious forms of instruction: "Our philosophy here . . . is that all students are gifted and talented. So all the activities that we do are for GATE students. . . . " Importantly, then, collective GATE certification served as one tool that teachers called upon to hold their students and themselves to high standards.

As a result of all this, although they might be labeled by those beyond the school (e.g., in media reports or state documents), Playa's students did not appear to suffer from the stigmatization that often accompanies labels (Cummings & Lau, 2003), or from the compounding effects that stigmatization can impose on students who identify with multiple historically marginalized groups (Artiles, 2013).

Promoting Capability Without Pedestals or Copious Praise

At Playa, the four pillars propping up teachers' anti-deficit stance cultivated feelings of safety and buoyancy among students, as well as opportunities for them to experience school as a humanizing space—a notable contrast to the denigrating treatment that they might experience in other schools (e.g., Daniel & Pacheco, 2015; Fine, 2002; Gándara et al., 2003). Certainly, this is part of what accounted for Kelsey spontaneously and sweetly complimenting Antonio—"you did it good, real good . . . "—when no adults were looking. Children at Playa seemed to see themselves and one another as capable and deserving at least in part because that was how adults so evidently saw them.

Together, these pillars contributed to an atmosphere that inspired confidence in students without putting any on pedestals in general or vis-à-vis one another, and also without requiring copious praise or cajoling of students insofar as their participation and academic performance was concerned.

"RAISE THE BAR" AS RIGHTEOUS AND RESPECTFUL

Playa's "high expectations for all" ethos intersected with CCSS implementation in consequential ways. Some have already been suggested; for example, the idea that externally derived standards should be read as a floor and not a ceiling for student learning primed teachers to take up and go beyond what the CCSS called for. In fact, that very idea of "going beyond" resonates powerfully with the central rhetoric of the CCSS—namely its emphasis on "raising the bar." Together, the "Playa Way" and the press to implement the CCSS colluded to advance a ramped-up definition of rigor that ultimately framed students' academic struggles as evidence of educators' anti-deficit thinking, and students' perseverance in the face of those struggles as evidence of, even a precondition for, learning. In the sections below, we explain how teachers ended up viewing the CCSS as fundamentally compatible with their own deeply held collective beliefs about teaching, learning, and equity for EBs.

Constructing Critical Compatibility Between Critical Education and the CCSS

In keeping with their anti-deficit perspectives, Playa's teachers emphasized the importance of social interaction, including student-to-student dialogue, around content. This isn't surprising, given their preparation for and professional expertise around teaching minoritized youth, and Latinx EBs especially. What is notable is that so many of them connected this emphasis back to the theorist Paulo Freire, and in particular to excerpts of *Pedagogy of the Oppressed*, which they had read together a few summers prior.

New to the school and profession at the time, 4th-grade teacher Justin recalled the intensity of those readings and "really deep conversations about how you shift this student–teacher relationship to where we are eliminating banking." It was from those conversations that a kind of "no banking" mantra took hold, to the point that we heard it every time we visited.

Because of such conversations, teachers reported experiencing, since joining Playa's staff, significant shifts in their thinking that deepened their anti-deficit orientations. For Rocio, "growing up . . . I was blinded by the idea that the teacher was always right, that adults were always right, and that that was the only way to see the world." After a few years at Playa, however, she had come to recognize even young students—like Kelsey and Antonio—as deep thinkers and powerful knowers.

Middle school teacher Miriam talked similarly about Freire's writing, particularly her understandings about no student being "an empty vessel" and teaching necessarily involving more than "pouring information in." Together, these statements summed up the espoused and enacted stance toward Playa's students: that all were brimming with knowledge, ideas, and resources for life and learning.

Somewhat surprisingly, teachers' desire to avoid "banking" and to enact the kind of dialogue-rich, humanizing, and anti-oppressive education that they associated with Freire also drove them into a deep embrace of the CCSS. On its surface, this might strike a reader as odd; indeed, it took us off guard the first few times we heard some teachers discussing what to them seemed like inherent compatibility between Freire's teachings and the Common Core. This sense of compatibility was especially evident during an exchange when the 4th-grade teachers enthusiastically described to us a presentation they had delivered at a recent regional conference. In their presentation, they linked the CCSS—especially the CCSS emphasis on academic talk and argumentation—with core ideas drawn from their own reading of

Freire—namely, dialogue, reflection, and what they called "pushing people's thinking." The ease and excitement with which the teachers mentioned these linkages admittedly took us aback, even though they offered insight into some of what we were already witnessing in classrooms.

So taken for granted was the perceived synergy between the CCSS and certain constructs drawn from critical pedagogy that some teachers were thrown off just by being asked to elaborate about them. The 4th-grade team, for example, admitted that synergy seemed, as Justin put it, "second nature for us," because of how the content had been presented "with those pillars in place." As it turned out, administrators—and in particular Dr. Ruiz, the much-loved and dynamic figurehead of the Playa *familia*—had introduced the CCSS in tandem with excerpts from Freire, focusing on the latter via a CCSS-inspired close reading process, while framing the former as secondary and essentially in sync with anti-banking education.

This account offers insight into how school conditions—administrative influence, especially—shaped teachers' understandings such that teachers came to see only compatibility, opportunity, and cause for optimism where others might see conflict, contradiction, and/or cause for concern. Ironically, the resulting perceived compatibility did not, in and of itself, reflect a critical pedagogical approach, which would have entailed teachers asking questions—such as: Who wrote the CCSS, why, and for whom? Whose voices and interests do these standards privilege and serve, and how? Who stands to benefit most? What conflicts might they represent and raise for educators of EBs, specifically?—and digging beneath the surface to unearth marginalized perspectives and alternative analyses.

Questions like those might have prompted Playa's teachers to consider, for example, the National Association for Bilingual Education's public opposition to the CCSS as late as 2012, before it cautiously committed itself as a resource in efforts to ensure teachers use the standards "in a manner that does not negatively impact the educational needs of ELLs" (National Association for Bilingual Education, 2013).

Lest the reader come away with the impression that these teachers were simplistic in their thinking or lax in their analysis, we want to underscore several points. First, there *are* potential areas of compatibility between, say, a dialogue-focused approach to instruction, and the CCSS's emphasis on student talk within its Speaking and Listening Standards.

Second, the examples offered above and below illustrate that Playa teachers, early in the study and the nationwide adoption of CCSS, had already worked hard together to develop familiarity with those standards. This was evident in the ease with which they spoke about them and drew on-the-fly connections between them and concepts from their close reading of Freire. For example, when asked, "How would you help somebody . . . see the way that you're bringing those two things [the CCSS and Freire] together in your minds and in your practice?" responses from Justin, Paco and Julie demonstrated that they spoke frequently to one another about the CCSS and had a sense not only of what the standards said (e.g., "all of this key vocabulary . . . like *justify, clarify, be able to critically analyze* . . . "), but what they did not say ("the dialogical component . . . and the mindset . . . not explicitly").

Third, it mattered very much to teachers that they experienced Playa's professional discourse as being, as Paco put it, "80% Freire . . . and then we have these new standards." Because of that breakdown, teachers felt more assured that, "we're not using standards to guide our instruction; we're using pedagogy to guide our instruction." This was a point of pride and professionalism; it was also part and parcel of their identity—namely, that they, as Playa-employed practitioners, got out in front of policy mandates so they could conduct themselves with professionalism and integrity on their own terms, rather than trying to comply or catch up.

Shifting the Onus and Holstering Help

In light of their overarching anti-banking aims, teachers across the grades sought to tip the balance of interaction and intellectual heavy lifting toward students and away from themselves. In particular, they strove to create classroom cultures, to use Justin's words, "where the kids are doing the learning and the kids are talking." It followed that dialogue—which teachers typically interpreted as time for learners like Kelsey and Antonio to converse with one another in semistructured ways aimed at "pushing their thinking"—became central to enacting the CCSS and making it "their own."

For teachers, dialogue represented a theoretically grounded, policy responsive, and locally sanctioned means by which to increase students' access to content, activate their assets for learning, and transcend dichotomies and distinctions that curtail deep learning. Indeed, just as Freire (1970) argued that in "true dialogue" there are "no utter ignoramuses nor perfect sages," only people "attempting, together, to learn more than they now know," Justin described dialogue as a space within which "you can have a kid that might be a striving student or a struggling student talking and calling out and pushing and changing the thinking of your 'top' student, and where they feel comfortable doing that. . . ." In this sense, dialogue was, to many at Playa, a means by which to make instruction more authentic and more CCSS-aligned, and engagement with one another more critical and more rigorous.

Teachers' efforts to shift the teacher–student talk ratio took varied forms, not all of which were successful in their eyes. Justin wisecracked about still needing to talk less himself and "give [students] some more time; they need to talk!" In Justin's classroom, like Rocio's and those of other teachers, opportunities for students to converse in whole and small-group settings were copious. Students often had ample time and space to share with one another their ideas and, thus, to produce and receive the kind of contextualized and accessible language that is widely recognized as essential to EBs' learning (Walqui, 2006).

More often than not, this dialogue orbited around topics of substance. Capturing schoolwide sentiment and anecdotes, Justin explained how "irksome" he and other Playa teachers found simplistic grade-based assessments of "intellectual ability and what you can get kids to do as a teacher . . . like, oh my gosh, you're having kids talk about that stuff?" Playa's teachers' decisions about curriculum and instruction proudly defied such assumptions. In fact, administrators expected teachers to cultivate students' engagement in part by planning units that reflected teachers' passions, and enthusiasm for which they could then convey to students. This helps explain why and how, for example, some teachers' concerns about the impact of environmental degradation on indigenous communities' ways of life came to inform unit topics as early as 1st grade.

Across classrooms, teachers also worked hard to holster providing "too much" direct assistance. There were, quite literally, countless examples of teachers redirecting students to resources when they stumbled or were stumped, as reflected in just a few minutes of instruction in middle school teacher Lynette's classroom. Noticing a student's mostly superficial character analysis of Piggy from *Lord of the Flies*, Lynette commented, before moving right along: "You're going in a different direction than I'd imagined. It's obvious he has glasses and is overweight—you're thinking at the surface . . . you need to be more analytical." When a student asked about the word *hoodlums*, Lynette simply quipped, "Maybe it's in Urban Dictionary?" The insinuation was clear: There are tools you can use to answer such questions yourselves, and so you should.

There were also examples of teachers, like Miriam, providing opportunities for students to direct and demonstrate their own learning. The terms of engagement required that students take the initiative to negotiate with her about things such as "What did you plan to do?" And there are examples of teachers, like Justin, imploring students to challenge teachers directly if the authentic purpose for learning was unclear: "If you guys ever, ever are thinking why are we doing this, why is this important, you better voice your opinion . . . you better start asking those questions. . . ."

Being "little" hardly seemed to factor. As the opening vignette shows, even teachers of young children expected them to do quite a bit on their own. Anything else, the thinking went, was an insult to their already-impressive intellects. In practice, this meant that much of what gets proposed as developmentally appropriate practice in the early elementary grades especially—singing, dramatic play, daily picture book read-alouds, and so on—did not feature prominently in 1st-grade classroom observations.

This was arguably a shortcoming of early childhood education at Playa. Yet it would also be wrong to disregard outright the teachers' concerns about infantilization as a form of "institutionalizing" EBs; schooling in the United States has a long history of empowering the state and its agents—teachers, too—paternalistically, while positioning non-White and working-class students as "wards" and "dependents," incapable of properly developing on their own or in the care of their families and communities (Spring, 2007).

Figuring It Out, and Failing

Nevertheless, the teachers at Playa admitted that teaching dialogically wasn't easy, despite their affinity for it and their sense that it was fundamentally CCSS-compatible. They were certainly not alone, as many have written about the inherent difficulties of "teaching against the grain" (Cochran-Smith, 1991), and in this policy climate especially (Au, 2007; Picower, 2011). Central to Playa teachers' "struggle,"

Ramón explained, was that "we can't bank . . . you can't impose your thinking on the students, so sometimes it is hard to find that balance" between offering students opportunities for intellectual heavy lifting and providing them with necessary support. Indeed, we found that it *was* hard for Playa teachers to strike "that balance" in practice, and that the balance they struck did not always strike them, and more often us, as particularly productive.

Playa's teachers tended toward opportunity for students to engage in dialogue and away from explicit instruction, modeling, and more tailored forms of support. This was often rooted in their fear of "giving them the answer" (Lynette) or "showing them how to do it" (Ana), and thereby over-scaffolding or "hyper-mediating" learning (Gutiérrez & Stone, 2002). It also reflected explicit counsel that teachers received from administrators who cautioned against modeling "too much" and relying on what they deemed "overused" instructional aids, including Venn diagrams.

These tendencies, which, as we show in subsequent chapters, generated considerable struggle on the students' part, were often connected, tacitly or explicitly, to an assumption—championed by some CCSS authors and proponents (Coleman & Pimentel, 2012)—that the most meaningful learning occurs when students are posed with challenging texts and tasks and left to "figure things out" on their own. Even if that leads to "failure," their logic goes, that failure can be productive of learning, and thus "productive failure" (Fisher, Frey, & Lapp, 2012; Kapur, 2008).

The press to let kids "figure it out"—and become more accustomed to failing "productively"—reappeared with frequency across Playa classrooms, implicitly in how teachers organized instruction and explicitly as the language Rocio uses in the chapter's opening vignette attests: "You and your partner are going to *figure this out. . . .*"

In 4th grade, for example, teachers spent the beginning of the year working with students to establish "what a critical thinker was" and explain why it might feel counterintuitive to think critically and feel comfortable to "be banked." Describing what this involved, Justin recounted watching video clips of psychologist Sugata Mitra's work with students in India:

> We watched the Sugata Mitra video at the beginning of the year and we took a couple of his catch phrases that they would use like, "What, you think I know everything?" "You're gonna come ask the teacher?" And so they [the students] would call one another out, like, "Don't ask the teacher." Like, "What, you can't think for yourself? You can't figure it out? C'mon man!" . . . So little things like that . . . funny little catch phrases for them to remind them of this deeper idea or this bigger idea that you have to be critically thinking for yourself.

For Justin, Mitra's example had become foundational to his ongoing attempts to strike the right "balance"—using the same wording as Ramón and others—between avoiding institutionalized didacticism and dependency on the one hand, and offering students adequate support on the other. As Justin explained, this was a problematic that teachers negotiated more than a problem they solved:

I question myself every day on that because kids will . . . you know, things will come up and it's like, do you think I know everything? Figure it out . . . and walk away. And that is a pedagogical practice . . . to sit with it and resist [the impulse to bank] . . . to find that balance.

In weighing that balance, occasions when students accomplished unexpected things seemed to take on a special power. These occasions in particular stoked teachers' concerns about their own institutionalized tendencies (e.g., sliding into low expectations), and they emboldened teachers to keep the level of challenge elevated and not interfere too much. The teachers' aim was in part to interrupt their own impulse to do what they felt effectively amounted to rescuing students from real instructional rigor and its central reward: learning.

To be clear, on its own, the move to create space for students to struggle in the service of learning is neither necessarily productive nor unproductive; its outcomes are contingent on the specifics of learners and contexts. Certainly at Playa, doing so contributed to some undeniably impressive interactions, but it also induced excessive struggle for some students—a trend we describe below and in subsequent chapters.

Seduced by Struggle

The interaction between Playa's ethos of unrelenting "high expectations for all"— as Mr. Pacheco put it, that teachers should ask of students, "always something else, something more"—and the CCSS's press to "raise the bar" led teachers to spend much of their time trying to avoid "watered down" curriculum (Sonya, Ramón) and "too simple" instruction (Rocio, Ana), and to design instead learning experiences that honored what they sensed students were capable of. Ana matter-of-factly described 1st-graders' experiences with complex texts like this:

> They might not understand it; they might understand 0, 20, 50, 80% of it, but we want them to first struggle a little bit. And after they've seen it once, then we'll process it together, so that they can eventually, if not understand it 100%, understand it 50%.

In the early grades, especially, teachers' efforts to induce struggle included looking to standards further up the gradespan and using texts that exceeded what even the CCSS "text complexity staircase" might prescribe.

The results of this were lessons often "targeting different concepts at the same time," moving students forward "very quickly," and leaving "many students . . . confused." In fact, "confused" was precisely how Rocio described much of her class after she "jumped" from using symbols with small single-digit numbers to comparing number sentences.

Her description was apt. Interactions like the one between Kelsey and Antonio weren't the only kind we saw with regularity. In fact, they weren't even the majority in the classroom that day. There were other pairs—roughly two for every one Kelsey and Antonio—for whom that exact same instructional stretch was far less productive, and a few for whom it seemed downright confounding. These pairs looked to one another and around the room, quietly conferred and wrote marks on paper, and engaged on the whole in a mix of sincere investment and pseudo-participation that gave off the appearance of close, meaningful work. Not surprisingly, then, two-thirds of students' work ended up incomplete or erroneous, despite the considerable time allotted to it. Observed exchanges indicated, too, that at least some students had only a fledgling grasp of how to use the focal symbols, never mind in relation to number sentences.

While acknowledged by Rocio in this instance as concerning, Playa staff often viewed fairly widespread confusion as a natural part of the learning process. To be sure, we saw teachers and students alike inspired by a sense of confidence in students' abilities; we also saw significant evidence of students struggling to figure things out, often in ways that extended beyond what even teachers thought productive. From our vantage point, this was not unproblematic, and it also was not surprising given the compounding impact of teachers working all at once to shift the onus of learning away from themselves, to grant students more opportunities to "figure it out" on their own, and to ramp up the level of instructional challenge. What was surprising, however, was that teachers mostly continued to pitch instruction toward the upper end of student performance and to gloss over students' struggles, so long as some students, like Kelsey and Antonio, gave credence to the notion that all could persevere to success.

To be fair, that students out of respect for teachers and the learning process persevered—or pseudo-participated—without much mutiny is partly what obscured for teachers connections they might have otherwise made between seemingly disparate data points: a slight uptick in tears and boundary-testing, droopiness and lethargy, undisruptive but still off-task behavior, repeated questions about snack or recess, and so on. Considering these data points altogether likely would have led teachers to more easily identify how some "resonant" emphases and "compatible" approaches they were importing from the CCSS appeared to not be meeting students' needs.

Instead, teachers' rationalizing of students' struggles as benign or even beneficial seemed to echo popular ideas about the importance of cultivating *grit*—perseverance, passion, and self-control—in students from outside the dominant group especially (Duckworth, 2013; Tough, 2012).

This idea of needing to cultivate grit among children who are likely to face obstacles in a system not built around their needs holds appeal for many, and it meshes well with the CCSS's college-ready, competitive-in-the-global-arena, rigor-for-all rhetoric. Yet the concept of *grittiness* also springs from questionable theoretical roots (e.g., Galton, 1869) and runs the risk in practice of placing an unduly heavy burden on young people (Anderson, 2014; Kohn, 2014).

Ultimately, the emphasis—in rhetoric and real time—on a mainstream and ramped-up definition of *rigor* and a related notion of *grittiness* seemed to place even these anti-deficit-oriented teachers at risk of explaining some students' "failure to perform" or persevere (i.e., their failure to "grit-it-out") as an indicator of weakness in character or will, rather than a pedagogical problem to solve. Though rare, a few particular moments stood out to us precisely because they so contradicted our triangulated sense of teachers' core commitments, as was the case when a loving 4th-grade teacher explained as "laziness" and a lack of "care" one student's disengagement from independently annotating an informational text far above his reading level.

LEARNING, MEDIATED AND MIRRORED

Many of these dynamics that defined students' learning experiences mediated teachers' experiences, too. Like students, teachers worked diligently and usually together, often for long stretches of time, and on tasks that induced significant struggle. That they did so was something about which they and their administrators felt a measure of pride. As Paco commented, glowingly, "They've always really pushed us." And as one administrator readily confessed, "We ask a lot; being a teacher here is no joke." Even just the simple practice of moving teachers from grade to grade every few years conferred on them substantial challenges.

In response to administrators' expectations, teachers generally went above and beyond, both dutifully and joyfully, motivated by deep love, respect, and trust for their colleagues. Little frustrations—like being sent on a release-day scavenger hunt without directions as an experiential exercise in the kind of "figuring it out for ourselves" that the school so prized, or "being told 2 weeks before you head on vacation, when you come back, you're teaching an extra period of language arts"—were taken in quiet stride. So, too, were larger fissures, such as leadership structures and approaches that seemed at times more hierarchical than dialogic. At one memorable instructional leadership team meeting, for example, the principal gave a passionate, somewhat chastising speech and then called for a fishbowl discussion with the purpose of checking for understanding; members engaged, seemingly upbeat, in discussion even though there only seemed one acceptable way of responding.

To be sure, no one at Playa would disagree that administrators wanted teachers —just as teachers wanted students—to find their passions and exercise their authentic voices, rather than just silently comply. In practice, however, this proved hard to actualize, in part because of teachers' respect for administrators' wisdom and sense of urgency, but also because of administrators' directness and definitiveness.

Playa's leaders tended to attribute bouts of silence on teachers' part to misunderstanding or to what one called "the pedagogy of silence: 'Let me just hear what's going on to really justify that my thinking is okay because I still have this fear of the institution telling me that I'm wrong.'" And teachers did admit sometimes feeling confused about decisions and requests, or nervous about being wrong. But they also admitted feeling disinclined to question or challenge out of faith that administrators had "good reasons," and/or out of fear of falling out of favor. In many ways, this dynamic seemed true for students, too, whose love and respect for teachers was palpable, as was their joy in being loved and respected by them. Thus, while remarkably open exchange was a Playa hallmark, it tended not to flow up as much as it did down or across.

A source of frustration for leaders, it seemed somewhat unsurprising to us that teachers might feel that it was high stakes to voice things that could be perceived as opposition or error, especially in the presence of leaders who routinely offered up, at least rhetorically, resignation. Mr. Pacheco, for example, drew on his own experience to make that very point: "If you don't really feel 100% . . . then you don't belong here. It's just like me. I didn't belong at that [prior] school because I didn't believe in the school. . . . I had to leave."

During our time interviewing and observing, the core tasks that produced struggles for teachers involved figuring out on their own how to bring the CCSS together with their established beliefs, their specialized expertise, and the new concepts administrators pressed them to consider. It was demanding, creative work to which they brought, much like their students, significant personal resources and perseverance.

Teachers described their collaborations, invariably, as "productive." And observations suggest that in so many ways they were. At the same time, teachers would have arguably benefitted from a discourse of professionalism that privileged struggle less and support more. Notably, the CCSS—versus California's prior standards—did treat teachers more professionally, holding high expectations for them in terms of having to translate fewer, more ambitious, and more abstract standards into robust, standards-aligned instruction. But they also contradicted some of Playa's teachers' professional expertise about equity-minded instruction for EBs and did so in a language framework (i.e., monolingual English) that invisibilized teachers' identities as bilingual educators and framed as an afterthought their EBs' needs (i.e., by addressing them cursorily and only in one of the CCSS's three appendices, rather than in the body of the document) (Common Core State Standards Initiative, 2010a).

In light of this, it can be argued that the high expectations set for teachers by the CCSS were especially high for teachers like Playa's on whom the CCSS conferred additional labor—labor involved in reconciling contradictions between universalistic policy and specialized expertise, and in working together to determine where and how English language standards should apply across disciplines and in Spanish. This is labor that most people probably don't even consider when they think about what it means for teachers to "implement" the CCSS. Although we would argue that it is unethical to construct policies that confer inequitable labor on teachers, it is nevertheless commendable that Playa's teachers took on that labor without complaint.

In this sense, the struggles teachers experienced in engaging in this labor both mirrored and fueled the normalization, discursive and otherwise, of students' struggles. In effect, teachers' struggles set a tone that permeated Playa's notions of work ethic and perseverance, and that tone was part of what permitted community members to expect so much of one another.

Teachers' struggles also commandeered a lot of their own time, both alone and together. As a result, teachers often ended up "figuring things out" mostly on an instrumental level—such as selecting challenging texts according to parameters set by the CCSS and administrators, or determining what prompts a graphic organizer should include. But they often didn't get to more critical conversations they reported hoping to have. For example, although our conversations with teachers frequently included comments about their CCSS-related concerns, such comments rarely seemed to surface in teachers' conversations with one another or factor in their instructional practice.

For example, although Rocio shared that Playa's focused efforts to "make our students be very critical and to expose them to complex texts" left her concerned about students' lack of exposure to art and music and "other ways to learn, or to support that literacy component," those "other ways" were never broached in meetings we attended, and they ended up running a distant second to traditional academics. The tendency to leave such issues unaddressed prompted Rocio herself to confess, "Sometimes I have to admit we don't reflect as much as teachers as we expect our 1st-graders to." This reality was less about teachers' desires and more about the many demands on their time and the limitations of not-so-dialogic leadership dynamics.

What unfolded in practice—at some points more than others, and for some teachers and teams more than others—indicated that teachers, like students, would have benefitted from more tailored support. Such scaffolding could have supported teachers to use their time more effectively, to ward off the exhaustion they experienced, and to identify instructional missteps and improvements, which they sometimes recognized only after the fact or not at all. Thus, the "figure it out" mantra and corollary faith in "productive" struggle, even failure, mediated teachers' experiences as it did students' experiences; indeed, the former seemed to legitimize and laminate the righteousness of the latter.

Of course, it is natural to hear sometimes, even from hardworking, accomplished teachers, "We thought it was gonna be excellent, and honestly it wasn't." It is also natural—at least for us, as teacher educators—for teachers to wrestle through bouts of working "harder and not smarter" (a phrase we don't particularly like, but fits colloquially).

It is something else, however, to observe dedicated educators laboring in ways that seem unsustainable over the long haul and that also are not yielding equity-oriented outcomes proportional to their exertions. Teachers' inspired engagement around policy and practice was a labor of love, but it was also a burden beyond what was needed to be "productive."

SUSCEPTIBILITY, DESPITE STANCE

Ultimately, these dynamics left teachers susceptible, first and foremost, to a rhetoric of righteous exhaustion that imbued discomfort—given consensus at Playa around "never to be comfortable" (Lynette)—with a kind of implicit moral character. At least some of teachers' pride in being at Playa was tethered to their sense that at least some of the school's transformation and success, according to its own narration, involved removing from the "bus" those who ought not be on it—the implication being that their stance and commitments, even their moral character, might not be adequately firm.

Second, these dynamics left teachers susceptible to deference, rather than dialogue, when it came to matters of instructional policy and the burdens that policy implementation placed on them and their students. Early adoption of the CCSS was never really a decision teachers made for themselves. Yet, it also wasn't a decision that teachers saw as problematic or deemed as conflicting with what they were already doing. This was at least partly because of the way their respected administrators presented the CCSS to them.

In addition, in keeping with Playa's prevailing stance toward policy, the CCSS were treated not as something being done to them, but as something they were taking up early and with agency; they weren't waiting to be subjected to the CCSS or considering resistance as a possible path. So it is not altogether surprising that teachers, when asked about the CCSS, tended to respond pragmatically and without evident philosophical or pedagogical concern. For them, CCSS implementation was an assumed wise decision. The uptake of it was part of what it meant to be an anti-deficit teacher and advocate of EBs. As Miriam put it,

> With Common Core, you're . . . knowing that it's for the betterment of the students. . . . That's always a better road [than to resist]. . . . That's always the philosophy. You're not expected to do everything. . . . The expectation is, you see it, and you adapt it. . . . Dr. Ruiz always talks about it. . . . "You make it your own. . . . "

Yet teachers' ready acceptance of the CCSS seemed to contradict Playa's espoused commitment to dialogue and distributed leadership. Though Dr. Ruiz claimed that he wanted teachers to "question" the CCSS and "make it your own," teachers were supported to do so only in narrow ways, not to interrogate the standards themselves or the broader initiative of which they were a part. One need only hear Justin's earnest questioning of us—for example, "I've been wanting to ask you . . . since you guys have your finger on the pulse more nationwide. . . . We know what's happening at Playa and at our district maybe, but what is the overall consensus? . . . Are people up in arms . . . ? Are people supportive of it? Or is it 50/50?"—to realize that underneath that acceptance some were uninformed, but not disinterested.

Third, and relatedly, teachers were susceptible to acquiescence and even si-lence, especially around matters of policy. Those who came to Playa after the school's ascendancy were somewhat wowed and cowed by the mythologies wrapped around the school's leaders, and thus, especially unlikely to question them or the discourses they advanced. Meanwhile, the more experienced teach-ers who witnessed the school's ascendency firsthand tended to have an admiring but more grounded sense of the administrators. Having lived with school leaders' idiosyncrasies for quite some time, they reported and demonstrated more com-fort pushing back and asserting themselves, though that seemed rarely necessary to them. More often, their responses were akin to Lynette's, reflecting trust in and responsiveness to administrative demands: "When one of the administrators comes to me and they say, 'I need this,' or 'I want you to do it like this,' it'll be done that next day."

Finally, and in part as a result of all this, teachers were susceptible to framing —or accepting others' framing—as fair an accountability system not organized in their interests or in those of their EB students. More than a few, for example, ex-pressed faith in the well-trafficked assertion (repeated by administrators) that "if you're doing things correctly, then it's gonna work out," even though the implica-tion is then that if and when things don't "work out" (e.g., students don't score well, or schools receive punishments for low performance), those outcomes are earned on account of "doing things" (i.e., teaching) incorrectly, rather than attributable to myriad other potential factors.

This meant that teachers sometimes, given pressures around raising achieve-ment at Playa, treated the lexicon and tools of the accountability system—such as "numerical scores" (as Rocio put it), Lexiles, and "low-performing" and "high-performing" labels—as more legitimate than they actually believed them to be. In this legitimation, they were pressed along by district and school leaders' drive to attain even more distinguished status in the accountability system, because "[those] schools are the ones that really get a lot of focus . . . and recognition" in terms of spotlighting and spreading what is "transformative and innovative"— arguably a problematic "carrot" to legitimate accountability systems, given what's known about its reliance on (English-only) measures deemed questionable for gauging EBs' learning, particularly within dual-language programming.

It also meant that even though Playa's teachers often came from families of educators and held teaching in the highest regard, they sometimes judged peers in the profession quite harshly in alignment with popular narratives. At times, this manifested in discounting other teachers' alternative perspectives on the CCSS as knee-jerk "negativity" and "resistance," or asserting without any direct knowledge that teachers' unions "get in the way" of good work, or attributing to "other teachers" a kind of recalcitrant "mindset" because "teachers as a group tend to not like change," or suggesting that principals should be able to get rid of "someone that is rocking the boat and isn't on board with the company's mission or a school's mission."

Of course, some of Playa's teachers had spent significant time working in other schools, so they spoke from their own experience. But what was striking was how these comments emerged more often in conversations with newer teachers who admitted having limited personal experience on which to draw and recognized at times how corporate logic had seeped unknowingly into their lexicon (e.g., reference to "the company's mission").

The compounded effect of all the above was that teachers were susceptible to a cheerily all-in approach to policy engagement. That said, none of it is meant to paint teachers as naive, or administrators as Machiavellian; doing so would violate profoundly our sense of who these educators are and how they approach their work. Taking up the CCSS less-than-critically does not make teachers fickle, simple, or "cultural dopes," to use the famed language of sociologist Harold Garfinkel (1967); it merely makes them human, especially in hard times for equity-oriented educators. We draw on discourse and positionality as constructs throughout this book precisely because of their complexity and purchase in moving beyond simplistic or essentialist claims about individual people.

Our hope with this chapter is to show how the high expectations and efforts of Playa's staff to prove their students' abilities and their school's deservingness often seemed to map almost seamlessly onto the CCSS's call to elevate instructional rigor and academic output in particular ways. In other words, Playa's particular anti-deficit stance offered a rather hospitable environment for the CCSS, enabling the standards to be taken up with ease once they entered Playa's activity system as a mediating artifact. Through this process, teachers began to appropriate the discourse of the CCSS (e.g., "raising the bar") to describe their own goals and values, eventually viewing them and the goals and values advanced by the CCSS as one and the same.

In this sense, reflecting dialecticism among elements of any activity system, the CCSS reshaped in certain ways Playa's anti-deficit stance, and it, too, reshaped the CCSS. In particular, teachers tended to privilege aspects of the CCSS that they felt resonated most with their established ideas about teaching EBs (e.g., engaging students in dialogue). This, in turn, furthered teachers' sense that the standards resonated with what they identified as essential to effective anti-deficit teaching. That resonance eased teachers' transition from prior state standards to new national ones, and made CCSS adoption less contentious at Playa than accounts suggest it has been elsewhere (e.g., Fink, 2014). However, it also made it challenging for administrators and teachers to view the CCSS critically, even when CCSS compliance—as we show in subsequent chapters—appeared to put some students' learning at risk.

CHAPTER 5

"Raising the Bar" and Responsive Teaching, in Tension

This chapter delves into the consequences in practice of Playa's teachers holding such elevated expectations while also laboring under the press to enact the Common Core State Standards (CCSS) and generate indicators of excellence via state-sanctioned measures. It begins by sketching key aspects of teachers' pedagogical coherence—or shared approaches to equity-minded teaching—that Playa's staff marshaled as they worked to enact the CCSS. These approaches build on the norms that we described in the prior chapter as so foundational to what we came to call the "Playa Way." In particular, this chapter explores—through descriptions and analyses of teachers' literacy instructional practice—the tensions that arose at the intersection of teachers' efforts to "raise the bar" on the one hand, and teachers' stated commitments to equity pedagogy on the other. In doing so, the chapter addresses some of the challenges and risks these tensions pose, even for teachers who hold anti-deficit, asset-based views of Latinx emergent bilingual (EB) students.

AGREED-UPON APPROACHES

Working at a "high-performing" charter school with a particular philosophical orientation, Playa's teachers experienced both the freedom and the pressure that came with planning standards-aligned instruction from scratch as opposed to drawing from prepackaged programs. Not surprisingly, given the significant coherence in Playa staff's ideological leanings, several pedagogical approaches emerged with relative consistency across their collective and individual efforts to act on their anti-deficit stances and actualize Playa's particular brand of high expectations. These included scaffolding in accordance with research-based pedagogies associated with language acquisition; planning thematically; contextualizing skill instruction; and striving to "teach beyond" the standards, in the name of both "rigor " and "authenticity."

Scaffolding, Rather than Sink-or-Swim

One of the ways that teachers expressed and acted on their high expectations was in their commitment to scaffolding students' developing multilingualism, rather than leaving students to "sink-or-swim." According to Ramón,

> You can't expect [kids] to just figure something out immediately . . . you have to support them, especially having language learners. . . . I can't just expect them to understand something I write on a chart. I have to give them visuals, I have to give them explanations, I have to use TPR [Total Physical Response]. I just have to use different strategies to have them access whatever I'm trying to say.

Others similarly emphasized the importance of scaffolding and named various methods for doing so, such as "gradually releasing responsibility" (Pearson & Gallagher, 1983)—for example, modeling expectations and providing guided experiences, before expecting students to complete tasks independently.

Many also spoke about the importance of using visuals in their standards-based instruction. First-grade Spanish instructor Sofia, for example, reflected positively on the guidance the GLAD—Guided Language Acquisition and Development—program offered around creating a "language functional environment" wherein wall-hanging resources—created to resonate visually and content-wise across classrooms—serve as scaffolds for learning in both languages:

> We have lots of visuals and . . . (pointing to a child standing in front of a wall-length chart) you see a little girl standing right there reading and making sense of what the *trama* [plot or storyline] is . . . they know where the resources are.

Justin, like Sofia and others, emphasized using "lots of visuals and [putting] lots of vocabulary up on the walls for [the students] to access," while also praising GLAD's and GATE's influence on Playa's commitment to students' "active participation" in all learning experiences.

Across classrooms, there was also evidence of students interacting meaningfully with challenging content and co-constructing the environment as they did. This kind of participation was neither deemed too advanced for young children, nor too childish for older ones. Young students were called to contribute substantively and publicly to collaborative meaning-making and environmental aids—for example, via Post-its, shown in Figure 5.1. Middle schoolers, meanwhile, were encouraged to take up markers, sentence strips, and poster paper and use them to create resources like cognitive content dictionaries to detail their evolving understandings of vocabulary words (e.g., Figure 5.2). They also created posters that depicted focal content and facilitated their own and peers' understandings about, for example, how to compare and contrast different characters from literary and informational texts, and how to recognize the language used to signal when comparisons are being made.

Many teachers identified active participation and collaboration as essential because they held the potential to infuse challenging standards-based instruction with social interaction and the kind of student-generated, accessible language received and produced through peer talk and text (i.e., comprehensible input and output) (Krashen, 1987; Walqui, 2006). Treating the "language aspect" of active

Figure 5.1. First-Graders' Collective Response to Literature

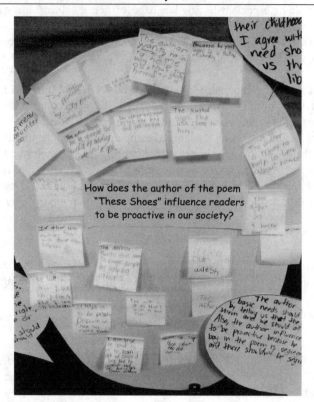

Students in 1st-grade classrooms contributed via Post-its and discussion as they worked to make meaning of a whole-class text, the poem "These Shoes."

participation as a "very important part" of instruction, Justin spoke, too, for example, about how he might support different learners' oral language production in dialogue. This might involve "finding a language broker or someone that's a really good model in dialogue to sit next to someone who is almost there . . . [who] can express really deep ideas on paper but . . . they're not real quick with the words rolling off their tongues." According to Justin and others, actively engaging students also enabled the sort of low-stakes environment that is critical for language learning. Using a term coined by linguist Stephen Krashen, Justin argued that the "whole dialogue component . . . has really helped to lower the affective filter" that might otherwise impede participation and learning.

Finally, given concerns for visual representation of complex content and for dialogue as a crucial component of active participation for EBs, graphic organizers —carefully created by teachers themselves—played a particularly prominent role and often functioned to scaffold student dialogue around focal content, the nature of which we turn to next.

**Figure 5.2. Middle Schoolers' Collaborative Charts Defining Key Academic
     Language**

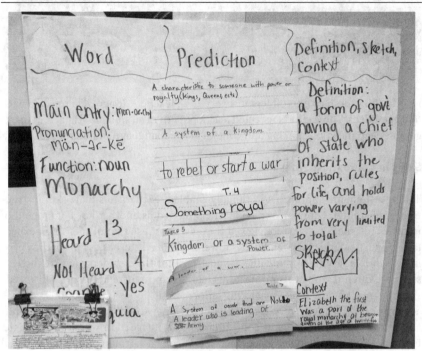

Seventh-grade students collaborated to create cognitive content dictionaries for
key concepts in their British literature units of study.

Big Ideas, Not Just Basics

Worth noting was Playa's schoolwide commitment to thematic planning—a tenet
of the GLAD program and a widely accepted feature of research-based instruction
for EBs, particularly because of its power to "cluster" meaning and better organize knowledge and learning (Walqui, 2006). From the 1st-grade unit focused on
human rights, to the 4th-grade unit on immigration (both referenced below), to
the 8th-grade unit on social injustice (featured in Chapter 6), teachers regularly
situated standards-based instruction in thematic units of study. The school was so
committed to these ambitious unit themes and their big ideas that teachers posted
them prominently, as in the 1st-grade classroom shown in Figure 5.3, to help hold
themselves and their students accountable for drawing connections to them.

Although wall hangings elsewhere might speak more to surface than to substance, and might not be made and/or decided upon by teachers themselves, time
spent in Playa classrooms made the centrality and familiarity of the displayed
themes clear. Teachers and students circled back to them routinely, before, during,
and after thematically linked learning experiences. In fact, we never once saw or

Figure 5.3. An Example of "Big Ideas" Anchoring Instruction in 1st Grade

heard of a random or one-off lesson; everything teachers designed connected back to bigger ideas. These efforts reflected teachers' faith in all students' capacities to engage in deep meaning-making and content-related language and literacy learning.

Skills in Context, Not in Isolation

Taking a thematic approach additionally enabled teachers to situate skill instruction in meaningful content, which teachers named as another key component of rigorous instruction. We, too, viewed this as a manifestation of their high expectations, particularly given tendencies toward rote, back-to-basics approaches in so many schools serving low-income, language minoritized students, where discrete skills are often divorced from meaning-making and where access to "advanced" skills is granted only after "mastering" more "basic" ones (Garcia, 2005). Playa's administrators made it very clear that they sought to depart from these trends and thus expected teachers to contextualize skill instruction whenever possible; teachers—not surprisingly, given their personal backgrounds and professional experience—touted the wisdom of these ways.

Teachers' efforts to contextualize skill instruction linked back to commitments to propel students above and beyond the high bar set by the CCSS—which Playa's teachers interpreted to mean offering instruction that was rigorous in a traditional sense and also showcased the standards' interconnectedness. In practice, this meant that while one or two standards might be at the fore of any lesson, they were never treated singularly; rather, standards from across CCSS-ELA strands were in play together—addressing, for example, critical reading, precise writing, robust oral discourse, and conventions, rather than just any one alone.

Surpassing the Standards

When Playa teachers talked with one another about the CCSS in grade-level and district-wide collaborative meetings, it was common for them to go beyond the CCSS in two ways. The first was literal. Teachers often looked across multiple grade levels, rather than focusing myopically on just one. Usually, this entailed looking up to the next grade level's standards to help inform what and how to teach. In some ways, this tendency on teachers' part responds to literacy scholars' concerns about the dearth of research supporting the ascription of individual standards to individual grade levels. It also responds to warnings issued against using the CCSS too "literally" and recommendations that teachers consider any grade level's standards in conjunction with those from "adjacent grades," noting the broader vision of "authentic, rigorous and worthy" literacy instruction included in the CCSS Introduction (Valencia & Wixson, 2013, p. 181).

Looking up the gradespan reflected one aspect of how Playa's administrators and teachers sought, as mentioned in earlier chapters, to get out in front of reform, "make the standards [their] own," and demonstrate the capabilities of Playa's students to exceed even that which was legislated.

The second way that teachers strove to go beyond the standards was in their efforts to use standards—even the most discrete ones—in ways that helped students see their real-world application. As Sonya put it, "I don't want to teach something that they have no clue why it's important . . . just because it's a standard, or whatever." We include below the voices of multiple teachers whose commentaries about their CCSS-aligned practice reflect this shared view.

Sofia, referencing an activity in which her 1st-graders hunted for adjectives in an assigned text said: "I want you to find adjectives to use them and make your writing beautiful and more descriptive with different words, not only *feliz*, but higher language, higher academic language . . . to be able to write clearly . . . to express everything. . . . "

Rocio described the rationale behind having her 1st-graders—like others schoolwide—annotate texts: "With annotations . . . it's not because we expect them to have marks on their paper but because it's gonna help them to better understand what they're doing, help them better understand the text. I think telling my kids like . . . 'why did you underline this?' [If they respond] 'I don't know,' [I might ask] 'Well, does it make sense for you? Is it important?' And they will say 'Yes.' [And I will ask them] 'So explain to me why do you think it's important?'"

Justin explained his practice of encouraging his 4th-graders to develop problem-posing and problem-solving skills as readers and writers: "So what do you do as a critical reader and as a writer that can transfer into your daily life? . . . Even when we're reading a text we'd say 'Okay . . . if I don't understand what this word means, why do I need to figure out what this word means? Why would I want to break it down and try to figure out what the prefix is, what the suffix is, or if there is one of those, and in context, how . . . ?' And then [we'd] say, 'Okay well if you do that, you better understand . . . the book, and then you better understand a topic or an idea or a perspective of this author.'"

Miriam reflected on her preference to provide her middle schoolers with project-based or inquiry-oriented learning experiences where they choose topics, readings, and methods for demonstrating knowledge: "My goal is . . . to prepare them to be able to access whatever information they need in order to either make an argument or build an opinion or be able to explain something. . . . So what tools do they need when they do come across something that they don't know? How can they access it?"

In the ensuing section, we offer examples of how some of these agreed-upon approaches unfolded in classrooms. First, we present examples that illustrate how teachers' anti-deficit, affective stances were woven through their enactment of the CCSS. At the same time, the examples point to tensions that can arise when teachers' anti-deficit, affective labor gets hitched to a reform like the CCSS grounded in market-driven, English-only, and universalistic, rather than equity-driven, multilingual, and particularistic assumptions about teaching and learning (Au & Waxman, 2015).

COHERENCE IN PRACTICE

In the middle of spring term, Playa's teachers and students—having already completed one narrative and two informational units of study—were well into their second and final narrative-focused, thematic unit of the year. Being that it was mid-April, it was highly likely that many schools serving EBs were spending much of each day preparing for standardized tests. At Playa, however, there was not a test-preparation booklet in sight. Instead, teachers and students were engaged in the intense teaching and learning we had come to expect, no matter the month, time of day, or grade level.

During this particular week, Playa's 1st-grade teachers—Ana and Rocio, the English and math instructors, and Ramón and Sofia, the Spanish and social studies instructors—were working across classrooms to engage students in a collaboratively designed unit of study on human rights. With direction from administrators, teachers had identified multiple ELA/Literacy standards that they aimed to address within the unit. The list that teachers were working with was extensive and varied and included multiple selections from the Reading standards for foundational skills and for literature, and from the Writing and the Language standards. A number of these standards were woven into teachers' lesson plans for this second week of the 4-week unit. In the project described below, for example, 1st-grade teachers Ramón and Sofia's instruction—again reflecting the 2nd-grade standards—aimed most concertedly to have students "acknowledge differences in the points of view of characters" (CCSS.ELA-LITERACY.RL.2.6). This expectation was a clear bump up from that expressed in the corollary 1st-grade standard, which asks students to "identify who is telling the story at various points in a text" (CCSS.ELA-LITERACY.RL.1.6).

Entering their classrooms, it was immediately apparent how closely Ramón and Sofia had been collaborating. Everything, from the arrangement of furniture, to the placement of resources and the posting of student work, looked similar. In each classroom, students' desks were clumped in groups of four or five to allow for teamwork. A kidney table in one corner and a rectangular table near the door awaited teacher-led small groups. Teachers' desks, meanwhile, were tucked against the back walls, fittingly, since Playa's teachers rarely spent time at them.

And it wasn't just the way things looked that made the classrooms seem so alike; the instruction was virtually identical, too. On the back wall of both classrooms hung large, butcher paper posters that had been created earlier in the unit. Each included a photocopy of an illustration from the picture book *Encuentro,* which students had been reading over the past week. Written by Jane Yolen, the book is set in 1492 and chronicles the encounter between European colonizers, including Christopher Columbus, and Taino Indians living on the island of San Salvador. In the story, the main character—an older Taino man—recollects how he attempted as a boy to warn his elders about the European settlers, and he reflects on what he, in his later years, now understands to be colonizers' destruction of his culture and people.

Ramón and Sofia drew on their understandings of "gradually releasing responsibility" (Pearson & Gallagher, 1983), as they guided students to respond to three of four prompts, which were distributed across the four corners of a piece of poster paper. During whole-class instruction, teachers scribed students' co-constructed ideas about different characters' physical characteristics, actions, words, feelings, and thoughts as students looked on. Students then worked in table groups to create posters on their own, responding to all four prompts, including the final one, which asked them to make a connection between their character analysis and "human rights." At project closure, teachers—together with students—drew on the small groups' responses to the final prompt to complete the whole-class model posters.

What is clear from looking at examples of students' posters (e.g., Figure 5.4) and what was said in conversation with their young creators is that the students were developing quite a command of the story and its characters' perspectives and experiences. As the image in Figure 5.4 conveys, this task involved far more than students merely copying content from the model poster; it involved the culling of important information, negotiating the wording and writing in each section, and collaboratively managing the necessary materials.

For example, the top right-hand corner of the model poster for *los extranjeros* (the strangers or foreigners) included among the *características físicas* (physical characteristics) particular facial expressions and emotions (e.g., *felices* [happy], *enojados* [mad], *serios* [serious]), as well as bodily/physical descriptions (*blancos* [white skinned], *grandes* [large], *poderosos* [powerful], *diferentes a las personas de la isla* [different from the island's people]). Meanwhile, as illustrated in the top right-hand corner of one of the student-made *el niño* (boy) posters, featured in Figure 5.4, the response to the same prompt describes the Europeans' physical characteristics more poetically and in ways that further convey their understanding of the book's content. Through their words, students showed how the strangers or foreigners were different from the (indigenous) people of the island (e.g., *Los extranjeros tiene piel blanca como la luna . . . y ojos como el mar.* / The foreigners have skin that is white like the moon . . . and eyes that are blue like the sea. *Los extranjeros cubran los pies.* / The foreigners cover their feet). Students additionally used physical description to communicate their sense that the foreigners were perhaps untrustworthy, even scary (*Los extranjeros tiene sonrisa de serpiente.* / The foreigners have snake-like smiles.).

Realizing that students now had some well-developed understandings of *Encuentro*, teachers aimed with this morning's lesson plan to use the story's text as context for addressing CCSS-specified skills related to verb tense (CCSS.

Figure 5.4. First-Graders' Collaborative Character Analysis Poster

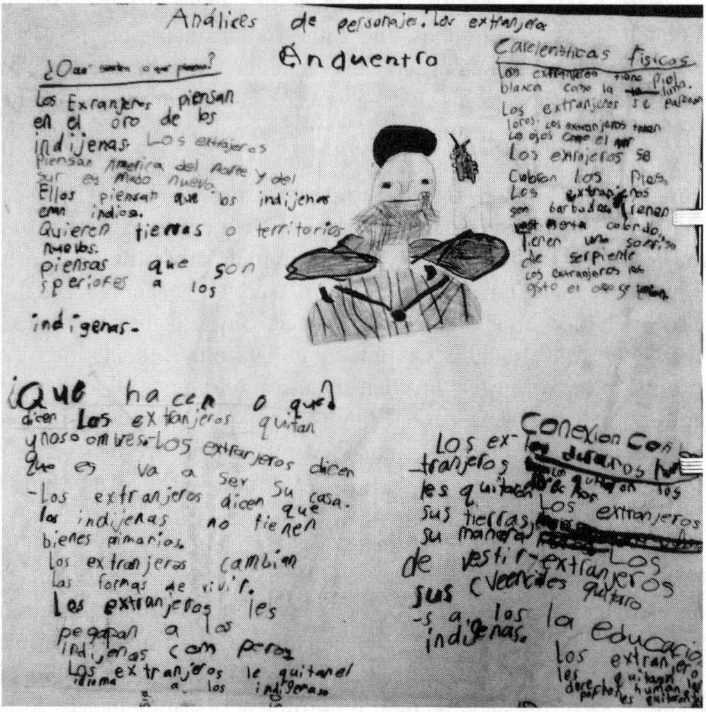

Students worked together to co-construct posters that identified key features, motives, and actions of the central characters in the book *Encuentro*.

ELA-LITERACY.L.1.1.E: "Use verbs to convey a sense of past, present, and future."). Intending to go beyond the standards, not only by situating skill instruction in familiar and meaningful content, Ramón and Sofia—along with Ana and Rocio—had looked ahead to see how this standard was extended in subsequent grades. Because the closest 2nd-grade standard focused on irregular verbs, teachers drew on the closest 3rd-grade standard, which required that students "explain the function of nouns, pronouns, verbs, adjectives, and adverbs in general and their functions in particular sentences" (CCSS.ELA-LITERACY.L.3.1a). In keeping with teachers' own views on language development and in alignment with what bilingual education scholars have advocated concerning CCSS implementation with EBs (Butvilofsky, Hopewell, & Escamilla, 2015; Seltzer & Ibarra Johnson, 2015), Ana and Rocio were addressing simultaneously in English the same standards that Ramón and Sofia were addressing in Spanish (albeit through different learning experiences), and so were communicating regularly about their lessons to ensure bidirectional connections across languages.

Reflecting all the standards in play, and using students' developing knowledge of *Encuentro* as context, the lesson Ramón and Sofia planned required that students consider how changing the tense of verbs within particular sentences from the story might change those sentences' meanings.

After calling students to the rug in their respective classrooms, Sofia and Ramón pointed to hanging banners that proudly featured the unit's big idea and led students in what appeared—noting students' comfort and fluency with the sentence—to be a practiced choral recitation: "Human beings have rules that they learn to follow in order to communicate effectively." Sofia and Ramón then distributed a handout they had created, and began reviewing the directions with students. The handout included six separate sentences from the book, and the task required that students identify each sentence's tense, change the tense of the verb, and explain if and how the change in tense changed the sentence's meaning. Underneath the instructions were the six sentences the teachers had selected directly from *Encuentro.*

After reviewing the instructions and asking if students understood what was expected, Ramón and Sofia sent them to their seats to "get started." As students moved from the rug to their desks, both teachers reminded them to work with their tablemates, since "dialogue" and "working together" would support them to do an "even better job" than they would likely do on their own.

In many ways, this lesson reflected what Playa teachers believed about their students' capabilities and what they valued instructionally, and thus it captured some of what we came to understand as relatively typical Playa instruction. Teachers addressed and went beyond standards for 1st grade and expected (if implicitly) students to engage with standards in ways that required basic understandings—for example, being able to identify a verb in context and recognize its tense—as well as applications of the focus skill—for example, changing a verb's tense and explaining how that change would, in turn, impact the sentence's meaning. Teachers elected to embed skill instruction in meaningful content that was linked to the broader unit theme, which itself addressed ambitious content and ideas. Teachers also opened the lesson by attempting to establish an authentic purpose for learning about verb tense—namely, framing verb tense as part of a set of rules that enable human beings, students included, to communicate effectively in the real world. Without a doubt, this lesson also illustrated teachers' high expectations for students, as well as teachers' professional understandings about particular dimensions of language acquisition and the kinds of instruction that hold promise for cultivating students' meaning-making competencies.

Nevertheless, once back in their seats, students showed signs of restlessness and waning focus. While they talked with one another as their teachers recommended, most seemed to discuss topics—like a grandparent's new pet or games to play during recess—that were unrelated to the assignment. And, with the exception of just a few, most students' papers remained blank, even though teachers provided what seemed like ample work time.

Why did this carefully and collaboratively planned lesson fail to generate teachers' desired results? This was the very question over which the 1st-grade team puzzled at their meeting the next morning.

Sitting around the conference table, Ramón and Sofia pulled out examples of the prior day's incomplete student work and placed them alongside their lesson plans. To their grade-level teammates, Ana and Rocio, and elementary co-principal Mr. Pacheco, also in attendance, they lamented how all the planning they put into the lesson seemed to have been for naught. Mr. Pacheco listened sympathetically and began to silently read through the student work. After a moment, Mr. Pacheco set the papers down, paused, and asked Ramón and Sofia which standard the lesson aimed to address. Pointing to the top of the lesson plan where the standard "Use verbs to convey a sense of past, present, and future (e.g., Yesterday I walked home; Today I walk home; Tomorrow I will walk home)" was written, Ramón explained that they hoped students would learn to identify, make meaning of, and manipulate verb tense. To this, Mr. Pacheco furrowed his brow and noted that the lesson seemed to go "above" the chosen 1st-grade standard. The teachers glanced at one another and nodded proudly, assuming they were being praised for adhering to what they and others had described as administrative pressure to "keep pushing" both themselves and their students "to the next level." As if to make this very point, Ramón explained that when he and Sofia consulted recent assessment data, they came away believing that "the [1st-grade] standard is far less complex than what students can do" and thus set out "to make it more advanced." Though Mr. Pacheco praised the teachers' "high expectations," he also reminded them that they "need to give students what they need to perform at that high level," which he argued entailed not just "guiding" students, as he acknowledged Ramón and Sofia were, but "supporting" them. Ramón and Sofia smiled meekly and agreed to rework the handout to increase the level of support it provided.

In this exchange, Mr. Pacheco offered little direction beyond affirming their decision, to borrow the language of Chapter 4, to "figure it out." He did not, for example, press them to reconsider the degree of authenticity in the assignment, which fell short of their espoused goals; the way they had structured students' work with the chosen sentences, which involved a somewhat counterintuitive and under-scaffolded, especially for 1st-graders, sequence of steps; or the sentences themselves—such as "*Un chasquido estruendoso de tormenta me despertó de mi sueño*" (A loud clap of thunder woke me from my dream), and "*Tomamos su idioma en nuestras bocas, olvidando el nuestro*" (We took their language in our mouths, forgetting our own), both spoken by the Taino boy and possibly excessively complex choices for an activity involving the manipulation of verb tense.

For the next hour, Ramón and Sofia worked, eventually deciding to include additional steps for each sentence so that each would "more closely follow the previous one" and would be "less abstract"; this involved asking students to identify each sentence's verb before asking them to identify each sentence's tense, as they had asked first in the original handout. They also included fewer sentences—four instead of six—and replaced some of the more challenging sentences with less challenging ones. Still, the challenging example sentence above, *Un chasquido estruendoso de tormenta me despertó de mi sueño* (A loud clap of thunder woke me from my dream) was the first one that students were expected to tackle in the new handout. Thus, despite changes, the core of the task and much of the text on which the task relied remained the same.

The next morning, Sofia and Ramón arrived ready to revisit the prior day's learning experience, this time using their revised plan. The teachers also approached the lesson's delivery somewhat differently on this second take, explicitly walking students through the steps and breaking them down further as needed, modeling each step using the first sentence on the handout, and checking for understanding in a more structured way that suggested a commitment to offer additional explanations should students require them.

Compared with the prior day, students were calmer and more confident. Most worked with greater focus. Several even finished the assignment within the allotted 30 minutes. The room hummed with the buzz of student voices, but this time, most were talking about the task at hand—for example, negotiating about which words were verbs, confirming their understanding of the sentences' original meanings, and dialoguing about if and how those meanings changed once the verb tense shifted.

And yet, at least a handful of students in each classroom still struggled just to complete the work as assigned. Without question, the day's additional support made it possible for more students to complete the assignment successfully. Still, we wondered why students whose needs appeared unmet by whole-class instruction were not offered targeted support. We also wondered about the absence of intervention for students who stalled on the handout's first challenging sentence and couldn't get any further. In other words, we puzzled that Sofia's self-described "student-driven" instructional approach, about which she reported always "trying to keep the students in mind . . . what they're interested in learning, [and] just the various ways that they learn," wasn't evident. Given the way things had gone initially, we couldn't understand why these wonderful teachers hadn't considered a more wholesale overhaul of the lesson rather than a mere tweaking.

The tendency we observed in 1st-grade classrooms to expect students to perform well above grade level, often without the necessary support, appeared in other grade levels, too, particularly in the elementary grades, where—simply because of the number of teachers—fairly intensive collaborative planning was the expectation and the norm. In these classrooms, as part of the effort to maintain high expectations and elevate academic rigor, teachers mostly worked together to design and deliver the same collaboratively planned instruction to all students. And they did so at a level of challenge that was arguably beyond many students' zones of proximal development (Vygotsky, 1978) and with universal forms of "guidance" and "support"—to borrow Mr. Pacheco's distinction—rather than targeted accommodations based on individual learners' needs, the tasks at hand, and the relationship between the two.

Consider, for example, how Justin engaged his 4th-graders in their study of character analysis, itself situated within a broader narrative unit organized around immigration themes and big ideas about the relationship between critical reading and precise writing. As was the case in the 1st-grade lesson described above, all students were expected to read the same text, and all were provided with the same whole-class instruction and instructional scaffolds—specifically, several related graphic organizers.

The texts and multiple organizers spread out in front of students depicted a familiar scene in 4th grade. Leading into this lesson, students had already completed multiple "close" or "cold readings" (see Snow, 2013) of *The Circuit* by Francisco Jimenez (e.g., Figure 5.5). This same text was mentioned in Chapter 3 for having been above grade level according to the Lexile system that the CCSS and administrators encouraged teachers to use, yet it was critiqued by a Playa administrator as not challenging or complex enough.[1]

In keeping with CCSS requirements and schoolwide emphases, Justin's 4th-graders had marked up mimeographed pages of the text with annotations,

Figure 5.5. A 4th-Grader's Close Reading of Complex Text

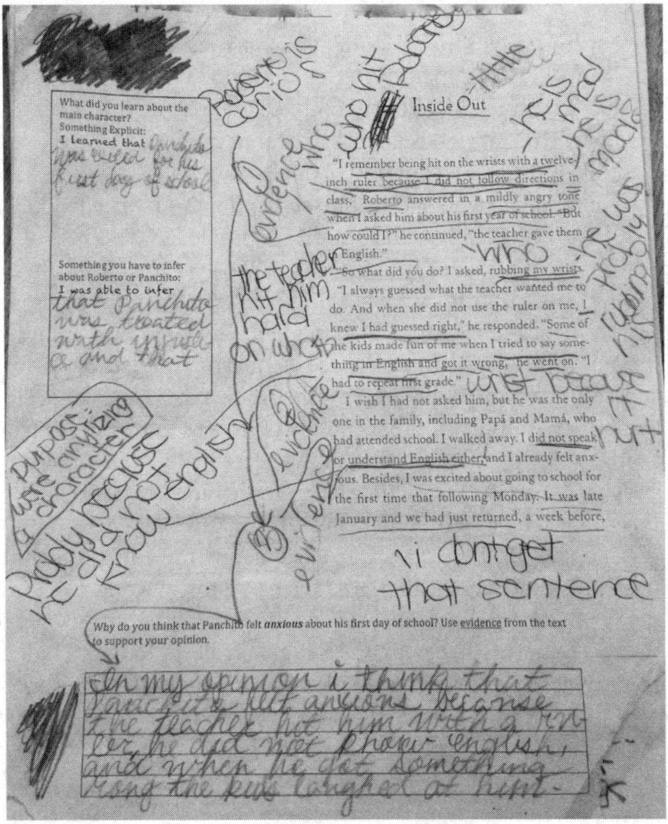

Students engaged in multiple close readings of *The Circuit*, utilizing different writing implements (e.g., pen and pencil) to show their multiple rounds of annotation; as a result, their texts often looked as marked up as this one.

which were now meant to assist them in independently completing a graphic orga-nizer designed around the standard that asks students to "describe in depth a char-acter . . . drawing on specific details in the text" (CCSS.ELA-LITERACY.RL.4.3). As Figure 5.6 shows, some organizers—like this one—were quite elaborate, reflect-ing the significant time that teachers—and especially Paco and Justin—spent col-laboratively crafting them in alignment with their aforementioned understandings of EBs' needs (e.g., embedding visual cues). In this case, the organizer included images to signify (using the language of the graphic organizer) "words" and "ac-tions" that indicate "explicit" details and "emotions" and "thoughts" that indicate more "implicit" details.

As was often the case, the first organizer used was not the last. These initial two steps—revisiting close readings and supporting a claim with textual evidence—served primarily as preparation for students to then engage in dialogue with their peers, supported by another graphic organizer.

In this third step, students completed with tablemates a creative, but somewhat cumbersome collaborative organizer that required them to—as two pairs—dialogue around their "initial ideas" concerning the character from their independent organizer (e.g., Figure 5.7). Figure 5.8 shows up close some of what students contributed to the organizer, which required them to write their "initial thinking" about the character's traits, and then glue their notes/opinions from the individual organizers where they provided textual evidence. Students then had to dialogue around their opinions and evidence and come to a consensus about the trait they believed best represented the character. In this case, the "final" piece of the organizer required that they record what they had settled on while dialogu-ing. Under "New Evidence" in the center of Figure 5.7, for example, one group's organizer read, "After having dialogue at our table we believe that the character trait 'anxious' best represents Panchito because . . . "

This type of graphic organizer—though more successful and, believe it or not, more simple, than some others we saw—was typical of what we saw across class-rooms. Like Justin had, teachers created and deployed organizers with particular standards in mind; for example, organizers often aimed to support students in meet-ing the CCSS's most heavily emphasized skills—namely, those specified in standards that ask students to (1) "summarize" texts, determine a text's "main idea" and "ex-plain how it is supported by key details" (CCSS.ELA-LITERACY.RI.4.2), and (2) "explain events, procedures, ideas, or concepts in a historical, scientific, or technical text, including what happened and why, based on specific information in the text" (CCSS.ELA-LITERACY.RI.4.3). Yet, teachers also created and used organizers in Playa-particular ways, like having students record how their thinking had changed after dialoguing with peers; in this sense, the organizers reminded students of focal standards, but also of the broader purpose toward which their work was oriented.

As the images in Figures 5.6–5.8 attest, these organizers sometimes seemed as complex as the complex texts they were meant to accompany. They also, at times, seemed even more complex than the dialogues and understandings they engen-dered. For example, soon after the prior lesson, Justin asked students to call upon

Figure 5.6. A 4th-Grader's Completed Character Analysis

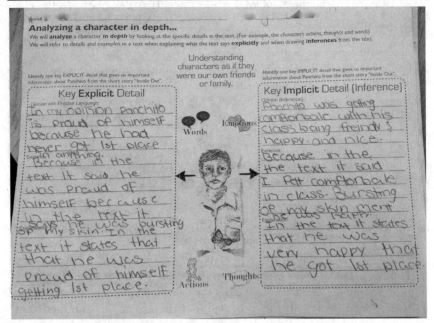

Students worked with teacher-made graphic organizers like this one to recount details and draw inferences about key characters in *The Circuit.*

some of the same content addressed in the organizers. He shared with students his goal: "to help you make a connection between what we've been learning about in terms of being critical readers and how we are becoming precise writers. . . ." And then he asked students to determine, using succinct and precise language, what they considered to be the story's central topic. Students launched into conversation. At one table, the exchange unfolded like this:

> *Jill:* I think the topic of *The Circuit* was about a school year because it starts at the beginning of a school year and ends at the end of the school year.
> *[Nodding]*
> *Eric:* Okay, so do we have a consensus that the topic is the school year?
> *All:* Yeah, okay.
> *Justin (who had been circulating and checking in on multiple groups, approached the table and bent down to address these students):* What topic did you decide on?
> *Eric:* We decided it was "school year."
> *Justin:* Well, I'm a little concerned because if you only tell someone the topic is "school year," they might not think the story is interesting enough

Figure 5.7. Fourth Graders' Collaborative Analysis of Complex Text

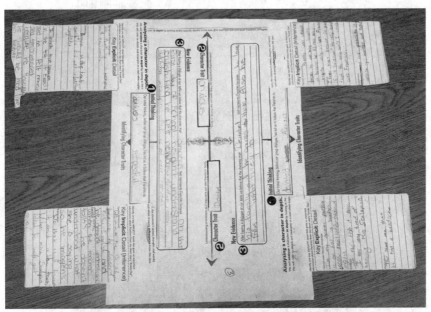

Two pairs of students worked together to co-construct this collective graphic organizer, which teachers designed to help them engage in small-group dialogue about
character traits they had identified as individuals.

---

to read. Maybe what we should do is explode the moment with details
about the topic so that it's not boring.
José: We could say that it's about a boy who has adventures during the
school year. *(At this, Justin departs to another table.)*
Jill: Yeah, but we should also say that it's about the boy's adventures
coming to a new school in a new country, too . . .

The exchange, despite all that led up to it, was more perfunctory than dialogic; the consensus was proposed rather than constructed; and the content
was superficial and simplistic even though the task called for more. As we often saw, even with universal scaffolds like graphic organizers in play, students
still required other supports—in this case, Justin's presence and affirming, but
also corrective probing—to get beyond the not-so-precise place where discussion
stalled. Exchanges like this one, and the long hours we knew teachers spent making graphic organizers, left us wondering whether they might be over-investing
in some (universal) approaches and under-investing in others, such as developing
more targeted scaffolds and supports.

Justin himself admitted: "How do we make sure that those lower groups are
making that next jump? . . . that's a good question." It was the kind of question, he

Figure 5.8. A Close Up of a 4th-Grader's "Initial Thinking"

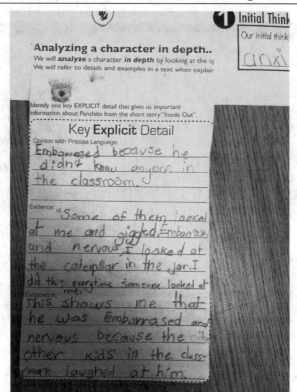

Students documented their own ideas about key characters' traits before they engaged in dialogue with classmates, and then these were incorporated into the collective graphic organizer.

also admitted, for which he felt there was often not adequate time to slow down and ponder, given all else that was part of the daily grind. And to us it was also a question that signaled, in its phrasing, the danger of a universalistic approach in contributing to situations that activated the very lens and language—that is, "lower groups"—that teachers were most trying to avoid.

As with Ramón and Sofia's students, and as the exchange above suggests, Justin and Paco's students often engaged in tasks such as these with different degrees of success, despite the mostly universal supports that Justin and Paco provided. When Justin and Paco noticed, for example, that a graphic organizer wasn't working as planned, their response tended to look like Sofia's and Ramón's; that is, rather than consider how to offer differentiated supports in relation to students' varied needs, Justin and Paco mostly revised existing or created new supports intended for use by the whole class. As was the case in Sofia's and Ramón's classes, while some students appeared to benefit from the supports offered, other students did not.

The same can be said for the universal use of "annotation" across grade levels and classrooms. It is worth noting the frequency with which teachers engaged students in the CCSS-endorsed approach of "close reading," usually using whole-class texts and annotation types. Here, too, though a whole-class approach—and day-to-day tweaks to it—appeared to buoy some students' meaning-making, for others it appeared to encourage simply going through the motions; for some students at least, there was little to no indication that rereading and annotating the text, regardless of how marked up it became, moved them closer to deep comprehension. So common was it for a subset of the class, especially in the elementary grades, to fly under the radar, so to speak, rather than reach the high bar, that it hardly seemed to strike teachers as strange.

This is not to suggest that teachers were untroubled when students seemed to flail. Indeed, while observations indicated that teachers tended to treat struggle as part and parcel of learning, interviews acknowledged that this did not always come easily. As Rocio commented: "I do feel like every child is capable. . . . I have to trust them, and it's been a battle . . . thinking or believing that, yes . . . I'm going to let you work on this [without intervening]."

Tensions around how much teachers should step in versus let students "figure it out"—in essence, how much struggle was enough or too much—bubbled up across classrooms and conversations. Playa's teachers were deeply committed and highly prepared to scaffold EBs' learning. But, as it turned out, CCSS-related and Playa-amplified calls for "raising the bar" in certain ways seemed to overpower or mute aspects of teachers' own expertise, leading them to holster some of the very supports known to be important for EBs.

RESPONSIVE INSTRUCTION AND RAISING THE BAR: IRRECONCILABLE DIFFERENCES?

How could teachers who otherwise demonstrated such care opt to teach the same lessons to all, even when some students demonstrated an observable need for additional and varied supports? Why might they be so susceptible to glossing over those needs? What role, if any, did the CCSS play in this dynamic?

Pondering these questions, we were reminded of the many research team meetings where we puzzled over what seemed—after long days of observation—like rather limited differentiation and learner responsiveness, despite teachers' stated commitments to responsive teaching. We were also reminded of teachers' mostly vague responses when, during interviews and post-observation conversations, in which we hoped to understand these tendencies through teachers' eyes, we asked teachers to talk about how they "targeted" or "scaffolded" instruction for particular students. Although teachers used words like *student-driven* to describe their approaches, more often than not they responded by emphasizing their efforts to maintain high expectations, avoid ranking or labeling students, and re-proving to the public that Playa's students were capable of big things and that the school was deserving of acclaim.

Ironically, in their quest to "raise the bar" for students and themselves, some teachers had come to enact—albeit inadvertently—a more one-size-fits-all approach to instruction than intended. In fact, in some cases, despite curricular and instructional autonomies afforded by Playa's charter and "high-performing" status, it was almost as if participants were scripting themselves and one another such that teachers were delivering lessons in the same ways to all students and felt inhibited from veering away from collaboratively developed plans, even in the interest of responsive-in-the-moment instructional moves. As Ana explained, "We're supposed to deliver everything the same way . . . from what we say to how we present it . . ." and so "the color coding, everything [laughs] . . . it's all planned," a kind of social contract among colleagues.

To be sure, teachers' instruction never seemed to be "cookie-cutter" in ways we might expect, based on experience, if derived from prepackaged programs. Rather, teachers demonstrated ownership over lessons and materials, respectively, in ways that made sense given that they had planned them and selected or created them together. Yet, despite this strong sense of ownership, the propensity to use a one-size-fits-all approach, with any group of students, offers some cause for concern. Applying the lenses of differentiated instruction, universal design, and equity pedagogy helps surface some of the implications of a one-size-fits-all approach, particularly in a school like Playa that serves students with a wide a range of academic strengths, needs, and interests, and many of whom hail from minoritized cultural and linguistic communities.

Differentiation Need Not Downgrade Expectations

Empirical and practice-oriented literature on differentiated instruction raises significant concerns about one-size-fits-all instruction (e.g., Subban, 2006; Tomlinson, 2004). Differentiating—designing instruction to accommodate students' varied needs—assumes that, in order to effectively facilitate learning, teachers must attend to differences, including differences in ability, culture, experience, language background, and interests, to name a few. In particular, scholars have highlighted "the dangers of teaching to the middle" (Subban, 2006, p. 938), in terms of lesson content, pacing, instructional approach, and challenge level—in other words, pitching instruction toward an imagined midpoint between those who would find a task most and least challenging. The failure to address the diverse needs and strengths in any classroom can have dire consequences, including students falling behind, losing motivation, and floundering academically.

As illustrated above, the CCSS-based instruction we observed at Playa rarely included variations in pacing, approach, content, or level of challenge, and typically oriented to an imagined "top" rather than "middle." Although such an approach might be accurately described as "standardized" or "undifferentiated," teachers tended to frame it as a means by which to hold all students to high expectations and, in particular, to "protect" or buffer students who might be struggling from the stigmatization that can accompany being labeled or singled out for "extra" support by a teacher.

Eighth-grade teacher Sonya, for example, explained that she expected all of her students to read the same text, regardless of reading level or language proficiency, in part because she didn't want them to "feel embarrassed" in front of classmates. Sonya was not unaware or dismissive of students' individual needs. In fact, her efforts to avoid stigmatizing students find credence in common wisdom regarding how evidently leveled texts can shape students' text selections and views of themselves as readers (American Association of School Librarians, 2011). Reflecting this perspective, Sonya chose different methods to accommodate students' needs—for example, "posing different kinds of questions during one-on-one conversations" rather than scaffolding students' learning in more public ways. Not surprisingly, observations indicated that this choice proved rather burdensome for teachers in that it forced them to do quite a bit of sometimes frazzled and on-the-fly individuation while it left other students' needs inadvertently unmet, as this method was contingent upon teachers' time management and organization, as well as students' absences, acting out, and/or assertiveness and initiative-taking abilities.

Universal Design for Particular Needs

From a universal design for learning (UDL) perspective, there are some upsides of teaching universally, at least superficially speaking. In particular, UDL proponents point to differentiation's limited capacity to respond to individual learners, highlighting teachers' tendencies to treat differentiation as an afterthought—that is, as something that can be tacked onto the "normal" lesson, rather than something that guides teachers to consider all learners' potential needs from the outset (Meyer, Rose, & Gordon, 2014). In addition, some kinds of differentiation—like leveling texts for struggling readers—can, as Sonya worried, diminish students' motivation to persist, particularly when doing so subjects them to texts that are not age-appropriate or of interest to them (Allington & Gabriel, 2012; Guthrie & Wigfield, 2000). However, it is important to note that UDL proponents argue that using the same text successfully with all students hinges on that text being used in conjunction with instruction that includes "built-in" or embedded supports or accommodations for the "widest range of learners" (CAST, 2011; Dalton, Proctor, Uccelli, Mo, & Snow, 2011).

Much of the instruction we observed at Playa included supports, but not necessarily enough or with adequate accommodations. For example, for students who struggled with different aspects of reading, such as decoding or comprehension, there were often no explicit supports—beyond dialoguing with a tablemate or, at times, completing the same work in a small group supervised by the teacher. As a result, for example, in the case of Sofia and Ramón's verb tense lesson featured earlier, some students found it overly challenging simply to read the sentences on the handout, let alone complete the tasks related to manipulating verb tense.

An Equity Pedagogy Audit

Looking through the lens of equity pedagogy (Banks & Banks, 1995) also yields insights regarding Playa teachers' propensities to rely almost exclusively on whole-class instruction. As noted already, Playa's school structure and instruction reflected several of equity pedagogy's core tenets. Teachers challenged deficit perspectives; incorporated into instruction cooperative learning structures and opportunities for students to co-construct knowledge; made explicit the authentic purposes for academic work and its potential application to the "real world"; and resisted the use of labels, ability grouping, and tracking.

Yet, despite teachers' stated commitments to responsive teaching, most instruction ended up rather unresponsive to individual learners' interests and needs. In addition, although students understood that the worthiness of the Standards depended on their real-world application, that premise was not taken as far as an equity pedagogy approach would encourage. In Sofia and Ramón's lesson, for example, there were numerous missed opportunities to have students draw connections between their own lives and the *Encuentro* narrator's experiences—for example, of coming from families whose traditions and practices are often framed by Whitestream culture as odd, exotic, and/or needing to change.

This is not to suggest that teachers discouraged students from talking about their families and communities and with pride. We often witnessed teachers encouraging such talk—for example, when Sofia gave one of her 1st-graders, Alfredo, the opportunity to share with the class a map of the Middle East and Africa that he had received from his father, who was stationed in Afghanistan, or when Justin had his students interview family members about their own immigration stories. As with the Alfredo example, however, connections like these tended to occur outside the official curriculum. Rarer were instances when topics of instruction emerged in relation to the specific "stuff" of students' home lives or community knowledge, their interests, or their experiences, rather than teachers' own passions or ideas about what constituted worthy content. And so, although social justice themes were fairly widespread across teachers' curriculum and instruction, there were also ample opportunities for stronger connections to the children's own worlds and for the deeper learning such connections could have yielded.

HOW CONTEXT MEDIATES CCSS ENACTMENT

Playa's prevailing collaborative approach to instructional planning, coupled with administrators' expectations regarding instructional coherence across and within grade levels, conferred numerous benefits, though it also made it challenging for teachers to design instruction that was open-ended enough to allow for the (spontaneous) centering of students' needs, knowledge, and experiences.

For example, being pressed to move from ambitious unit to ambitious unit at a somewhat set pace limited opportunities for teachers to engage students' questions. The result of this was, as Rocio put it, that "sometimes we don't take what the students are asking . . . it's like, yes, that's interesting, but let's leave it on the side because this is the question that we're looking at." There were, likewise, limited opportunities for students to bring their developing knowledge to bear on the world beyond the classroom. For example, 1st-graders wrote impassioned essays about Pakistani youth activist Malala Yousafzai as part of their unit about human rights, but they did not share them beyond the classroom walls, connect them to their own local context, or take action inspired by Malala's example. So while an emphasis on authenticity was woven through the rhetoric of teachers' instruction, it was less a feature of the instructional reality.

Administrative feedback on teachers' practice was also a contributor in that it functioned especially to encourage ambition and challenge, more than introspection and instructional reflection. As the exchange between Mr. Pacheco and Ramón and Sofia suggests, teachers did receive feedback that at times pressed them in the general direction of greater responsiveness to students' needs. But where feedback tended toward most, and most specifically, was "bar raising," for both teachers and students alike. For example, although Mr. Pacheco described Justin as "a model teacher" and his classroom as "a Common Core lab . . . what the Common Core classroom should look like," he still made sure to "push back" on Justin as much as he would on any other teacher, insofar as high expectations were concerned. For example, he recounted —as referenced in prior chapters and above—pressing Justin to question whether he was asking enough of his 4th-graders.

> I had that conversation with Justin where I said, Okay Justin, I love everything that you do, but I'm gonna question a little bit the way you're using *The Circuit* to convey the concepts that you're teaching. . . . So can you give the students a different type of text and see how they are applying what they're doing with *The Circuit*? Can you give them a higher-level text and see if they're able to do the same thing? So that would be an example of trying to push on that idea that we can move . . . a constant sense, not of an uncomfortableness, but . . . what else can I do?

This press for "what else can I do?" encouraged teachers to look beyond what they were doing, rather than to look closely at how they were doing and the way their instruction was affecting all learners.

These schoolwide factors help explain why teachers gravitated, seemingly without much consternation, toward a one-size-fits-all instructional approach. The enthusiastic embrace of "high expectations" at Playa often served to obscure how "raising the bar" for all contributed to varied degrees of disconnect between a uniformly high bar on the one hand and the diversity of student needs on the other. This, in turn, clouded teachers' vision when it came to considering the implications of such disconnection and offering students the necessarily varied supports they needed. In essence, teachers' own learning environment placed them at significant risk of practicing in ways that fell short of the equity-oriented high expectations they held for themselves.

That said, school conditions fail to explain entirely teachers' tendencies to overlook the potential and the actual shortcomings of their instruction, particularly as these pertained to some of their own cherished convictions. This was initially quite surprising to us because of how strongly teachers voiced their equity-oriented commitments, how strenuously they labored (affectively and otherwise), and how wide the disconnect still was, at times, between their stated values and actual practices.

CONTRADICTION AS (HUMAN) CONDITION

Of course, human activity never fails to be exceedingly complex. Well-documented dissonance between peoples' beliefs and behaviors is but one example of this complexity, and research indicates that teachers are no exception (Pajares, 1992). In this respect, Playa teachers' behaviors reflect what we know to be true of all teachers, ourselves included—our beliefs and practices hardly ever align perfectly. Rather, their alignment is better understood as the kind of "horizon"—to borrow the language of CHAT scholar Yrgo Engeström—toward which teachers might consciously chart progress, rather than seek arrival or (impossible) perfection. That said, the nature of the disconnect between Playa teachers' stated beliefs and actual instruction suggested to us that something more was going on and compelled us to dig deeper into the potential roots of this disconnect.

Part of understanding complex human activity involves considering varying motives for engaging in an activity, such as educating youth, and how those motives then shape the activity's outcome—for example, what youth experience, learn, and do as a result of that educating. In other words, and as articulated in Chapter 2, human activity is fundamentally object related (Engeström, 1987; Leontiev, 1978). Certainly, Playa's teachers' core motives for doing their work—for engaging in the activity of teaching—were rooted in their beliefs about young people in general, and Latinx, EB, and immigrant youth specifically. These motives were evident in individual teachers' comments and personal–professional trajectories, and also in Playa's own genesis in keeping with the idea that Latinx, EB, and immigrant students deserve better—deserve a "dream school"—and can do better than typically expected.

But, as described in Chapter 3, over the years, Playa administrators and teachers also became increasingly motivated by their sense of capability in overcoming a "low-performing" label and by their desire to retain their status as high performing. This makes sense in so many ways. The institutional press on teachers—in this case, to become and stay high performing—intersected with teachers' owns beliefs and practices, and the boundaries between them seemed to blur. They became more intertwined, more co-constitutive: what we might think of as two once-separate streams joining together.

According to Leontiev (1978), although it is typical for activity systems to have multiple objects or motives for engaging in activity, it is also true that such objects or motives rarely exist on a level plane. In Playa's case, the ceaseless press to achieve, fueled by the introduction of the CCSS, seemed to disrupt the "hierarchy of motives"—or competing "streams"—among its educators. This reordering might explain why teachers gravitated toward a mostly uniform, undifferentiated approach to instruction, while simultaneously claiming allegiance to a student-centered, dialogical one. While neither stream disappeared altogether, one overpowered the other to a degree.

The perceived resonance between teachers' anti-deficit high expectations and CCSS rhetoric around "raising the bar" aided in this. In particular, it obscured the reordering of motives, rendering less visible to teachers certain contradictions between their beliefs and practices that were evident to us and, we argue, would have been to them as well under different circumstances. Most especially, this occurred in relation to teachers' approach to curriculum and instruction, which they unanimously described as critical and transformative, but which appeared in practice to be oriented toward compliance with a certain interpretation of the CCSS as legitimately and unproblematically bar-raising. In the following two chapters, we explore these dynamics through a closer look at teachers' responses to the CCSS-informed expectation that they engage their students in "close reading" of increasingly "complex" texts.

CHAPTER 6

"Close Reading" of
"Complex Text" in Middle Grades

One of the hallmarks of the Common Core State Standards (CCSS) is their focus, across disciplines, on language and literacy. No two aspects of this focus have received more emphasis—in CCSS documents and related teacher guidebooks—than calls for "close reading" and increased "text complexity." Unsurprisingly, Playa's teachers and administrators dedicated significant time and energy to both. In fact, there wasn't a day during our more than 50 days at Playa when we didn't overhear a conversation about these emphases—whether in grade-level meetings, instructional leadership team meetings, after-school professional development sessions, additional CCSS implementation-related workshops, and/or informal exchanges—or witness at least one teacher attempting to engage students in close reading of "complex" text.

Given their prominence in popular education discourse and our data, these emphases—and Playa teachers' uptake of them—take center stage in this and the following chapter. This chapter explores how Playa's teachers brought their equity orientations into conversation with the CCSS, thereby making visible some of what's possible instructionally, even in the face of demanding and often constraining policy demands, and illuminating key school conditions that mediated teachers' CCSS enactments.

Toward the chapter's end, we also highlight some of the struggles that Playa's teachers faced in their efforts to take up text complexity and close reading in ways that would benefit emergent bilingual (EB) students. These struggles, in turn, become the focus of Chapter 7.

INTERTWINED CCSS EMPHASES:
CLOSE READING AND INCREASING TEXT COMPLEXITY

The 10th anchor standard in the CCSS for English language arts (ELA) stipulates that students will "read and comprehend complex literary and informational texts independently and proficiently." This standard aims to "place equal emphasis on the sophistication of what students read and the skill with which they read" in order to improve students' "college and career readiness" (Common Core State

Standards Initiative, 2010, English/Language Arts, p. 8). Although this anchor standard recommends that students engage with complex literary and informational texts, the CCSS are emphatic about increasing the use of informational texts, particularly in the early grades where literary texts have typically been featured more frequently than informational ones.

This 10th anchor standard privileges text complexity through "a grade-by-grade 'staircase' of increasing complexity that rises from beginning reading to the college and career readiness level" (CCSS Introduction, p. 8). To aid teachers in identifying the "right" complex texts for students, the CCSS offer example texts and suggest that teachers, when making their own determinations, apply three approaches: those that rely on quantitative measures, those that gauge qualitative dimensions, and those that consider the reader–task relationship.

Quantitative measures—such as the Lexile Framework for Reading (Lennon & Burdick, 2014), the Renaissance ATOS readability formula (Milone, 2015), and Pearson's Reading Maturity Metric—use algorithms to calculate a text's complexity by accounting, for example, for the number of syllables in each word, the use of low-frequency words, and the length of sentences. Qualitative measures gauge a text's complexity based on the text's levels of meaning, structure, language conventionality and clarity, and knowledge demands. Approaches that take into account "reader–task relationship," meanwhile, treat a text's complexity as contingent upon a text's use with a particular reader. In such approaches, factors internal to the reader, along with supports provided to the reader, also contribute to a text's complexity.

As Hiebert (2014) has noted, although the CCSS recommend using multiple approaches to determine a text's complexity, quantitative "benchmarks" are described with greater specificity than other criteria. Indeed, the development of the grade-by-grade staircase relied on "quantitative benchmarks in the form of Lexiles (in the initial CCSS documents) as well as five more quantitative systems [identified] in a supplement to the Standards" (p. 1).

In addition, Common Core authors introduced the idea that students should be presented with texts complex enough to facilitate "struggle." Specifically, they recommended that teachers use texts that do not lend themselves to easy understanding and instead require persistent, reiterated efforts to unpack texts' basic and underlying meanings (Coleman & Pimentel, 2012).

This idea—that teachers should select texts complex enough to induce a degree of struggle—has been adopted and expanded upon by some well-known authors of literacy instruction guidebooks (e.g., Fisher, Frey, & Lapp, 2012; Jones, Chang, Heritage, & Tobiason, 2014). Two such experts, Doug Fisher and Linda Frey, published seven guidebooks on the CCSS in 2012 and 2013, several of which we regularly saw in Playa teachers' classrooms. Considering their tattered covers, dog-eared pages, and frequent mentions by participants, we came to view these authors and their ideas as particularly influential in Playa staff's standards navigation.

Like authors of the CCSS, these authors urge teachers to introduce texts that are above students' current reading levels—at levels that even approach student thresholds for frustration—in order to bring about "productive failure" (Fisher et al., 2012). This assumption that the "right" amount of academic struggle can be "productive," presses teachers to intentionally assign texts that students won't likely comprehend, and to have students read independently in order to make them more "receptive" to "subsequent instruction" (Fisher et al., 2012, p. 83). These authors also argue that having students struggle with "rigorous" texts ultimately helps them build academic stamina and construct identities as perseverant readers—both of which students arguably need in order to meet the "higher bar" set by the CCSS and develop "college- and career-readiness."

In addition to encouraging teachers to present students with text that is complex enough to generate "productive struggle," the CCSS offer various other instructional guidelines for engaging students around such texts. These guidelines are articulated explicitly, for example, in the CCSS's first anchor standard, which stipulates that students must "read closely to determine what the text says explicitly and to make logical inferences from it" and "cite specific textual evidence when writing or speaking to support conclusions drawn from the text" (Common Core State Standards Initiative, 2010a, pp. 10, 35). Calls to engage students in "close reading" and text-based argumentation are emphasized across the full gradespan of the CCSS.

Notably, although the CCSS suggest that marshaling textual evidence to support a claim depends upon having engaged in close reading, a recent National Council of Teachers of English (NCTE) policy brief challenges this premise. The brief argues that "any approach to reading can insist on warrants for interpretations of texts"; thus, "by itself, then, close reading cannot ensure that students will develop deep understandings of what they read" (National Council of Teachers of English, 2012, p. 2).

In "close reading," which has also been called "cold reading" (see Snow, 2013), students are given a text with which they have little to no familiarity. Without substantial pre-reading activities, students are asked to independently read the unfamiliar text and "annotate" those features or sentences that they do not comprehend. Only after they struggle through this first reading are students offered scaffolds such as partner discussion and teacher-led rereading. Subsequent discussions are expected to focus on ideas contained "within the four corners of the text" or page (Coleman & Pimentel, 2012, p. 4); in other words, teachers are urged to discourage students from connecting ideas from the text to their personal experiences and instead to encourage text-dependent meaning-making.

CCSS authors and supporters (Coleman & Pimentel, 2012; Fisher et al., 2012; Jones et al., 2014) argue that cold reads force students to rely on reading strategies rather than prior knowledge or experiences to make sense of complex texts. Fisher and colleagues (2012) additionally speculate that by wrestling with unfamiliar texts, students learn how to identify whatever is tripping them up when they read and practice persevering through challenging material. Meanwhile, Coleman and Pimentel (2012) argue that cold reads with little to no pre-reading or "early" scaffolding (e.g., generating predictions, providing context, activating students' prior knowledge, etc.) prevent teachers from doing the "heavy lifting" for students or diminishing the "excitement" that can come from a reader's anticipation about a new text.

Although the CCSS claim that they are designed to "help ensure that all students are college and career ready no later than the end of high school" (Common Core State Standards Initiative, 2010a, p. 3), they offer little direction when it comes to using the standards with culturally and linguistically diverse learners. Indeed, discussion regarding learner diversity is mostly limited to the general recommendation that teachers should offer "extra scaffolds" during instruction (Fisher & Frey, 2013). Regarding what such scaffolds might look like within the parameters of cold/close reading, no further details are offered.

Scholars have become increasingly vocal about the potential benefits and risks of putting the close reading of complex text into practice with diverse learners, including emergent bilinguals (EBs). As discussed in this book's Introduction, some experts offer tepid praise for the CCSS given its potential to increase the likelihood that EBs will be held to higher standards and given more opportunities to develop academic language, particularly through accessing more complex text (Wong Fillmore & Fillmore, 2012; Wong Fillmore & Martinez, 2015).

More common, however, are cautionary accounts about potential risks for EBs. These tend to problematize the language demands associated with having students read complex texts (which are also often above-grade-level texts) (e.g., August & Shanahan, 2015; Bunch, 2015) and the call for teachers to withhold scaffolds during close reading, despite clear evidence of their importance for EB students especially (Au & Waxman, 2015).

When mapped against their expertise about teaching EBs, as well as their more general equity-oriented goals, Playa's teachers' enactment of close reading and text complexity was at times exemplary and at times troubling. This dynamic is not altogether surprising given (1) ongoing debates about close reading and text complexity within literacy and bilingual education scholarly communities, (2) ambiguities concerning the implementation of these CCSS emphases with culturally and linguistically diverse students, and (3) a complex array of factors, outlined in prior chapters, mediating Playa's teachers' work and learning.

EFFORTS TO MERGE CLOSE READING, COMPLEX TEXT, AND EQUITY PEDAGOGY

Several months into Playa's adoption of the CCSS, 4th-grade teachers Justin, Paco, and Julie gathered around a rectangular table for their regularly scheduled collaborative meeting. With 2½ hours allotted for planning and reflection, they reviewed the agenda that Paco—the grade level's instructional leadership team "rep"—had crafted following their meeting that month. The agenda included several substantial items, including establishing grade-level literacy and mathematics benchmarks, checking in about specific struggling students, and thematic unit planning. Topping the list that morning, however, was one word: *annotation.*

The term *annotation*—as used at Playa and in this book—refers to the practice of marking up a text while reading it. Teaching about annotation generally involves instructing students how to respond to text in various ways, and to indicate such responses on the page using a symbol and/or accompanying note. Annotation is often used to help students develop habits of mind related to critical reading, to acquire strategies for use in supporting their own meaning-making, and to develop their note-taking skills.

Paco shared that, in response to administrative mandate, he and other instructional leadership team reps had spent most of their previous meeting in grade-level bands—K, 1st–2nd, 3rd–5th, and 6th–8th—trying to identify three areas of "focus for our annotation work," which administrators now considered a required schoolwide practice.

Despite the chock-full agenda, teachers launched into a lively 45-minute dialogue about annotation. Topics ranged from the logistical, such as determining which marks or symbols students ought to use; to the philosophical, such as contemplating annotation's authentic purpose; to the pedagogical, such as considering what students were "getting out of [the practice]" and whether informational texts called for different kinds of annotation from literary ones. Teachers also discussed how math and science teachers, like Julie, might incorporate annotation into their instruction, too.

The teachers came to agreement about several issues, such as a shared definition of annotation, what Justin described as "physically interacting with texts," and a shared sense of some "starting" targets for annotation at their grade level—including, in Paco's words, to "summarize major points, identify unknown words and phrases, and point out evidence of opinion." Still, various issues remained unresolved when the teachers, noting the time, moved on to remaining agenda items.

Before transitioning, Paco reminded them that they were expected to have students do close readings involving annotation as often as possible, and that they would return to these topics at their next collaborative meeting.

We share this vignette because it speaks to teachers' willingness to engage deeply around the CCSS. It also points to the varied and numerous resources that teachers summoned as they strove to make meaning of and act upon even just a few CCSS emphases—in this case, annotation as a key component of close reading. Exchanges like the one above also provide further insight into the kinds of coherence teachers worked to construct, the ambiguity they wrestled with, and the hard decisions, trade-offs even, they made along the way.

Despite ambiguity and complexity, teachers' policy enactment efforts were coherent in various ways—for example, especially pertinent here, in the careful and sustained attention to annotation across the gradespan. Indeed, almost every time we stepped into classrooms, we encountered students annotating challenging texts, often for extended periods of time. From 1st-graders annotating informational texts about human rights and deforestation, to 4th-graders annotating literary texts about immigration and migration, to middle schoolers annotating articles about race and religion, there was no doubting that Playa's teachers had taken up annotation as a schoolwide practice, even in the early stages of CCSS adoption.

Yet, there was also considerable variation in how teachers put CCSS-sanctioned instructional emphases into practice. Despite their best efforts, teachers at times struggled to comply with the CCSS's call for close reading of complex text—and with their administrators' interpretations of that call—while simultaneously attending to the authentic learning goals they held for students (e.g., in the example below, developing literacy practices that matter for real life and facilitating a deep and nuanced understanding of segregation and its historical significance). Teachers balanced these concerns—which often played out as competing demands—with different degrees of confidence and success.

MAKING MEANING IN MIDDLE SCHOOL

Playa's middle school teachers demonstrated a degree of comfort, relatively speaking, when it came to integrating their sense of what the CCSS were calling for with their sense of what equity-minded literacy instruction should entail. In light of this, in the next section, we offer an extended account of how one teacher, Sonya, interpreted the CCSS emphasis on close reading of complex text and enacted a close reading cycle with students. We follow that account with more succinct descriptions of Lynette's and Miriam's approaches to close reading of complex text.

Across all three accounts, we highlight how these teachers scaffolded EBs' engagement and learning: Sonya, through multiple close readings about school segregation situated within a unit on social injustice; Lynette, through structured collaborative work supporting close reading of narrative and informational texts related to British literature broadly defined; and Miriam, through students' close reading and presentation of self-selected texts connected to the study of Islam, one component of their broader exploration of world religions.

Relevance, Responsiveness and Rigor in Close Reading

It was a breezier than normal winter morning when Sonya's 8th-graders filed through the classroom door. Many seemed sleepy—it was first period, after all—but that didn't stop students from greeting Sonya, most of them cheerfully. Sonya was also quick to welcome students, and in doing so, she indicated the depth with which she knew and cared about them. With one student, she inquired about a sick relative; with another, she joked about messy hair the result of either the blustery weather or having woken up a few minutes prior.

Students demonstrated similar warmth and familiarity with one another, too. A gaggle of laughing girls talked excitedly, hugging one another as they entered the classroom and exchanged gifts for one of their birthdays. Meanwhile, several boys talked animatedly about a movie they had seen over the weekend.

Once everyone had found their seats, just a quick look from Sonya led students to quiet themselves and turn their attention to her. In response, Sonya explained that they would continue with the unit theme "Racial, cultural, and socioeconomic differences can lead to misunderstandings, prejudice, and violence" by further examining the topic of school segregation that they had begun addressing the previous week. Notably, given teachers' commitments to bilingualism and critical pedagogy, we understand explorations of similar topics across grade levels as reflecting teachers' efforts to develop students' conceptual understandings and increasingly sophisticated associated academic language, rather than as curriculum redundancy.

Although the study of segregation was a relatively new one, Sonya and her students had been exploring the broader unit theme for some time. Earlier that morning, before students arrived, Sonya had shared with us details about her prior instruction, in which students had traced instances of injustice over time and compared and contrasted "the idea of the American Dream with the reality that is experienced by many, particularly immigrants to the U.S." She had also walked us along and talked about her classroom walls, where student work took center stage (Figure 6.1). In accordance with Playa's emphasis on thematic instruction, the topics represented were related, yet wide-ranging, and included, for example, Japanese internment; indentured servitude; and racial profiling, with specific focus on the United States post-9/11, Arizona's immigration laws, and the murder of Trayvon Martin. A central CCSS-based approach that Sonya utilized for exploring these topics was close reading. Figures 6.2 and 6.3 capture some of the many ways that Sonya had done this. Students had additionally completed various persuasive and analytical essays about these topics as part of their effort to meet standards, identified below, focused on argumentative writing.

Sonya had launched the study of school segregation the prior week by presenting students with an informational text entitled "Historical Perspective: Segregation in Public Schools," which offered a historical overview of seminal school segregation cases filed by different racial groups over an approximately 100-year period. On the bottom of this article, as well as others she would use in subsequent days, Sonya identified standards that students would be expected to meet, a practice she engaged in regularly so that her students would always "have a clear purpose for what they're doing."

In this instance, Sonya included the following from one of the standards concerning the reading of informational text: "Analyze a case in which two or more texts provide conflicting information on the same topic and identify where the texts disagree on matters of fact or interpretation" (CCSS.ELA-LITERACY. RI.8.9). Although Sonya argued that including the CCSS's actual language helped focus students, she purposefully avoided using numbers to represent standards because she believed that doing so undermined possibilities for using standards "authentically."

On this morning, Sonya's goal was to build on student understanding generated through reading this text the previous week. Thus, she opened the lesson by posing questions so that students might recount prior learnings and establish common understandings from which to build. Students seemed ready and prepared for Sonya's line of questioning; several jumped organically into conversation, co-constructing responses regarding why *Plessy v. Ferguson* "was so important." Together, students conveyed that *Plessy* set a precedent that positioned

Figure 6.1. A Snapshot of Sonya's Classroom Wall

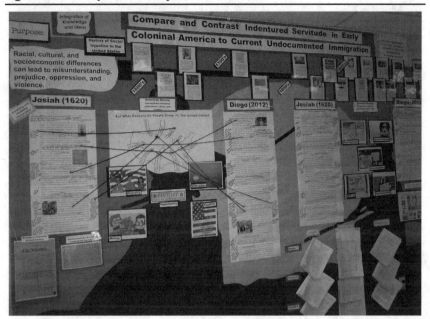

Teachers like Sonya displayed on their classroom walls unit themes, model texts, and student work.

the separation of different racial groups as acceptable, so long as the facilities and services available to different groups were equal.

Following this opening discussion, Sonya referred to the movie *The Help*— which, from looks of recognition among students, was a shared point of reference—and asked students to consider why the maid in the story was required to use separate facilities from the family for whom she worked. Students were quick to respond.

Using *Plessy* and *The Help* as common referents for the concept of segregation, Sonya then asked students, as was standard Playa practice, to mark the connection of new material to the unit's "big idea"—"Racial, cultural, and socioeconomic differences can lead to misunderstanding, prejudice, oppression, and violence"— which she had them read chorally. This set the tone for the introduction of three new informational texts, each of which offered a different perspective on school segregation, and which Sonya asked students to read and annotate multiple times.

Two such texts addressed the same subject. One was an article offering an in-depth account of *Mendez v. Westminster* (1945), the famed California school desegregation case filed on behalf of 5,000 Mexican American families; the other was a faded copy of a 1945 newspaper article reporting on the *Mendez* court ruling. During our conversation earlier that day, Sonya explained that she selected these articles because she believed they met the expected level of text complexity

Figure 6.2. An 8th-Grader's Annotation of an Informational Text about Muslim Bias

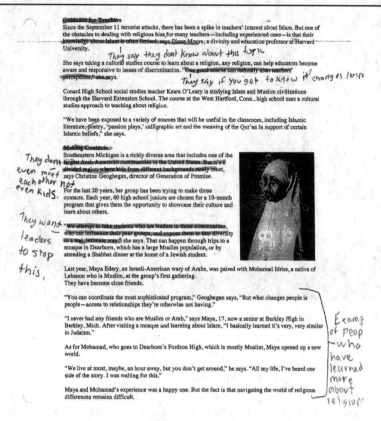

One page—annotated by 8th-grader Lionel—of a multipage article titled "Combatting Anti-Muslim Bias" (Shah, 2011). This particular page, as any others would, shows a range of annotations—in this case, restatements of key points (e.g., "They say if you get to know it changes perspective"), syntheses of main ideas (e.g., "They want leaders to stop this"), and features used by the author to substantiate an argument (e.g., "example of people who have learned more about religion").

for 8th-graders as per the parameters set by the CCSS (CCSS.ELA-LITERACY. RI.8.10): "By the end of the year, [8th-graders will be able to] read and comprehend literary nonfiction at the high end of the grades 6–8 text complexity band independently and proficiently."); however, she explained that her selection was also based on the texts' capacities to "challenge common assumptions about *Brown v. Board of Education* being the first school desegregation case and (de)segregation primarily affecting Black communities." Sonya additionally felt the text would have relevance for Playa students because the content "took place in Southern California" and "involved Mexican people."

Figure 6.3. An 8th-Grader's Argument Map

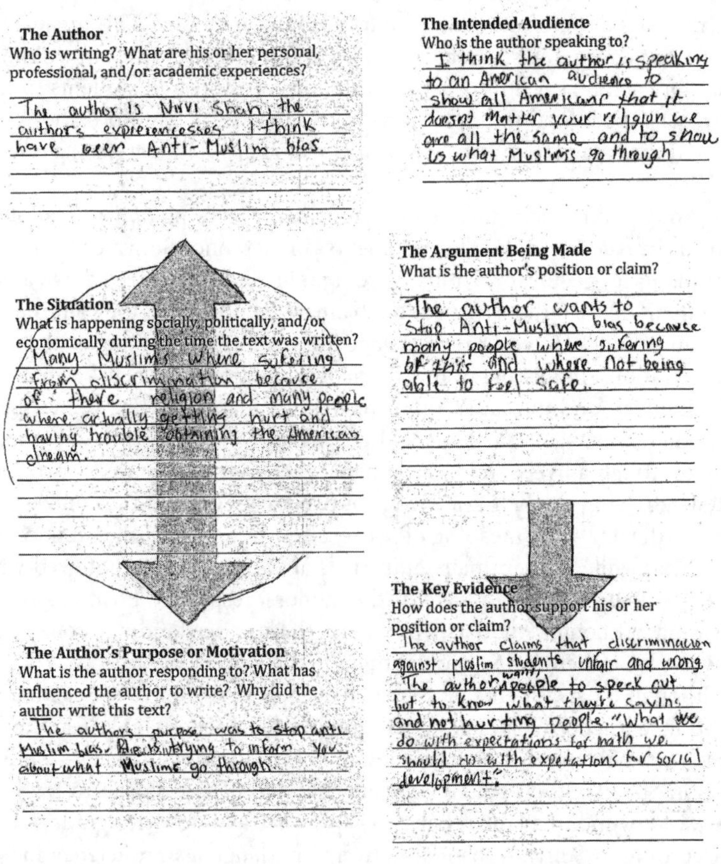

The Author
Who is writing? What are his or her personal, professional, and/or academic experiences?

The author is Nivi Shah, the author's experiences I think have been Anti-Muslim bias.

The Intended Audience
Who is the author speaking to?

I think the author is speaking to an American audience to show all Americans that it doesn't matter your religion we are all the same and to show us what Muslims go through

The Situation
What is happening socially, politically, and/or economically during the time the text was written?

Many Muslims where suffering from discrimination because of there religion and many people where actually getting hurt and having trouble obtaining the American dream.

The Argument Being Made
What is the author's position or claim?

The author wants to stop Anti-Muslim bias because many people where suffering of this and where not being able to feel safe.

The Author's Purpose or Motivation
What is the author responding to? What has influenced the author to write? Why did the author write this text?

The authors purpose was to stop anti-Muslim bias. By is notifying to inform you about what Muslims go through.

The Key Evidence
How does the author support his or her position or claim?

The author claims that discrimination against Muslim students unfair and wrong. The author wants people to speak out but to know what they're saying and not hurting people. "What we do with expectations for math we should do with expectations for social development."

An "argument map" completed by the same student, after reading and annotating the article featured in Figure 6.2, in which he communicated his overarching textual understandings and analyses, in alignment with prompts posed by the graphic organizer Sonya provided.

The other text, a 2005 *Chicago Tribune* opinion piece entitled "Chicago's Segregated Schools," chronicled the opening of Urban Prep Charter Academy, an all-boys high school established to serve "primarily Black youth," as part of a broader discussion about the 50th anniversary of *Brown*, and what the piece characterized as the reintroduction of "segregated schools in the name of reform" (Turley, 2005). Sonya told us she had chosen the piece because it presented a contrasting perspective on school segregation and was likely to appeal to Playa students, who, like students described in the piece, attend a public charter school that was designed to advance particular, and some might argue, community- and culturally specific goals.

As the texts were distributed, Sonya presented students with a graphic organizer that she designed to scaffold them toward mastery of the aforementioned standard, which she included again in each text's footer: "Analyze a case in which two or more texts provide conflicting information on the same topic and identify where the texts disagree on matters of fact or interpretation." This organizer, "Analyzing Conflicting Texts," included a two-column table, with one column designated for each text. Within each column, prompts pressed students to identify each writer's "position," multiple "facts" and the writer's "interpretations of such facts," and the "major areas of disagreement" that arose in comparing one text to the other.

Although Sonya administered no guidelines regarding *how* to read, her lack of explicit instruction didn't deter students. In fact, once Sonya cheerily encouraged students to "get to work," most dove right in. Some hunkered down alone and read to themselves. Others turned to tablemates, with whom they alternated quietly reading aloud. However they engaged in reading, most blanketed their texts with annotations, indicating prior experience with this approach.

Walking around the classroom revealed that many students were supporting one another to navigate the texts and complete the standards-based graphic organizer. Through a lively and rich bilingual exchange, for example, two boys negotiated—drawing on their knowledge of two languages and the contextual clues offered by the text—the meaning of *per se,* a word they encountered in one of the pieces. Meanwhile, student pairs and triads at various tables conferred with one another—usually bilingually—about the authors' respective positions on school segregation. Although students worked out their understandings collaboratively, each wrote his or her own version of them in the graphic organizers.

Although most students participated at their seats, Sonya also gathered four students for a teacher-facilitated, small-group conference at a table near the front of the classroom. Two such students—newcomers to the United States—were strong readers in Spanish, their native language, but had been exposed to English only in the past few months. The other two—both "struggling" with grade-level reading, according to Sonya—possessed strong oral language proficiency in Spanish and English, as was immediately apparent in the way they moved fluidly between languages. These kinds of hybrid language practices abounded in the small-group interaction, as they did elsewhere at Playa.

The heterogeneity of this small group, by Sonya's design, positioned students to support one another with close reading. Sonya, in turn, leveraged these conditions by facilitating a text-based discussion that encouraged students with more developed English to pull examples directly from the text, while encouraging newcomer students to draw on prior knowledge to contribute to high-level sensemaking of the text's content, while building basic and more academic vocabulary along the way. In the context of this teacher-facilitated talk, students were willing and able to riff off and respond to one another's ideas and questions about what they were reading—in essence, engaging "effectively" with "diverse partners on grade 8 topics, texts and issues" and citing "textual evidence" to support both explicit and inferential interpretations as stipulated in grade-level Speaking and Listening standards (CCSS.ELA-LITERACY.SL.8.1 and CCSS.ELA-LITERACY.RI.8.1).

However, as soon as Sonya turned her back to attend to other students, the enthusiasm of those in the small group waned; their sinking posture alone suggested they were beginning to experience the texts and task more as something to slog through than stimulating. Although Sonya had written tailored questions in the margins of the four students' texts—a support others, who were expected to annotate texts with self-generated questions, did not receive—the small group didn't respond to them. And although they stared down at the pages in front of them, there was no indication that they were, in fact, reading, never mind comprehending and critically interrogating.

Always attuned to classroom dynamics, Sonya noticed that the small group had lost focus; but just as she circled back to check in with them, the class period ended.

Picking up where she left off, Sonya began the next morning's class by asking students to take out their texts from the prior day. She then followed with 15 minutes of explicit CCSS-based instruction regarding how authors craft text-based claims and effective argumentation (CCSS.ELA-LITERACY.W.8.1A; CCSS.ELA-LITERACY.W.8.2A; CCSS.ELA-LITERACY.W.8.2B). Essentially, Sonya was laying the groundwork for students to later draw evidence from across texts to write their own well-argued essays about school segregation.

Using undocumented immigration as her focal topic in order to avoid modeling "too much," or "hypermediating" (Gutierréz & Stone, 2002) students' eventual writing about segregation, Sonya then offered guidelines—via PowerPoint slides and an accompanying mini-lecture—about the role of "strong" introductory paragraphs in argumentative essays. Specifically, slides focused on the importance of students "preparing readers" by "defining the claims" of their argument—claims they would be expected to substantiate by "incorporating textual evidence." In these ways, Sonya's instruction reflected the CCSS call for students to "introduce a topic clearly, previewing what is to follow" (CCSS.ELA-LITERACY.W.8.2A), and to "support claim(s) with logical reasoning and relevant evidence, using accurate, credible sources and demonstrating an understanding of the topic or text" (CCSS.ELA-LITERACY.W.8.2B). Once Sonya finished, students returned to the texts from the prior day. For the remaining 35 minutes of class, students reread the texts and added new annotations. They also referred to those texts and their annotations to determine which arguments and details they might incorporate into their future essays.

The next day—the third in this close reading cycle—Sonya again greeted students warmly: "Okay, take out your graphic organizers and stuff—oh, and good morning!" Students laughed in response, ruffling through backpacks in search of readings and all else. Meanwhile, Sonya distributed a new collaborative graphic organizer that we also observed Lynette use with her 7th-graders—titled "Conversational Round Table Organizer." Depicting a circle divided into empty quartiles, the organizer encouraged table groups to discuss and then document their joint understandings about segregation, based on the texts they had been reading over multiple days. The completed organizer, with space for four group members to write their respective ideas, would serve eventually as the group's "exit ticket."

Before students jumped into the work together, Sonya reminded them of the overarching unit theme and reiterated this week's focus: identifying conflicting information across texts. As we saw while circulating the room soon after, the students' lack of hesitation in getting started, despite not receiving any instructions from Sonya, suggested that they had used this type of organizer before. The kaleidoscope of colorful annotations splattered across most texts also suggested that many students had completed multiple close reads of all three.

Only 5 minutes later, however, students' focus seemed to wane, much like it had for the small group the day prior. The hum of attentive collaboration we had come to expect in Sonya's classroom gave way to louder, more animated, and off-task interaction.

While off-taskness can be frustrating for teachers, in this case we sympathized with students. After all, and as we and others have questioned elsewhere (Beltramo & Stillman, 2015; Winograd, 2015), how much undivided attention to the same texts can we reasonably expect of students? Shouldn't we assume that multiple readings of the same texts, and with little variation in how those texts are approached, might generate boredom and distraction? To be frank, we were impressed that adolescents had remained so focused over the course of multiple days and numerous readings of the same pieces, particularly given the privileging of annotation over all other reading approaches.

True to form, Sonya seemed to anticipate this moment and announced that she would be showing two short videos with the purpose of "supporting [students'] understandings" of the texts they had been reading (and rereading). Students, excited and relieved to momentarily set their texts aside, quickly quieted themselves for the screenings.

After the first video, Sonya asked students to discuss in table groups the video's content, specifically a school board member's efforts to incorporate the *Mendez* case into her district's official social studies curriculum. Students immediately launched into conversation, moving with ease between Spanish and English as they considered the pros and cons of such a policy. Before asking students to share their ideas with the whole class, Sonya screened the second video, a more recent 3-minute promotional video for Chicago's Urban Prep Academy Charter, the very school whose founding was described in one of the texts students had been reading. Her goal, she explained to us while the video ran, was for students to draw across a range of texts—written articles and videos—to complicate their understandings of school (de)segregation.

Once the second video ended, Sonya posed multiple questions to the whole class that stimulated a 20-minute stretch of student dialogue. This dialogue—excerpted below—showcased the kind of engagement, comprehension, and analytical competency that had been generated over several days through Sonya's particular uptake of close reading.

To open the discussion, Sonya asked, simply: "Is it okay to have schools like Urban Prep that are just for African American males?" Students clamored to respond, initially talking over one another in their efforts to be heard but then yielding to a few particularly passionate voices, not all of whom were the most frequent speakers in the room. At first, students seemed mostly to agree with one another that schools like Urban Prep ought to exist. The discussion became more contentious, and also more substantive and nuanced, after Sonya interjected at a critical point to ask students if they considered Urban Prep a segregated school.

> *Elena:* In the 1940s, they—the schools—segregated between the races. But now, they're trying to make it look good. They're trying to make it look as if segregation is something good. But even though it's not. They're segregating the African American males, but why don't they just get other teachers that care about all of them [the students] instead of just segregating them?
>
> *Sonya:* Who agrees with Elena about that?
>
> *Carlos:* Well, you can't necessarily call it segregation because, um, I mean segregation is basically hating on a certain race. They're not hating on a certain race. They're focusing on African American males . . .
>
> *Elena:* They're targeting . . .
>
> *Carlos:* They're targeting them to help them grow and have a better life. And I'm sure as Elena said that there are other races, other genders that need help. But it's like, one problem at a time. They have the statistics that African American males have more problems graduating from high school, more dropouts. And it's just helping—they're not necessarily segregating.
>
> *Cristina:* It's not like the 1940s segregation where they put 'em in a different school because they can't speak the language . . .
>
> *Carlos:* Or because of their skin color or . . .
>
> *Cristina:* Now they put 'em in a different school because they can't, um, they can't succeed in life by themselves. They need that extra push . . .

This idea that some students may "need an extra push" took hold in the discussion. Some students argued that those who had been forced to attend poorly resourced schools and had limited access to high-quality teachers deserved opportunities to attend a school like Urban Prep. In particular, they noted that it was almost always students of color and students from lower-income areas—indeed, students much like themselves and their peers—who were relegated to "bad" schools and subsequently held responsible for their own academic struggles, even when adults—namely, teachers and other staff, according students—ought to bear responsibility, too. Students also noted similarities between their own school and Urban Prep, highlighting, for example, Playa's "press" on them to "step it up" and their families' beliefs that they—given racial and socioeconomic discrimination—would not be held to Playa-level expectations in other local schools. Many students agreed with this perspective until Sonya complicated the issue further.

Sonya: Okay, so the Urban Prep school focuses on African American males. What if I'm from the same neighborhood and I'm one of those students' sister? Can I go there?

Students: No, because . . .

Sonya: Why not? We have the same upbringing, we have the same background, we live in the same neighborhood . . .

David: Because you're a woman.

Students raised a few clarifying questions about this scenario. A previously quiet young woman then posed a question that bumped the level of conversation up further, pressing the class to wrestle with complex issues like structural versus individual attributions of educational inequity; intersections of race, gender, and other identity markers; school reform, including the privatization of public education; and the difference between segregation imposed by others and separation affirmed or even introduced by one's own community.

Ceci: It is segregation because you have the same characteristics as your brother but you couldn't get in.

Josue: Or, if it's a different race, like say, myself.

Ricardo: It would be discrimination in a way, but today's segregation is a little more justified because they're the ones who need the help. It wouldn't be fair to put them aside and accept women just because people would consider it segregation or discrimination. It wouldn't . . .

Ivan: Yeah, but, she said she came from the same . . .

Sonya: The only difference is my gender.

Carlos: Exactly. So how is that fair . . . ?

Ricardo: It's discrimination.

Sonya: Yeah, no, I mean, you have a point—you have a valid point. You're just saying that this specific school is just targeting this specific group of people. There is a need for other minorities and other subgroups to get this additional help also. Right? We all agree with that, right?

Students: Yeah.

Sonya: There's no right or wrong answer here. This is your opinion and how you are supporting your opinion. Whether it's your personal experience or something that you've read—statistics. That's whatever it may be. What is your opinion when it comes to segregated schools? What I hear from most of you is segregation from the 1940s, '50s, '60s, that was unjust. That was an injustice that happened here in the United States and it should not be repeated again. Is that correct?

Students: Yes.

Sonya: Segregation that is happening now . . . hmmmm? It's a fine line. Is it acceptable?

Students: No.

Paloma: I say it's not.

Sonya: You say it's not? Because?

Ricardo: Yeah, because not everybody is living the American Dream . . .

Paloma: I say it's not because how do you know that the African American women are not struggling also? How do you know?

David (Gesturing toward the texts on his desk): The statistics [in these texts] don't show that . . .

Ceci: They shouldn't, like, separate them and make them feel different and put them in a completely different school. They should give them more support—more moral support, more educational support, instead of just separating them. Like, "We'll teach you and you, but forget about you."

Ivan: Well, maybe it's the school's fault—

Carlos: It's the people that they hire.

Ceci: Exactly! They should just hire other teachers that support you . . .

Manuel: But there's no money for that.

David: How do you know?

Paloma: Yeah, there's money to build that new school but not . . .

Ceci: If there's money enough to build another school, then why is there not enough money to pay the teachers?

Sonya: So, it sounds like you're saying that it's not an issue with the students but it's an issue with education and educational reform.

Gabi: It's the teachers.

Elena: We need to get teachers that care and that offer us support, in any school . . .

Ceci: Just like in this school. If you're failing a class, you have a one-on-one. They're telling you—they give you the support here. So that's what they should do in other schools.

Sonya: So your solution would be: Don't focus on one particular group. Just change the whole education program.

David: I kinda agree with Ceci, but the problem is that public schools are getting too big. There's way too many students for teachers to be able to give one-on-one.

Paloma: Then make more schools. But not through racial discrimination.

David: But budget cuts don't let us. Urban Prep is a private organization—somebody got money to build that school. It wasn't the district.

Maria: Well, couldn't they have built one school for everybody?

David: No, because they're not a part of the school district. The school district has to be able to pay for that.

This stretch of dialogue prompted students to grapple with issues surrounding the privatization of public education. In particular, they wondered—and ultimately disagreed about—whether individuals have the right to open schools that reflect their personal or political agenda. Some students argued that Urban Prep's founder, a Black man, had knowledge and life experience that ought to inform educational decisions. Others, however, were uncomfortable with the premise that any wealthy individual could open a school to serve only certain students, particularly when the funder is perceived as caring about advancing only his own community, or in the words of one student, Carmen, "only wants his own race to succeed." Responding to that comment, Sonya asked Carmen, "You're inferring that?" When Carmen nodded, Sonya added, "Interesting . . . she's more for educational reform and restructuring how the educational system works in the United States to support and target all students. Is that a possibility?" Many students called out affirmative responses; when Sonya asked who would make these sorts of changes, students shouted that it would be themselves, with one boy adding, "After we get an education!"

Students were observably energized at this point, with many jumping out of their chairs to insert their two cents. A loud "Awwwww" rang out when Sonya announced there was no time left in the period to continue the discussion—a discussion that students were so committed to pursuing, they continued debating with one another as they filed out the door.

Although we, too, would have liked to see the discussion unfold further, we left Sonya's classroom that day impressed by what we had witnessed and heartened by the cumulative and also unfinished nature of the conversation. Indeed, the discussion was arguably even more powerful in its incompleteness—as if grappling with challenging questions was Sonya's central purpose, rather than coming to any particular answer, at least not one sanctioned by her.

What had Sonya done to generate these high levels of interest, engagement, understanding, and academic discourse in the context of the CCSS charge to engage students in close reading of complex texts? For starters, Sonya utilized magazine and newspaper articles as core informational texts, a move that, because of their manageable lengths and power to entertain and inform, arguably offered students greater access to content than other forms of informational text might have (Hiebert, 2013a). Sonya also selected texts that would advance students' learning about a broader a theme—one that students had been exploring for some time prior to using the three texts detailed here, with which they were already knowledgeable, and in which they were already invested. Students' references in the above dialogue to texts read the prior week and to the American Dream were but two of many more times when we witnessed students making connections between assigned texts and broader themes. Importantly, the unit of study within which this close reading work was situated was also one of genuine interest to students and offered opportunities for real-world application, as did the topics addressed in the assigned articles themselves.

Adding to this relevance was Sonya's encouragement that students look beyond "the four corners of the page" to draw connections across written texts and, for example, popular culture artifacts (like *The Help*) and mainstream media sources (like the video about Chicago's Urban Prep High School), as well as between those varied texts and students' own lives (like their families' expressed reasons for choosing Playa). In one illustration of this encouragement, for example, Sonya equated the validity of text-based arguments, where students might use "something [they've] read" like "statistics" to support an argument, with the validity of arguments supported by personal "experience" or opinion. As the dialogue demonstrates, students confidently enlisted both types of evidence as they contributed to the discussion, participating in ways that align with and arguably extend beyond CCSS demands, such as those stated in CCSS.ELA-Literacy.SL.8.4: "Present claims and findings, emphasizing salient points in a focused, coherent manner with relevant evidence, sound valid reasoning, and well-chosen details; use appropriate eye contact, adequate volume, and clear pronunciation."

Sonya's encouragement to look beyond the "four corners of the page" also manifested in the many instances when Sonya allowed students to bring in their own ideas, and then also directed them back to the assigned texts, holding them accountable for the ideas therein, as well. This was evident in the above dialogue when Sonya attempted to connect a student's seemingly opinion-driven comment that Urban Prep's founder only wanted "his own race to succeed" to broader text-based arguments about school reform, and the role of charters specifically. And, although she had students do multiple reads of the three informational texts—an approach that could have led to disengagement (and at times did)—Sonya mostly seemed to anticipate when the process might become boring or unproductive, and employed other tools (e.g., graphic organizers, student talk) and texts (e.g., video clips), which observably augmented student engagement and understanding.

It is worth noting here that, at times, classroom dialogue still did privilege students' opinions over textual evidence, and not without issue. As illustrated at various points in the featured dialogue, Sonya—like most other teachers at Playa—sometimes folded students' opinions into dialogue without pushing them to deeper levels of (critical) analysis. One could argue that this tendency undermined opportunities for students to meet standards requiring that they use textual evidence to substantiate arguments. More troubling to us, however, was that this tendency often compromised teachers' stated commitments to criticality. This was arguably the case, for example, when Sonya left unchecked students' framing of "bad teachers" as the root of (systemic) educational inequity and individual choices as the driving force behind widespread segregation, rather than engage students in analyses that would bring them closer to nuanced, structural understandings of societal inequity.

Returning to positive features of Sonya's instruction, it is important to underscore how Sonya's thematic approach to close reading of complex texts also supported her to enrich and contextualize her standards-based skill instruction. For example, her efforts to have students "analyze conflicting information on the same topic" across multiple texts (CCSS.ELA-Literacy.RI.8.9) and to prepare students to write argumentative essays using text-based substantiation were specified by pertinent standards (e.g., CCSS.ELA-Literacy.RI.8.1: "Cite the textual evidence that most strongly supports an analysis of what the text says explicitly as well as inferences drawn from the text"; CCSS.ELA-LITERACY.W.8.1: "Write arguments to support claims with clear reasons and relevant evidence"). In addition, students did not complete close reading as a stand-alone activity; rather, it was but one—albeit often used—component of their broader thematic learning. Students thus came to the texts with some key pre-reading experiences, which helped them navigate new, challenging material. As mentioned earlier, though pre-reading experiences, including tapping into readers' background knowledge, have long been held up by literacy and language acquisition scholars and practitioners as essential to literacy development (Echevarría, Vogt, & Short, 2016; Levin & Pressley, 1981), CCSS authors and supporters have deemed them generally unnecessary, even disruptive, to learning (Coleman & Pimentel, 2012: Fisher & Frey, 2013).

Sonya additionally provided students with opportunities to collaborate and make choices about their own learning, including about which language(s) to use with one another. These opportunities supported students to "do bilingualism" (as opposed to "have bilingualism")—in other words, to communicate authentically as bilinguals "do" (García, Flores, & Woodley, 2015); it also helped them make meaning of the texts on their own terms and in context (García & Hesson, 2015). High levels of student participation in small- and whole group discussions, including discussions mediated by graphic organizers that encouraged students to "'talk aloud' their thinking" (Gibbons, 2008, p. 166), additionally suggest that these collaborative learning experiences provided low-risk contexts for oral and written language production (e.g., Gibbons 2003, 2006).

That students had so many and such varied opportunities to work with one another and to collaborate in meaningful endeavors was also foundational to students' literacy learning and to the learning community, or community of practice, that Sonya cultivated (e.g., Almasi & McKeown, 1996; Guthrie, Rueda, Gambrell, & Morrison, 2009). This kind of participative approach helps in general—and helped in Sonya's case specifically—to lay groundwork for establishing the norms necessary for productive peer-to-peer and whole-class conversation (Alvermann et al., 1996; Hynde, 1999)—practices valued by both Playa faculty and the CCSS, and used by Sonya to scaffold students' learning vis-à-vis writing-heavy standards, such as those involving text-based argumentation (CCSS.ELA-LITERACY.W.8.1 and CCSS.ELA-LITERACY.W.8.2). In Sonya's case, it also clearly bolstered students' engagement, supported them to take ownership over their textual analysis, and facilitated purposeful learning (Au, 1998).

Finally, Sonya held high expectations for students at every turn and in ways that illustrated her embrace of mutual accountability. For example, although she selected difficult texts for close reading, Sonya provided students with varied resources—such as small-group work structures, peer talk, graphic organizers, explicit instruction, and video clips with relevance to students' lives—for navigating them. On multiple occasions we saw Sonya push students to higher levels of performance—for example, by pressing them to substantiate their opinions and arguments more fully. When appropriate, she also noted in academic terms when students were already demonstrating mastery over higher-order skills, like "inferring" information from text. Although Sonya was undoubtedly proud of students' accomplishments in such moments, she also resisted administering excessive praise, choosing instead to treat students' contributions as expected, the norm for Playa middle schoolers.

Scaffolding, Student Interest, and Structured Collaboration

Many of these same practices were evident in other middle school classrooms, too. In Lynette's 7th-grade ELA class, for example, we observed her take students through a week-long, scaffolded close reading cycle also designed to support students' progress toward multiple standards. In particular, Lynette's instruction drew from standards focused on having students "read and comprehend literary nonfiction in the grades 6–8 text complexity band" (CCSS.ELA-LITERACY.RI.7.5); "determine" a text's "central ideas" and analyze their development . . ." while "providing an objective summary of the text" (CCSS.ELA-LITERACY.RI.7.2); "cite . . . textual evidence to support" literal and inferential textual analyses (CCSS.ELA-LITERACY.RI.7.1); and "engage . . . in a range of collaborative discussions . . . with diverse partners on grade 7 topics, texts, and issues, building on others' ideas and expressing their own clearly" (CCSS.ELA-LITERACY.SL.7.1).

Like Sonya, Lynette had chosen text with relevance in mind. Working within the bounds of British literature, her assigned focus, Lynette explained that she sometimes struggled to find topics that were compelling to her students. During the previous (narrative) unit, students had "loved" reading *Lord of the Flies* and studying British poetry that spanned works from the 16th century, including Shakespeare's sonnets and Sir Walter Raleigh's "Ode to Queen Elizabeth," to contemporary songs composed by British artists, such as Adele's "Rolling in the Deep" and Sir Elton John's "Candle in the Wind." For Lynette, however, selecting engaging informational texts for the subsequent (nonfiction) unit was more challenging—that is, until she came upon an unexpected area of student interest.

The class had been exploring the dynamics of British royalty as part of the context-setting for their study of British literature. Students had engaged in a range of reading-related tasks—for example, annotating a 1939 speech delivered by King George VI, as well as an article arguing for the abolition of the monarchy. During those readings, Lynette learned that students were passionately curious about Princess Diana's death and especially the possible role of the paparazzi therein. Determined to resist reliance on easier-to-find, "boring" texts, Lynette happily followed students' lead. Like Sonya, she located a mass media article—in this case, a relatively involved *Time* magazine article from the 1990s—that explored the topic at hand.

As per CCSS emphases and Playa mandates, students first spent time reading and annotating the article independently and with little instruction from Lynette. After doing this for 2 days, students spent the final 3 days of the 5-day cycle participating "in a range of collaborative discussions" in table groups (CCSS.ELA-LITERACY.SL.7.1) in order to identify each section's and the overall article's "central ideas," and to explore their "development over the course of the text" (CCSS.ELA-LITERACY.RI.7.2).

To do this, Lynette assigned each group a section of the article, from which she had removed all subheadings in order to encourage students to "figure out on their own" the central ideas. She then asked groups to work together to write on one sentence strip their section's main idea, and on additional sentence strips three pieces of textual evidence that support that idea. Once students completed that task, they then worked across groups, drawing from sentences they had crafted to construct a single paragraph synthesizing the article.

As they engaged in this activity—which Lynette drew from a GLAD strategy called "cooperative strip paragraph" that involves using a similar process to structure students' collaborative paragraph writing—students worked smoothly together, as they had in Sonya's class. In one group, which had gathered on the ground around their sentence strips, two girls debated the meaning of one of their sentences. Scissors in hand, one offered to cut the strip and combine part of it with another to increase clarity. Another group member then suggested reordering two sentences, arguing that they would flow better if one followed the other. After a brief conversation during which the five group members came to consensus about these suggestions, students changed the sentences' wording and order. As they worked, they spontaneously complimented one another's ideas (e.g., "That is such a good idea—we should write that!"), supported one another to take on leadership roles (e.g., "I think you should write on the sentence strips since you have the best handwriting!"), toggled fluidly between Spanish and English, focused simultaneously on the minutiae of mechanics and more holistic matters of meaning, and took responsibility for their own and one another's individual participation (e.g., "Hey, why don't we each contribute [a supporting detail]?")—all this, while sharing accountability for the group process and product. Only after completing this scaffolded activity were students asked to write an argumentative essay about the media or paparazzi, in which they had to draw from various texts, including the one at the center of this activity, to offer supporting evidence for their opinions and ideas. That they could do so at a high level was testament to the close reading cycle that Lynette had taken them through in preparation.

Miriam, the 6th-grade Spanish language arts (SLA) and social studies teacher, also privileged scaffolding, student interest and ownership, and collaboration in her uptake of close reading of complex text. Across a broad unit on world religions and sub-unit exploring the Islamic Empire, for example, Miriam positioned students as historians and archeologists in an effort to develop their content knowledge and literacy skills in tandem. Throughout, students engaged with and produced a variety of texts, including annotating readings and creating their own maps and timelines depicting the rise and fall of major religions. (See, for example, Figure 6.4.) As suggested by the comic strip included in Chapter 1, featuring a dialogue between Jesus and the Prophet Mohammed (see Figure 1.6), Miriam offered students a menu of options for further engaging this material and showcasing what they were most interested in and had learned.

As depicted in Figure 6.5, once context had been established through experiences like those already described, students used iPads to search for accessible online texts related to Islamic history, including Islam's contributions to different fields, such as medicine, mathematics, and astronomy. Supported by

Figure 6.4. A 6th-Grader's Annotation of Informational Text

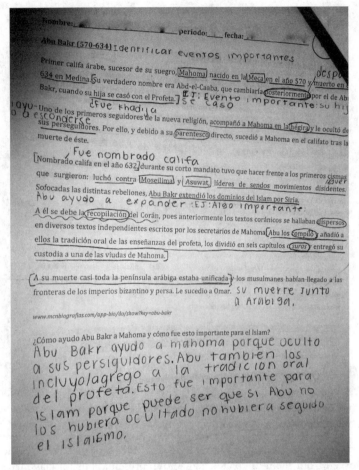

As noted atop her text about Abu Bakr (i.e., the Prophet Mohammed's advisor, father-in-law, and successor), 6th-grader Amanda has focused her annotations on "important events," as per Miriam's directions. Although Amanda does not annotate all such events (e.g., that Abu Bakr succeeded Mohammed as the first Caliph of Islam), her underlining illustrates attention to several, including Abu Bakr's birth and death, his role in fighting dissidents and in helping Islam spread, and his contributions to the Quran. Her handwritten notes likewise reflect the assigned focus (e.g., *"Abu ayudo a expander EI: algo importante* / Abu helped to expand: IE: something important"). In her response to the question at the bottom of the page, Amanda has drawn on these annotations to explain that "Abu Bakr helped Mohammed because he hid him from his persecutors. Abu also took on the oral tradition of the prophet. This was important for Islam because if Abu hadn't hidden Mohammed, Islam wouldn't have continued."

Figure 6.5. A 6th-Grader Conducts Online Research

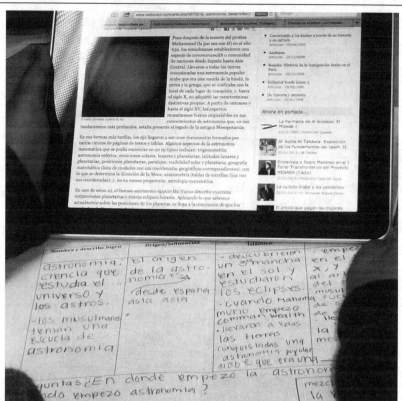

Students completed research on unit-related topics of their own choice—in this case, about Islam's contributions to astronomy.

graphic organizers, students engaged in close readings of those self-selected texts and worked from them to create small-group presentations for classmates about specific contributions and their influences and impacts within and beyond the Muslim world. Here, especially, Miriam's practice reflected literacy experts' recommendations about making close reading more student centered than is currently advocated by the CCSS (NCTE, 2012), particularly by offering students opportunities to select texts from among a menu of options (Calkins, Ehrenworth, & Lehman, 2012) and inviting students to identify texts that can be offered as close reading selections and analyzed and re-presented in some form (Seiler, 2011).

Notably, even though this unit was taught in Spanish, Miriam—demonstrating her already well-developed knowledge of the CCSS—drew both on ELA and on complementary disciplinary literacy standards for social studies instruction. In particular, she drew on standards that focused on students "integrating," "gathering," and "assessing the credibility" of information from multiple sources, including complex texts (CCSS.ELA-LITERACY.RI.6.7; CCSS.ELA-LITERACY.RI.6.8;

CCSS.ELA-LITERACY.RH.6-8.7; CCSS.ELA-LITERACY.RH.6-8.10), so that they might then "conduct short research projects to answer a question, drawing on several sources and refocusing the inquiry when appropriate" (CCSS.ELA-LITERA-CY.W.6.7). This aspect of Miriam's practice was representative: All other teachers instructing in Spanish also demonstrated familiarity with and commitment to enacting the CCSS, even though they were not written to guide Spanish-language instruction.

IMPRESSIVE INSTRUCTION THAT ALSO RAISES CONCERNS

We offer the above examples because they provide some insight regarding how teachers can engage the CCSS without abandoning equity-minded principles or expertise about teaching diverse learners, including EBs. They also offer opportunities to identify some of what—beyond anti-deficit stance (Chapter 4) and agreed-upon approaches (Chapter 5)—enabled impressive aspects of teachers' instruction.

One need spend but a few minutes in Sonya, Lynette, and Miriam's classrooms to notice how they differed from "typical" U.S. middle schools and their "institutionalized" norms. Gone were rows of individual desks historically intended to retain order and minimize socializing. Instead, students sat at tables, where they were encouraged to talk with peers in academic collaborations and social activities designed to build community.

All three teachers also held a special place in their hearts for adolescents, whom they named as their preferred age to teach. That preference informed the authentic care cradling each classroom—evident, for example, in the ease with which teachers and students interacted around challenging academic material. And although students, like typical adolescents, showed a strong desire to connect with peers, that tendency didn't undercut the respect they showed their teachers or schoolwork. This overall atmosphere was not coincidental or tangential, but intentional and essential to the instruction teachers offered.

Importantly, each teacher also had many years of experience in teaching and at Playa, where they reported having stayed because of its mission and the relationships each had built there. Given Playa's penchant to reassign teachers every few years, Sonya, Lynette, and Miriam had also all taught multiple grade levels, in and beyond middle school.

This experience mattered, both because it conferred a degree of pedagogical confidence and a repertoire of practice on which to draw, and also because it amplified teachers' sense of agency vis-à-vis policy and those in positions of relative power, like administrators. Whereas newer teachers were somewhat wowed and cowed by their accomplished administrators and thus unlikely to question them, Sonya, Lynette, and Miriam—all of whom had witnessed the school's ascendency firsthand—had an admiring but grounded sense of administrators, whose idiosyncrasies and imperfections they knew well. These three teachers, in turn, reported and demonstrated more comfort than others with challenging administrators if they felt it was needed.

In the above examples, teachers also named their own high expectations, friendly "competitiveness" with one another, and freedom to design curriculum "from scratch" as critical factors enabling them to integrate close reading and complex texts into instruction in responsive, scaffolded ways.

Despite their impressiveness and their enabling factors, the above examples also leave some cause for concern—especially in light of, rather than despite, teachers' expertise and experience. First, reflecting the almost normative-at-Playa resistance to instructional differentiation (described in Chapters 4 and 5), students in each example—as was true more broadly, too—read the same texts, regardless of their reading levels or language proficiencies. Even Miriam's students, who were afforded agency over text selection during iPad research, ultimately read the same texts as their tablemates, despite the groups' heterogeneous makeup.

In most cases, teachers eased the close reading process by, for example, selecting texts written for a general audience about topics of interest to students and providing task-aligned graphic organizers. These moves supported students to make more meaning from assigned texts than they would otherwise. Still, we couldn't help but wonder why teachers weren't employing a greater variety of texts, or a wider range of strategies to help students access them.

Take, for example, moments of disengagement among Sonya's students, which, as at other times, seemed to occur in part as a result of some students not yet being ready to read assigned texts on their own. Noting this, we asked Sonya why she opted to use the same texts with all learners. This was a pressing question for us because of the evident diversity in students' reading strengths and needs, and especially because of indications that texts may have been too difficult for at least some students. These indications included some students' slow and stumbling progress through texts; reluctance to talk with peers about texts; and scarce or superficial annotations, including mark-making that seemed more perfunctory and performative than reflective of real engagement.

As mentioned in Chapter 5, Sonya initially attributed her decision to use the same texts to concerns about leveled texts' stigmatizing potential:

> I do use the same text [for all students]. . . . It wasn't logical for me to say, "Okay, well, we're gonna study the American Revolution, and you're gonna study this text, and you're gonna study this different text." . . . Why are we gonna water down or dumb down lessons for our kids when they should all [learn]? I mean, if we're talking about the [state] test, it's the same test for all kids . . . so I felt that [not using the same text] was a way of watering down a lesson, or even dumbing it down . . . my kids deserve better than that.

Without question, Sonya's sentiments reflect first and foremost her care and high expectations for the young people she teaches. However, CCSS-related accountability expectations played a part, too—specifically the standards themselves, which state that 8th-graders should "by the end of the year, read and comprehend [texts] at the high end of the grades 6–8 text complexity band independently and proficiently." Also playing a part in Sonya's decision were the Playa-wide administrative mandates, which charged teachers with asking more of students than policy or prior performance, however "high," and impending standards-based and standardized tests, which would impact students' educational trajectories, administrators' interpretations of teachers' instruction, and Playa's performance status. Resulting pressures—not all of which were unwelcome, given perceived resonance between the CCSS and the "Playa Way"—confirmed Sonya's and other teachers' sense that to maintain the same high bar for all was a fundamentally anti-deficit move, and informed teachers' specific decisions to have all students read the same complex texts in the same time frame.

That the most experienced teachers among participants confirmed this, both explicitly and otherwise, is especially notable, because they are arguably those teachers best positioned at Playa—for reasons addressed above—to push back against pressures and resist on principle if deemed necessary.

To explore further the interplay between experience, grade level, and positioning vis-à-vis power dynamics, the next chapter returns to 1st grade, where close reading of complex text emerged across almost all data as the most concerning manifestation of the CCSS, in light of its impact on EBs at the start of their formal learning experiences and during especially formative stages of literacy development.

CHAPTER 7

The Common Core State Standards and Compromised Practice in the Early Grades

In this chapter, we build on the prior chapter's account of teachers' efforts to merge their knowledge of equity-minded teaching with two key dimensions of the Common Core State Standards (CCSS): increasing text complexity and engaging students in "close reading." Here, however, we highlight the challenges, and especially those that 1st-grade teachers faced, as they worked with these dimensions of the CCSS. Specifically, we illustrate how 1st-grade teachers' enactments of "close reading" of "complex text" frequently resulted in what we call "compromised practice," with all the meaning implied by the term *compromised*: exposed or vulnerable to danger; reduced in quality, value, or degree; having accepted something less than what one originally wanted or sought, often because what was wanted was unattainable; and so on. As in prior chapters, we partially attribute 1st-grade teachers' tendencies to engage in compromised practice to the CCSS press to "raise the bar," especially when that press is interpreted—as it was at Playa—as providing all students with the same accelerated instruction. We also consider the contributing role of Playa teachers' resistance to "banking" (or teaching that treats students as empty vessels into which teachers deposit knowledge), their commitment to "dialogue," and their privileging of "productive" struggle—each of which manifested most pointedly, and most problematically, in 1st-grade instruction geared toward addressing the CCSS's emphasis on close reading of complex texts.

It is important to note that we do not attribute 1st-grade teachers' compromised standards-based instructional practice to the teachers themselves. Doing so would grossly oversimplify how and why these teachers ultimately took up the CCSS as they did. Instead, in this chapter we illustrate how certain contextual factors, including school conditions—and even the Common Core standards themselves—limited 1st-grade teachers' opportunities for standards-related professional learning, while also adversely shaping their CCSS enactments.

Nevertheless, we don't view the 1st-grade teachers' CCSS engagement in fixed or static ways. Indeed, in the final portion of the chapter, we illustrate how, when conditions for teachers' professional learning changed, so did teachers' responses to the standards.

PRIMARY CONCERNS

Literacy instruction in 1st grade, as in middle school, often involved students annotating complex text, usually multiple times, and over multiple days. Teachers Ramón, Ana, Sofia, and Rocio, like their counterparts further up the gradespan, typically assigned a single complex text to the whole class and had students annotate independently or with tablemates. Although teachers sometimes pulled aside small groups to provide extra support, the norm was undifferentiated, whole-group instruction. This was the case despite the fact that assigning all students the same text departs quite significantly from exemplary and even just more typical 1st-grade reading instruction, which, given the emergent nature of many 1st-graders' reading, favors teacher-facilitated, small-group learning experiences.

Beyond bins of leveled texts from which students could choose during independent reading time, individual reading competencies didn't seem to factor prominently in text selection. For whole-class texts, teachers tended to make selections primarily based on two criteria: (1) how well texts helped advance content area understandings within thematic units of study, and (2) how well texts, in the words of Ramón, met the "expectation that we present complex text," an administrative directive grounded at least partially in concerns about preparing students for the kinds of text passages they would encounter on CCSS-aligned tests—in the case of 1st-graders, 2 years later.

Although teachers were clear that this was the expectation, they were less clear about what text complexity meant and how to select the "right" texts. As Ramón reported, "I don't think we've been able to find that balance of having a text that is complex at the right level for everyone, or for the majority of them." In the face of uncertainty and administrative press, teachers mostly operated as if "more difficult text was better text," often erring on the side of selecting "very complex" or "too complex" texts, without fully considering—or being urged to consider—complex interactions among readers, texts, and tasks.

Their prevailing interpretation of more difficult text as necessarily better text perhaps explains why 1st-grade teachers so frequently looked beyond 1st-grade standards for instructional direction.

We can understand why administrators like Playa's might feel pressured to encourage teachers to use complex texts, even for young students. We also can empathize with teachers who, given these pressures, felt compelled to use complex texts so that their 1st-graders wouldn't be underprepared for upcoming academic challenges—even though the CCSS's text complexity staircase does not begin, and standards addressing text complexity are not introduced, until 2nd grade (CCSS.ELA-LITERACY. RI.2.10). However, this approach to literacy instruction, not surprisingly, yielded several concerning trends—namely, that 1st-graders often struggled and disengaged when expected to complete close readings of overly complex texts. In addition, when 1st-graders were expected to engage in peer dialogue in relation to overly complex texts, the quality of that dialogue often diminished.

Below we describe these trends and then illustrate with some examples.

The Excessive Challenge of Overly Complex Texts

First, observations in 1st-grade classrooms suggest that teachers frequently assigned students too-difficult, whole-group texts, and that such texts presented excessive challenge for many students. Students' resulting struggles were especially
apparent when they participated in small-group instruction, where, under their
teacher's close gaze, their actual capacities with, and responses to, complex texts
were more readily detectable than when they were working on their own. We noticed on multiple occasions, for example, that students who were pulled aside by
teachers struggled to demonstrate basic understandings of the text, even when,
over a 30-minute period, they zeroed in on just one paragraph, and with the teacher's encouragement and assistance, disassembled it, sentence by sentence.

The same tended to be true in 4th-grade classrooms. As Figure 5.5 (a sample
of student work featured in Chapter 5) illustrates, even when students annotated
extensively over multiple close reads, annotations themselves often offered little or
no evidence of comprehension improving over time. Although not visible in the
black-and-white image, it is worth noting that the student used pencil to annotate
during one reading, and pen during another. This use of different writing instruments offers a potential glimpse into how the student's reading might have evolved
over the course of engaging the article twice. For example, though the student
wrote, "I don't get that sentence" in her initial reading, no clarifying notes were
written in response, and so it seemed—and observation confirmed—that multiple
readings did little to enhance her understanding.

At times, annotations also seemed not to assist students with, and to maybe
even distract them from, focusing in on a text's key ideas. For example, this same
student wrote in the margin that the main character "was probably rubbing his
wrist because it hurt." Although this was factually correct, a close look at the text
reveals that this student has focused attention on less crucial details (i.e., the character's wrist hurt) rather than the main idea (i.e., the character is being mistreated
by a teacher for being a non-English-speaking immigrant student). In short, while
a lot of annotating was under way, and some was possibly helpful, this student's
misunderstandings were mostly not resolved through this process, despite the student being asked to engage in it repeatedly.

Despite evident—and for some, acute—academic struggle, teachers mostly
viewed students' experiences with complex text neutrally, assuming that students
would ultimately benefit from pressing—and being pressed—through struggle.
This manifested most evidently when teachers had students complete multiple,
un-scaffolded "close reads" of complex texts. During such readings, students were
expected, per CCSS guidelines, to make meaning of the text by relying exclusively
on the text itself—what the CCSS refers to as remaining within the "four corners
of the page." They were also expected to "annotate," or mark up those features or
sentences from the text that they found difficult to comprehend.

Although students often covered their papers with annotations during these close reads, teachers rarely addressed such annotations directly; rather, teachers structured lessons in ways that treated students' struggles through the texts—that is, their (often superficial) rereading and re-annotating—as a step, or even the key step, toward greater comprehension. This perhaps explains why teachers so often required students to reread texts multiple times, but often without any changes in the instruction they provided.

Once in a while, teachers questioned the productivity of such struggle for learning. For example, after teaching a lesson they had planned together, Sofia and Ramón worried that their text selection had been overly ambitious: "I talked to Ramón," recounted Sofia, "and I said . . . yesterday they had a really hard time when they were doing the close reading. We did text that was [at a] pretty high [level] and he told me the same. . . . "

Concerns like these notwithstanding, the belief expressed by the CCSS and many of their supporters that learning occurs through struggle seemed to supersede teachers' reservations that complex texts and close reading, in Ana's words, "might not be working." Ultimately, teachers persisted with them even when doing so felt "wrong" or seemed to them to be undermining students' engagement and learning.

Student Disengagement

A second concerning trend was that when asked to annotate complex texts independently at their desks, 1st-graders frequently disengaged from the process and often failed to complete assignments as a result. Some students simply stared into space until the period ended. When we asked one seemingly disengaged student what she doing, she answered, a far-off look in her eye and intoning a question, "Reading?" Meanwhile, other students seized every chance they could to take breaks—for example, by leaving their seats to visit with classmates, sharpen a pencil, or drink water from the fountain, which together comprised a sophisticated repertoire of strategies for coping respectfully with the tedium or stress of the task.

It was also common to see students making superficial changes to annotations they had done during previous readings of the same text. This involved, for example, darkening an already there underline or circle, or adding a word or two to a previously written question. One little boy added nothing new to his annotations as he made a fourth or fifth pass through the same text; instead, he traced over all his preexisting ones. This made it challenging for us to discern what he was getting from reading the text, or if he was indeed reading at all. Circling back to Figure 5.5, we can see that the 4th-grader underlined the same sentences and phrases with both pencil and pen, and that some of her notes, although written with different writing instruments, are identical across readings (e.g., "he is mad" in both pencil and pen).

Evidence of students' disengagement also became apparent when teachers asked students to draw on their annotations to engage in substantive text-based exchanges—oral and written—only to be met by a lack of understanding or interest on students' parts, even after they had spent extended time "reading" the text in question. For example, during a typical morning in a 1st-grade English language arts (ELA) class, Ana asked students to draw connections between two informational texts, one on deforestation and one on the water cycle, both of which they had annotated multiple times already over the past several days. Although Ana had asked the question in earnest, students stared blankly at her. Despite her subsequent probes, students remained silent, looking genuinely confused about what she had asked them to do. Only when Ana asked students to discuss, more generally, deforestation's many impacts did they begin to offer ideas. They enthusiastically conjectured about the dangers deforestation might pose to animals, even though deforestation's impact on animal life was not part of the reading.

When Ana tried again at the end of the lesson to steer students away from using their own experiences and interests to make meaning of the text, and instead pressed them to contain their responses within the assigned task of making connections between the two informational texts, students were again unresponsive. Stumped by the high-level texts and the connections they were supposed to make between them, as well as the parameters of the assignment, which condoned only the meaning-making that occurred within "the four corners of the page," a good number of students became confused or lost interest.

In many cases, tendencies to disengage seemed to result from students' apparent boredom with the close reading process. Although doing close reading almost every day led students to become adept at the process, at least superficially, the monotony of reading and annotating the same text so many times chipped away at students' motivation, particularly during third, fourth, and fifth readings. Indeed, circulating through a 1st-grade classroom on a morning when students were expected to annotate the same text for the nth time, we overheard an otherwise eager little girl say to no one in particular, "We're reading this again?"

Observations of students' disengagement additionally affirm cautions administered by early childhood experts about the potential inappropriateness—developmentally speaking—of the CCSS for young learners (Alliance for Childhood, 2010; Miller & Carlsson-Paige, 2013). At Playa, we regularly watched 6-year-olds squirm in their seats as they spent upwards of 90 minutes annotating texts, with little if any time allotted for physical movement or varied forms of instruction. Relatedly, 1st-grade teacher Sofia, recounted how students had struggled with the CCSS-driven expectations they faced upon entering 1st grade:

> At the beginning of the year I had some that cried because (crying voice) I don't understand anything, teacher! . . . It is becoming more normal, I guess, for them to get exposed to this type of text. . . . They don't say, oh wow, that's a lot of reading. No. They don't complain at all now. At the beginning "all this?" because they came from kindergarten and they're like we have to read all this? But now they just take it as normal. Okay we'll read it. And then we answer these questions right? Yeah. Oh, okay.

Although Sofia spoke with some pride about some students' new ability to persevere "without crying" through long stretches of rereading and re-annotating, her words were also tinged with sadness, suggesting that she, too, had reservations about what the CCSS and administrators were pressing her to do. Ironically, in this push to develop students' "college and career readiness," students were, in fact, potentially losing momentum on the path to becoming lifelong readers (Appatova & Hiebert, 2013). Reading, as Sofia's quote suggests, had become something to do and get through, an academic and *ascetic* act, rather than the kind of pleasurable and *aesthetic* experience critical to developing a love of reading in early childhood.

Diminished Dialogue

A third and related concern is that teachers' tendencies to select and press students through overly challenging texts seemed to diminish the quality of students' discourse. Playa teachers were exceptionally committed to having students engage in dialogue with one another, particularly as a way to deepen understandings and support students' capacities to think critically about texts of various kinds. First grade was no exception; students had daily opportunities to talk with peers in both structured and unstructured ways.

Although students clearly enjoyed these opportunities, when they were asked to talk with one another around complex text to elicit text-based evidence in the crafting of an argument, the quality of their oral exchanges often withered. Two examples of student dialogue from one morning in Ramón's Spanish-instruction classroom illustrate this concern and its interconnectivity with the prior two concerns, as well.

That morning, Ramón warmly greeted his 1st-graders as they entered the classroom and explained they would continue reading an informational text about the *lacandones,* the Maya people who, for millennia, have resided in the jungle in the Mexican state of Chiapas. Reflecting the teachers' struggles to provide "just-right" levels of text complexity, he and Sofia had adapted an above-grade-level article—aiming to make it 1st-grade appropriate, while still presenting sufficient "difficulty." With its focus on the jungle's inhabitants, Ramón and Sofia hoped the text would offer "a humanistic approach" to thinking about the broader unit theme of deforestation, thereby leading students to become invested in deforestation's many impacts.

The five-paragraph article featured dense expository text to describe how the *lacandones* draw on various local natural resources to survive. Accompanying the text were five images—one for each paragraph—illustrating how the *lacandones* engage with those resources. Eight text-based questions, some recall oriented and some more inferential, accompanied the text.

Over the prior few days, students had had multiple opportunities to annotate the article. This morning, Ramón began by asking students to work in pairs to answer the text-based questions. Reflecting CCSS reading standards for 1st grade, some of these questions asked students to offer descriptive answers about "facts" from the text (CCSS.ELA-LITERACY.RI.1.1) and to "demonstrate understandings of key details of the text" by drawing connections between their own lives and ideas and those of the *lacandones*; these questions reflected standards for 2nd grade even more than for 1st (CCSS.ELA-LITERACY.RI.2.1).

Before releasing them to their pairwork, Ramón stated for students—warmly, firmly, and gesturing for emphasis—the broader goals they were working toward and the specific skills they were meant to demonstrate:

> *Estamos analizando que recursos utilizan los lacandones de méxico en la selva tropical. Recuerda niños, tenemos que utilizar lenguaje académico . . . para poder usar nuestra voz, y poder comunicar nuestras ideas. Así que, el enfoque de hoy es que tu busques los detalles espicíficos del texto que te dice o que indica que recursos utilizan la gente de los lacandones de méxico.*

> [Today, we are analyzing the resources that the Lacandon people who live in the Mexican rain forest use. Remember, boys and girls, we have to use academic language . . . so that we can use our voices and communicate our ideas. So, today's focus will be to look for specific details from the text that indicate which resources the Lacandon people of Mexico use.]

In keeping with the schoolwide commitment to dialogue, he reminded students, that "*el diálogo es tan importante como tu escritura*" ("Your dialogue is just as important as your writing"), especially for helping them develop deeper understandings of the material. In this sense, Ramón's framing of the task arguably reflected, as well, his consideration of 3rd-grade standards, like those calling for students to cite in their own discussions "specific details from the text (CCSS.ELA-LITERACY.RI.3.7), as well the Speaking and Listening standards for 1st grade and beyond.

As students turned toward their partners, Ramón called a small group to the kidney table at the back of the room, where they worked with him while others responded to the questions without his assistance. Circulating to observe students' collaboration, we were drawn to Verónica and Heather, who seemed especially animated and on-task from afar and who Ramón identified earlier as some of his most advanced students. Based on their densely annotated texts and lively exchange, we assumed we would find them immersed in dialogue about the text and text-based questions. As it turned out, they were engaged in a different kind of conversation—one focused on which writing implements they should use, how they should take turns, and who would do what when it came to the assigned work. Meanwhile, Verónica read aloud (and loudly) for Heather, even though Heather was already writing answers to the questions and didn't appear to be listening.

Undeterred, Verónica finished her read-aloud and then returned to the top of the page, only to begin reading the text again, robotically enunciating each word, and with little expression or intonation. After Verónica completed two consecutive read-alouds, the pair checked in with one another, again in a manner that might look from afar like substantive text-based dialogue—each leaning in toward the other, looking at the text, speaking, poised as if ready to write or writing. This time, the girls were simply alternating in reading, with clear enunciation but little affect, the questions aloud. Given their focus on reading the questions (without attempting to answer them), and correcting one another's pronunciation, accuracy and fluency seemed to be their central goals. This tendency for students to privilege "form over content" is something literacy experts have highlighted as one of close reading's central shortcomings (NCTE, 2012).

An hour later, during what Ramón's agenda designated as "phonics time," the same group of students participated in a different assignment that again required peer dialogue. Reflecting Playa's commitment to situating even skill-based work in meaningful content and connecting it to units of study (in this case, deforestation), students were working with a text describing *murciélagos* (bats) and their rain forest habitat. Comprised of fewer and shorter paragraphs, the text was structurally less complex than the one about *lacandones*; it likewise included more familiar, less high-level academic vocabulary.

Ramón asked students to read the text in pairs and discuss its meaning, but also to discuss the difference between the Spanish sounds *r* and *rr*. By design, the text featured a high proportion of words incorporating these sounds—for example, *murciélago, ratones, agarrar, tropicál*, and *horrenda*, to name a few.

Almost immediately after hunching over this text with their partners, the same students who were engaged in superficial paired conversations just an hour before jumped eagerly into animated, substantive dialogues about the text's content and the focal phonemic elements. As they worked to craft arguments, students excitedly offered examples of words in context and used verbal emphasis and hand gestures—sometimes emphatically—to communicate meaning and support their partners' understanding. For example, Hector, a student Ramón described as struggling with Spanish-language development, took the lead in a dialogue with his Spanish-dominant-speaking partner, Diego. As the two discussed the specific features of a tree where bats nested within the rain forest, Hector argued emphatically for a specific pronunciation of the word *capoquero* (Capoc Tree), explaining, "*No es capoquerro*" (rolling his *rs* in an exaggerated fashion), "*Es capoquero!*" Pointing to the page as he spoke, he attributed this distinction in pronunciation to *capoquero*'s spelling (i.e., that it includes *r* rather than *rr*). Like Hector and Diego, most pairs were engaged meaningfully with one another, talking about the text and its content and features, and communicating an overall sense of ownership over their discussions.

It is with some reservation that we offer up these examples in order to raise questions about the potential for less complex text to support richer and more complex dialogue. To be fair, teachers selected these texts for different purposes and with different goals in mind. And neither we (nor they) would want to imply that simply using a more basic text and focusing on a discrete skill, as we see in the *murciélagos* example, would necessarily make for better instruction, let alone richer discussion. Rather, our aim in juxtaposing these examples is to offer a window into students' differential engagement with texts and with one another when texts reflected different levels of complexity and when texts and tasks together presented different cognitive and linguistic demands.

In our time at Playa, we noticed that the more difficult the texts, the harder it seemed for students to engage productively around them on their own or in dialogue with one another, even when the related tasks were relatively straightforward. Using more manageable, grade-appropriate texts, meanwhile, seemed to free up cognitive and social–emotional resources, enabling students to grapple more actively and deeply with texts and with one another, even when the tasks at hand were themselves quite complex (e.g., multimodal, multilayered, or multistep). Notably, these trends manifested equally across Spanish- and English-instruction classrooms and, again, most acutely in the lower grades.

NAVIGATING A RISKY ALPHABET SOUP: CCSS, EBs, AND ECE

In some respects, the findings reported above aren't surprising, given clashes between much of what the CCSS (and its supporters) have recommended—especially with respect to text complexity and close reading—and what we know about effective literacy instruction, particularly for EB students. Research, for example, suggests that the standards potentially position teachers and students to struggle in just the ways we saw them struggle at Playa. Like others (e.g., Au & Waxman, 2015), August and Shanahan (2015) have raised questions about the CCSS's call for students' focus to remain within the "four corners of the page," noting that discouraging the building of background knowledge disadvantages students like "ELs," who may lack the vocabulary and background knowledge needed for making sense of English-language texts. They also question the CCSS's presumption that all students can and should make meaning of texts primarily through close reading, especially when a strict application of the text complexity staircase would result in "ELs" typically being expected to "read texts at least two grade levels above their instructional reading levels" (p. 156). Thus, although the CCSS might afford "ELs" opportunities to "read and think about content and ideas that are consistent with their intellectual abilities" (p. 156), the authors urge teachers to "balance" students' needs with the demands the standards impose.

Others have similarly highlighted the burdensome linguistic demands presented by the CCSS's press for complex text, and likewise implore teachers to offer more scaffolding for EBs than the CCSS currently recommends (Flores & Garcia, 2015; Hopewell & Escamilla, 2015). After all, at the most basic level, research indicates that requiring students to read too-difficult texts limits their development as readers (Allington, 2002). Even those scholars who underscore the opportunities for literacy learning extended to EBs by the CCSS's emphasis on text complexity agree that teachers must remain vigilant in the face of the standards' monolingual bias (Wiley, 2015), in part by offering EBs "special" academic support (Bunch,

2015; Kibler, 2015; Kibler, Walqui, & Bunch, 2015). Moreover, literacy scholars have suggested that when students show signs of struggle while working with complex texts, teachers ought to interpret such struggle as a signal to learn more about students in order to choose texts that better suit their interests and needs (NCTE, 2012).

In light of the risks imposed on young learners by the CCSS and highlighted in earlier chapters, it is also relatively unsurprising that the trends described in this chapter seemed to be especially acute in 1st grade. Indeed, studies suggest that, of all the CCSS's emphases, the press for more complex text poses the greatest threat in the early grades (e.g., Hiebert & Mesmer, 2013). Fitzgerald and colleagues (2016) add that this "raising of the bar" stands to disadvantage struggling readers especially. They explain, "Historically, while many students have achieved a reading level at or above 820L by the end of 3rd grade, struggling readers have attained on average, only about 400L" (p. 60). Expecting 1st-graders to reach this CCSS-set "bar" thus seems unreasonable, even for those who aren't considered struggling readers.

Recent research additionally suggests that we shouldn't be surprised by Playa teachers' struggles to select the "right" complex texts for their 1st-graders. Fitzgerald and colleagues (2015, 2016) highlight the particular challenges of selecting complex texts for young readers because the CCSS's four indicators of text complexity (i.e., levels of meaning, structure, language conventionality and clarity, and knowledge demands), which may offer some useful direction for upper-grade texts, fail to capture the full range of complexity characteristics that are unique to texts designed to support emerging readers' progress. This leaves primary teachers especially vulnerable to confusion about which texts are "just right" for students, particularly when such students are from nondominant linguistic backgrounds (Hiebert, 2012, 2013b).

Although they used the CCSS in good faith and embraced opportunities to expose EBs to complex texts, rarely did Playa's teachers—including those teaching 1st grade—offer the sort of "special" support deemed essential for EBs' success. They mostly expected students to navigate complex texts on their own and they did so mostly in accordance with CCSS direction to privilege close reading as a— or really, *the*—core instructional strategy; and, in many cases, they also did relatively little to capitalize on a fuller range of students' meaning-making resources (i.e., allowing or encouraging them to go beyond the "four corners" of the text in order to understand its content on their own terms).

As a result, students who could independently read universally assigned texts appeared to develop increasing comfort with close reading; those who struggled, meanwhile, appeared to fall further behind in their ability and desire to work with such texts. These challenges were exacerbated for 1st-graders, who were regularly expected to read texts that, although properly leveled for some, often were inappropriate for others. In short, some teachers' efforts to align instruction with the CCSS contributed to a learning environment that was—for their beloved EB students—in some ways "optimal" and in other ways "at risk" (Ruiz, 1996).

CAPTURING, CONTEMPLATING, AND COUNTERING AT-RISK-NESS

Even early on in the study, to get at the instances of CCSS-related "compromised" instruction described above with teachers, we posed numerous questions about them—for example, "How does a teacher know if a text is too complex for her students?" and "What do you do when you see students struggling with a particular text?" Yet, even when questioned, Playa's teachers, especially in 1st grade and to some degree in 4th grade too, often seemed to overlook, accept, or explain away examples of students struggling, especially in relation to the CCSS-encouraged approach to close reading and to "reading" texts that presented arguably too much complexity. That teachers who were so accomplished, so committed to "putting students first," and so determined to be "critical" accepted as natural students' struggles perplexed us and also compelled us to try and learn more about teachers' understandings.

Thus, a year into the study, we asked teachers if they would be open to our using video artifacts of their teaching to anchor conversations with us about their standards-based instruction. The resulting video-mediated interviews became one of the most generative parts of the study. In essence, engaging with teachers around video clips of their teaching helped illuminate previously unreachable dimensions of their CCSS enactment as well as harder-to-see conditions that mediated those enactments.

Perhaps the most illuminating outcome across teachers' video-mediated interviews was that teachers, without direct prompting (apart from whatever prompting clips alone might represent), began to question instructional practices that, prior to these experiences, they had seemed to accept or take for granted. Much of teachers' spontaneous talk and questioning circled around particular practices, such as annotation, related to close reading of complex text. Their commentary mostly focused on the quality of student dialogue in relation to the texts at hand, their concerns about texts being too difficult and possibly undermining engagement and learning, and the definition of text "complexity" and its place in text selection.

During Ramón's interview, we screened four clips, including one of Heather and Verónica discussing the *lacandones* and another of Hector and Diego dialoguing about the *murciélagos* text. As Ramón watched the first time through, a range of emotions registered on his face and body. He shared that the clips confirmed and refined a concern that had come up repeatedly among the 1st-grade team—namely, that the texts they were using, as a result of pressure from the CCSS and administrators, were too complex and potentially impeding, rather than facilitating, student learning. It was the first time such reservations had been stated so definitively.

Ramón lamented the girls' rudimentary discourse, which he believed resulted from them missing "that they had to get those key details from the text." Ramón attributed this to "text complexity" and suggested it was "something to definitely think about during collaboration with my team." When asked why and how he would bring this example to his colleagues, he elaborated, "Like, how is it possible that two of my high [highest-performing] students are missing pretty much the purpose of the lesson and [not] collecting those key details from the text? . . . What are we doing wrong as teachers for them to not understand?"

Rewatching the clip featuring Hector, meanwhile, Ramón identified the kind of interaction he was hoping would occur while he worked with the small group at the back of the classroom. "I love how he's explaining to Diego the sound that it's supposed to make," Ramón explained. "They're dividing the words into syllables. . . . And they're engaged, they're focused. . . ." Interestingly, he added that the text, which he and the other teachers had deemed "appropriate for 1st grade," was critiqued by administrators who dropped in during instruction; as he put it: "They were like, 'That's too basic.' And we're like . . . 'Really?'"

To a degree, the clip of Hector and Diego made the clip of Verónica and Heather even more troubling to Ramón because it reinforced for him the capacity he knew all his students—not just the most advanced—had for productive dialogue. It also made clear that high-level discourse around certain texts was not necessarily occurring, even for "high-performing" students, in part because the texts seemed to demand so much of students just to make basic meaning of them.

In future weeks, Ramón would circle back, unprompted, to the experience of watching those clips—the joy he felt seeing students teach one another around a text, and the dismay he felt seeing others, equally capable of reciprocal teaching, "just copying out of the text." Text complexity, it seemed to him, was undermining the very kind of student dialogue that Playa worked so hard to cultivate, and that teachers considered a crucial and positive aspect of what the CCSS stood to encourage.

Ana had a similar experience while watching a clip of an instructional exchange, when she noticed new aspects of a text's linguistic demands, described earlier in the chapter, wherein students labored through an informational text about the water cycle. After watching herself pause mid-text to discuss with students some key terms and text features, she noted that although the text's vocabulary and structure had posed challenges in the moment that she had not fully anticipated, those challenges were more visible to her now. As she debriefed with us, she referred back to a sentence that described how people "made demands on the land," and asked: "What does 'demands on the land' mean? . . . Just the word *demands*, what does *demand* mean, you know, for them? Demand. I can demand something from you, but demanding something from the land?"

Moments later, Ana also began questioning potential connections between what she viewed as students' lack of engagement, interest, and motivation, and the focal text's level of complexity. Describing the text as "very complex," but also on par with "the [administrative] expectation that we present . . . that type of text," Ana then commented that she wished students featured in the clip were showing "more enthusiasm," particularly given how excited they were about the topic when it was introduced the prior week. She recollected, "When we started the unit last week, they're like, 'Yeah! The water cycle! . . . and the forest!'" Given their initial interest, Ana said she thought the level of complexity, not the content, was turning them off:

They're in 1st grade. . . . They're like, "Oh my gosh, I'm gonna go and struggle with this text." So maybe that could be one factor that makes them not be that engaged or that enthusiastic about what we're doing. . . . It's the complexity of the text that is not making them, you know, "Oh! I'm gonna read about the water cycle."

Meanwhile, for Rocio, watching a clip of students responding to complex text led her to suggest that part of what made the text selection process so challenging was the contrast between the administration's messaging, which often treated text complexity somewhat simplistically, and what teachers saw as a broader range of ways to think about complex literacy instruction and the role and even definition of complex text therein. Rocio recounted how "our administrator told us . . . to use a Lexile to define what complexity is." And then she explained, "But as I was doing my research on close reading, and going back again to . . . what the purpose of [text complexity] is . . . it's . . . how complex do *you* want to take it . . . in a way that you're gonna make your students successful."

With this comment Rocio began to question out loud, and for the first time with other educators, core aspects of the mainstream discourse around text complexity. She also began to voice agency that she was coming to realize she and other teachers had in determining how complex a text was, or could be, for their own students. Having researched the Lexile Framework herself, Rocio shared her skepticism about the measure's usefulness and the idea that complexity could ever be a property of text itself, rather than a product of the interaction between a particular text and particular readers. Speaking about her grade-level team, she elaborated:

> We were so taken by . . . the word *complex* . . . [but] how do we get into a consensus that this [holding up paper] is complex for the students? . . . We know every group of students is different . . . they have other experiences, they have other skills and abilities, so now let's use what they know, what they can do, and make it complex to them. . . .

For Rocio, "complex to them" hinged on recognition of her students as cultural beings and language learners, and what might make a text complex for them as a result. She offered *The Lorax* as one example. About it, she asked rhetorically, "What makes it so complex, is it the rhyming . . . the concept . . . the structure of the sentences . . . ?" She then recounted having learned that *The Lorax* received a lower Lexile score than *Where the Wild Things Are*, which "you can finish in 5 minutes." Rocio understood that Dr. Seuss's writing, with its deeper themes and made-up words, might bring for her students a kind of complexity that a Lexile wouldn't fully capture.

Rocio's text complexity reflections also took into account the kinds of meaning-making, analysis, and discourse she imagined wrapping around text. She described the potential to focus conceptually on *The Lorax*'s message about socially just action *and/or* on "the phonetic part . . . foundational skills" *and/or* on the author's craft (e.g., "how Dr. Seuss used rhyming, and for what purpose . . . looking at the patterns more carefully").

Unbeknownst to Playa's teachers, the questions they raised during video-mediated interviews were akin to those raised by literacy scholars, who have challenged the conflation of *text complexity* with *text difficulty* (Mesmer, Cunningham, & Hiebert, 2012). Gauging a text's *difficulty* for a given student in relation to a given task, they argue, depends upon first understanding the text's *complexity*—those aspects of the text that can be "analyzed, studied, or manipulated," and by whom (p. 236). This kind of nuanced interplay is part of what was somewhat lost in translation as Playa's administrators and teachers worked to enact the CCSS emphases as they understood them, and also part of what teachers started coming to deeper consciousness around during video-mediated interviews. We address some of the reasons why this may have been the case in the next and final chapter.

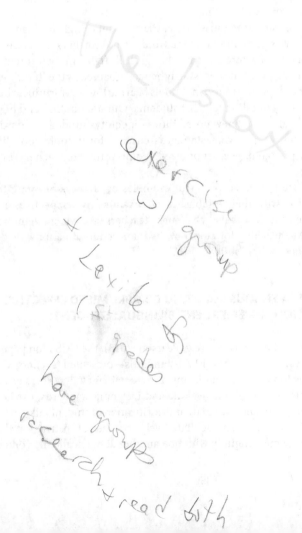

CHAPTER 8

Teaching for Equity in Complex Times

In this final chapter we share our study's most valuable takeaways to shed new light on the Common Core State Standards (CCSS) and to illuminate the complexities of teachers' policy navigation over a decade into this era of high-stakes accountability. While no written account can do justice to the magic of accomplished teaching and the multidimensional relationships on which it relies, it is our sincere hope that practitioners, researchers, and policymakers will find this account insightful and worthy of reading.

A central reason for situating our study at Playa was its "high-performing" status. We thought such a setting might offer a window into teachers' experiences navigating policy in a school where reforms, though still "tight" in their intent to impact the "technical core," wouldn't necessarily be accompanied by the "tight" regulation and surveillance typically found in schools bearing low-performing labels and serving Latinx emergent bilingual (EB) students. Our assumption and hope was that this setting would reveal new possibilities for equity-minded standards-based reform—in other words, what standards-based reform could look like if taken up by well-prepared, well-supported, equity-minded teachers in a high-functioning school.

And indeed our study yielded powerful examples of teachers bringing the CCSS into conversation with their established equity-minded perspectives and practices. At the same time, it revealed challenges teachers face when attempting to enact the CCSS while teaching for equity at the intersection of nationwide demographic, political, and policy "shifts."

HOW THE CCSS-ELA ENCOURAGED AND COMPROMISED EFFECTIVE INSTRUCTION FOR EMERGENT BILINGUAL STUDENTS

As scholars have suggested might occur (e.g, Pearson, 2013), the CCSS "on paper" —vis-à-vis prior English language arts (ELA) standards—presented teachers with promising possibilities for some crucial forms of robust literacy practice. For example, partially encouraged by CCSS Speaking and Listening standards, teachers at Playa were able to maintain and extend their prioritization of student talk—what they called "dialogue"—and, in turn, facilitate lively stretches of instruction that supported EBs to engage meaningfully with one another about academic content and text. This affirms researchers' identification of the CCSS's emphasis on student talk as promising in light of its potential to (1) challenge the prevalence of superficial "IRE"-driven discourse wherein teachers initiate (I), students respond (R), and teachers evaluate (E); (2) cultivate students' comprehension capacities and their capacities to "organize" their post-reading thinking (Bunch, 2013; Horowitz, 2015); and (3) provide low-stakes opportunities for EBs especially to "rehearse" their ideas and language, to use language about the same topic for varied audiences and purposes (Gibbons, 2002), and to engage in highly contextualized exchanges (Wong Fillmore & Valadez, 1986).

In addition, in its departure from a discrete skills-based or "building block" conceptualization of literacy learning—a conceptualization championed by California's prior ELA standards (Sleeter & Stillman, 2005)—the CCSS supported teachers' propensity to embed skill instruction in meaningful content and around real, content-rich texts rather than, say, encouraging them to treat critical thinking as contingent on students' mastery of foundational skills such as phonemic awareness. It also supported teachers' propensity to offer all, instead of just some, students language-rich content area instruction, rather than, say, treating disciplinary literacy as contingent on English mastery.

For Playa's more experienced teachers, and especially for those teaching the upper grades (i.e., middle school), where calls from the CCSS for "college and career readiness" were perhaps most appropriate, the CCSS provided the most promising guideposts for facilitating students' content-area learning. In particular, middle school teachers frequently and fruitfully drew on the CCSS in their efforts to have students explore complex topics in depth and develop text-related arguments.

Despite these CCSS affordances, however, students' well-supported forays into content-area literacy were guided mostly by teachers' preexisting understandings about teaching EBs, rather than the new standards themselves. For example, as experienced teachers of EBs, middle school teachers were equipped and felt emboldened to offer students rich pre-reading experiences prior to "close readings" of unfamiliar texts—for example, by having them engage in extensive discussion, thoughtfully use multimedia, and engage around visual tools such as maps—even though the CCSS called for them to forgo such activities. They also offered students opportunities to make meaning of challenging texts by drawing from all of their available resources—personal and academic—rather than only the text itself (i.e., "the four corners of the page") as the CCSS recommend.

Despite these positive points, our findings also speak to problematic influences of the CCSS on instruction for culturally and linguistically diverse learners. Indeed, as examples throughout our book show, the CCSS-aligned instruction of Playa's teachers was frequently compromised—meaning that it did not live up to their stated understandings of equity-minded teaching and/or fell short of what scholars would consider effective literacy instruction, especially for EBs.

In particular, the press to increase text complexity—as encoded in the CCSS itself, and as interpreted and enacted at Playa—frequently led teachers to select whole-class texts that were excessively challenging for at least some students. Advice from administrators to rely on the Lexile system—a CCSS-advocated system for quantitatively measuring text complexity—encouraged this, as did the privileging, in the CCSS and in related guidebooks (e.g., Fisher, Frey, & Lapp, 2012), of academic struggle and/or failure as necessary preconditions for learning. These dynamics give credence to scholars' concerns about the potentially adverse impact of the CCSS on EBs especially (e.g., August & Shanahan, 2015; Bunch, 2013, 2015).

In response to encouragement, even pressure, from the CCSS and school administrators to engage students in a particular kind of "close reading"—or "cold" reading of unfamiliar text—at least some teachers complied by (1) having students holster preexisting knowledge in favor of exclusively text-dependent meaning-making and (2) emphasizing close reading over other instructional strategies. As a result, students too often ended up "going through the [reading] motions" and without evidence of enhanced comprehension. In short, these dynamics increased for students the risk of experiencing too much challenge and too little scaffolding.

These CCSS-driven, schoolwide instructional patterns echo literacy and language scholars' concerns about the standards' implicit rejection of extensive reading research, particularly research noting essential connections between readers' existing knowledge and their comprehension of new text (August & Shanahan, 2015; Au & Waxman, 2015; NCTE, 2012). They also echo scholars' concerns about the CCSS's implicit rejection of scholarship indicating the likely-to-be-adverse effects on student interest and motivation if students are pressed to read the same text again and again, potentially with little variation in approach (Guthrie, 2015).

Notably, tendencies to comply with the CCSS- and administrator-induced press to increase text complexity and emphasize close reading were most pronounced in 1st grade. There, teachers collaborated almost to the point of standardizing instruction across their own classrooms, thus leaving little room for responsive or adaptive approaches. In addition, three of four 1st-grade teachers had been teaching for only 1 or 2 years. Predictably, they were more reluctant about questioning administrators than their more veteran counterparts at other grade levels; they were also less confident in their own assessments of the CCSS, particularly when their assessments countered administrators' messages about the "right" or "best" way do things. That compliance-oriented behaviors were most acute in the same grade level where the CCSS presented the most misleading and difficult-to-decipher recommendations regarding reading instruction (Fitzgerald, et al., 2015, 2016) only compounded the risks to EBs' learning. In fact, so complex are the clashes between young students' developmental needs and the expectations imposed by the CCSS—particularly concerning the types of complexity captured in the CCSS text complexity staircase versus those typically featured in texts designed for emergent readers—it would be challenging for even the *most* experienced early elementary teachers to bridge the gap between what the CCSS are asking of them, and what they know to be effective instruction for young learners.

These risks were arguably only ramped up further by the CCSS's exclusive focus on English, the standards' accompanying failure to recognize EBs' linguistic resources, and their alignment with English-only, high-stakes standardized tests, a known contributor to the privileging of English language development over bilingualism (Menken, 2015; Wiley, 2015). To be sure, teachers' commitment to their bilingual program was never in question; that was a testament to Playa's people more than any (monolingual) policy with which they grappled. In fact, working to apply the CCSS as monolingual policy to their bilingual program commandeered significant resources (e.g., time, labor, etc.), which might have been invested more productively otherwise. For example, the CCSS's inattention to how the standards might be used to support EBs and the corollary onus teachers felt to cover all of the standards in each language mostly reinforced Playa's language separation model, wherein teachers served as "pure" language models by teaching in only one language (i.e., Spanish or English). Rather than harness for program improvement teachers' expertise concerning bilingualism as a unified system (Garcia & Wei, 2014), CCSS-implementation press corralled their energies into the program mostly as it was rather than as it could be.

TENDENCIES FOR TEACHERS TO "MISS" INSTANCES OF CCSS-DRIVEN COMPROMISED INSTRUCTION

Although aspects of the CCSS frequently compromised instruction for EBs in ways that were visible to us, they often weren't obvious to teachers. In fact, teachers mostly treated the CCSS uncritically, and accepted as inevitable their own somewhat uncritical enactments of them. This was the case even when we asked teachers directly about such instruction, and when teachers themselves recognized that their instruction was falling short of their intended goals.

In the following sections, we draw on our theoretical framework (cultural-historical activity theory, or CHAT) to explore why, in some cases, teachers seemed able to marry the principles of equity-minded teaching with standards-based reform, while in others, teachers struggled to engage critically with the CCSS, or to note when the standards contributed negatively to students' opportunities to learn.

MAJOR MEDIATORS OF TEACHERS' CCSS ENGAGEMENT AND ENACTMENT

Just as important to us as insights about the CCSS themselves are insights about how and why teachers took them up as they did. Therefore, below we discuss how certain "major mediators" shaped teachers' CCSS engagement. Specifically, we focus on the mediating roles of the following: Playa teachers' backgrounds, including their professional preparation and anti-deficit ideologies; the onslaught of educational policies that teachers nationwide are expected to implement; and schoolwide norms shaped by Playa's particular history and cultural context.

Playa's Teachers: Special Subjects, on Their Own and Together

Findings summarized above highlight CCSS features that both hold promise for, and put at risk, EBs' learning. Taken together, they underscore the importance of supporting teachers to think critically about policies and how to navigate them with agency. This navigational labor is complex and consequential. Indeed, as policy "arbiters," teachers "hold one of the most important keys to educational opportunities for bilingual children"—namely, their capacity to control how policy influences classroom life (Palmer & Martinez, 2013, p. 270). In many ways, Playa's teachers' backgrounds, professional knowledge, and commitments positioned them to do this work well.

The previous chapters' accounts of Playa teachers' interpretations and enactments of the CCSS offer evidence that Playa teachers' shared understandings about teaching EBs helped them recognize as positive CCSS features—such as emphases on student talk and contextualized skill instruction—that stood to benefit EB students. And because teachers were attuned to students' ethnolinguistic resources and understood how development in one language could inform development in another, they treated the CCSS—despite its monolingual focus—as a resource for instruction in ELA and SLA classrooms, and they allowed students to draw fluidly on both languages, despite Playa's language separation model.

Many teachers traced these shared understandings back to preservice teacher education. Several referenced asset-based orientations of faculty and peers toward Latinx EBs, coursework pertaining to language acquisition, and theorists such as Lev Vygotsky. Those who did also confirmed that their orientation had been fortified by early on-the-job learning at Playa and ongoing professional development.

The composition of Playa's staff was also crucial, and far more so than any formal preparation experiences. Those in our study—a mix of men and women, many Latinx, some who were immigrants and had experienced school as "ELs"—expressed repeatedly their desire to work with Latinx EB youth and in Playa's community. They were quick to note their students' brilliance and potential to achieve at high levels and in multiple languages. Many forged family-like bonds with those in their charge, which helped develop trust and inspire students' hard work.

All told, teachers—individually and together—set a powerful, affirming tone and then actualized it through the anti-deficit, affective labor they exerted every day. In this sense, Playa's faculty cultivated fertile ground into which they could plant the CCSS or any other policy.

In particular, Playa teachers' "ideological clarity" (Bartolomé & Trueba, 2000)—their understandings of how students were situated inequitably vis-à-vis the structures of schooling and society, and how they ought to teach in turn—powerfully shaped or "mediated" their CCSS engagement. Contrasting deficit-oriented discourses about Latinx EBs, the humanizing relationships Playa's teachers brokered and the high expectations they held meant that their students experienced a challenging curriculum and received positive messages about their capacities to tackle it. Given the CCSS's lack of direction regarding the standards' usage with culturally and linguistically diverse learners, it is easy to imagine that other teachers might be hard-pressed to use the CCSS to similar ends.

The same can be said about the role that teachers' ideas about language, specifically, played in their uptake of the CCSS. Playa's teachers viewed students' languages as resources to be cherished and cultivated (Ruiz, 1984), and our findings indicate that these "additive" language ideologies represented powerful protective forces in the face of the CCSS's monolingual bias. Indeed, Playa's teachers did what bilingual education scholars advise: They thoughtfully drew on the CCSS to guide SLA instruction, too (Brisk & Proctor, 2015; Butvilofsky, Hopewell, & Escamilla, 2015).

Yet, teachers' "ideological clarity" often also seemed somewhat uneven or "clouded over" in certain areas, which undermined teachers' capacity to view the CCSS more critically. In particular, teachers tended to apply their critical, anti-deficit perspectives to students' language rights and the related role of language policies, exclusively; in doing so, they left unquestioned other ideologies or the proliferation of charter schools and policies—such as the adoption of national, monolingual standards—that stood to inflict harm.

For example, tendencies to focus narrowly on language (and language policy) made it difficult for teachers to view their charter status—which, following the passage of California's 1998 "English-only" initiative, was one of the only available mechanisms for teaching bilingually—in anything but positive terms. This seemed to obscure for teachers how at-will work and anti-union cultures at many charter schools, including their own, might lead them to uncritically accept administrative mandates. It also likely foreclosed opportunities for Playa's teachers to learn from others who might have analyzed the potential impact of the CCSS in ways they hadn't.

The same can be said about teachers' tendencies to accept, seemingly without question, neoliberal notions of achievement and failure. In practice, this involved attributing Playa's "success" compared to other schools to their own "harder" work, and treating other schools' underachievement as the product of an imagined dearth of effort, ingenuity, or "grit." Certainly, such attributions may have propelled Playa teachers to work harder and even to reap the reward of "high-performing" status. Still, failing to recognize these attributions as ideologically laden did little to challenge the broader educational system—a system that has been shown to broadly disadvantage Latinx EBs (Gándara & Hopkins, 2011). It also put Playa, and thus its teachers, in a kind of contradictory posture: reveling in its disavowal of "institutionalized" labels, while reifying its own "high-performing" status and quest for higher levels of distinction.

Insofar as the CCSS were concerned, teachers seemed placated by their sense that they, given their additive language ideologies, had addressed already the CCSS's central shortcoming (i.e., its monolingual bias). This, in turn, defrayed any sense that the standards could impose harm, and made teachers less inclined to question other CCSS features that might disadvantage EBs and/or violate aspects of their expertise (e.g., tapping into students' background knowledge, which the CCSS downplay or even discourage). This offers some explanation as to how such dedicated and accomplished teachers came to enact the CCSS in less-than-optimal ways.

Policy Churn, Teacher Burn

A second factor that contributed to teachers' mostly uncritical CCSS engagement was the inundation of policy demands that teachers faced in their everyday work. The sheer volume of these demands frequently oriented teachers toward CCSS compliance and coverage, leaving little room for critical reflection.

To be sure, teaching today necessarily involves navigating rapidly shifting policies, many of which aim to hold schools and teachers more accountable for education outcomes, which are influenced by far more than teachers alone (e.g., Heineke, Ryan, & Tocci, 2015). Increasingly, various scholars have written about the range of (negative) impacts that accountability policies—and the pressure, surveillance, and competition they bring, often by design—can have on teachers and teaching. We know that, particularly in schools experiencing the greatest pressure to improve, these policies often narrow the curriculum by encouraging teachers to teach only those subjects that fall within standardized tests' purview (Crocco & Costigan, 2007; Winstead, 2011), and compel teachers to game the system—for example, by funneling attention toward students anticipated to be the biggest "score bumpers" (Booher-Jennings, 2005; Neal & Schanzenbach, 2010). We also know that such policies can leave teachers feeling alienated from their own teaching (Kostogritz, 2012), leading some to show signs of demoralization (Santoro, 2011), and increasingly, to leave the profession (Santoro & Morehouse, 2011).

Such outcomes have been especially pervasive in schools serving EBs, where discriminatory, monolingual assessment practices regularly (and inaccurately) lead to determinations of low academic performance (Escamilla, Chavez, & Vigil, 2005; Hopewell & Escamilla, 2014) and where subsequent pressure to improve performance typically involves pressure on teachers to embrace instructional practices best described as "backlash pedagogies" (Gutiérrez et al., 2002), including privileging English over all other subject areas (Palmer & Rangel, 2011).

Although some such trends manifested overtly at Playa, more striking was how policy demands seemed to subtly undermine teachers' opportunities and capacities to engage the CCSS critically and adaptively. Policy-related demands at Playa, for example, cultivated what we came to call "churn and burn": Teachers were "burning" the candle at both ends simply to keep up with, let alone make meaning of, the "churn" of policy mandates, especially those related to the CCSS.

This might seem innocuous enough, since working with and learning about new policies necessarily requires sustained time and effort. What we found, however, was that performing in the face of policy churn oriented teachers toward CCSS compliance and coverage, leaving little room for critical reflection. For example, given time spent selecting complex texts and developing graphic organizers to support students' way through them, teachers had limited space to even "see" their own practice, let alone map it against their vision for effective equity-minded instruction.

Because the conditions at Playa were in many ways "better" than those typically found in "tight-tight" school contexts, where "tight" reforms are "tightly" regulated, and where most teachers of EBs work (Gutiérrez, 2006), this finding initially surprised us. After all, on paper Playa had in place structures associated with supporting critical reflection and learning among teachers (e.g., Little, 1993), particularly about literacy (Hoffman & Pearson, 2000), and in the context of standards-based reform (Hargreaves, Earl, Moore, & Manning, 2001). Teachers, for example, enjoyed the autonomy of developing standards-based, bilingual units—luxuries, relatively speaking, afforded by their administrators' vision and school's status. They also enjoyed regular collaboration, ensured by weekly release time and resourced through enrichment classes and quiet meeting spaces meant for serious, meaningful work. Teachers additionally participated in what they described as "useful" professional learning, tailored to Playa's mission and population. The schoolwide summer reading assignments—which participants described as reflecting and refining their commitments to equity and social justice—engaged them around seminal texts by renowned scholars of critical pedagogy. These, taken together, seem like optimal conditions for critical policy engagement.

Yet, even these school conditions and teachers' critical orientations were undermined by policy churn. Reflecting research on the impacts of high-stakes accountability policies on teachers' work (Masuda, 2010; Mausethagen, 2013), teachers' collaborative planning time and instructional autonomy was almost always colonized by policy demands. Teachers, in one way or another, spent the vast majority of collaborative and professional development sessions we observed over a 2-year period working to align instruction and assessment with the CCSS. For example, in numerous meetings teachers spent hours making sense of the CCSS and its constituent features (e.g., the text complexity staircase, Lexile system, role of annotation in close reading), which required departures from how they were expected to teach previously. In none of these instances were the CCSS the subject of critique. Rather, the focus was almost always on better understanding what the CCSS were asking, how teachers could address standards thoroughly and efficiently, and whether—and how to ensure—students were "meeting" or "exceeding" expected benchmarks.

Adding to the general sense of churn were pressures that teachers experienced in relation to standardized tests. Even though teachers had, per school and district mandate, relinquished California's ELA standards to use the CCSS exclusively, CCSS-aligned tests were still under development. Thus, teachers were expected to administer California's existing standardized assessments, aligned with California's state standards, while also preparing students for CCSS-aligned assessments, about which they knew little, but anticipated would be implemented the following year. Not surprisingly, Playa's teachers reported feeling they needed to "address everything," which ultimately encouraged compliance and coverage. That Playa's highly public, "high-performing" status depended upon teachers and students weathering this transition exacerbated these dynamics.

Phoenix and *Familia:* School Culture and Identity

Playa's norms and values—what we've referred to elsewhere as the "Playa Way"— shaped or "mediated" teachers' CCSS engagement, too. As we've illustrated throughout the book, Playa's history and identity as a beacon of bilingual education in a sea of monolingual bias, and as a low-turned-high-performing school—a phoenix of sorts—cultivated firmly rooted schoolwide norms. Ironically, these norms often undergirded teachers' uncritical CCSS engagement, as well as tendencies for them to miss instances when their CCSS enactments engendered compromised instruction.

Early in its history, Playa embarked on a grueling journey to overcome a "low-performing" label. Those present at the time reported that this experience bred even stronger convictions and work ethics than they had held previously. In response to their deep sense of dismay that students "weren't getting the education they deserved," Playa's practitioners determined they must always "put students first." This involved working extremely hard to ensure that students had more and better educational opportunities, and never becoming complacent about students' achievements. It also came to mean holding exceptionally "high expectations" for students and developing a more competitive spirit, expressed by many as a desire to "be the best," among fellow Playa teachers, but more important, when compared to other teachers and schools.

These norms—holding high expectations for students and wanting to be the best—could certainly contribute to an agentive, critical approach to working with the CCSS. At Playa, however, these norms mostly propelled teachers and administrators toward seeking success within the existing system, rather than toward resisting, disrupting, or transforming it. For example, teachers often read their commitments to high expectations as aligning with the CCSS's call to "raise the bar," even though the "raising of the bar" advocated by the standards was derived without considering EBs, and therefore often pressed teachers to withhold scaffolding; design whole-class, undifferentiated instruction that presented excessive academic challenge; fear that "too much modeling" might amount to "banking"; and view "struggle" as generative of learning. Teachers similarly often equated their own drive to "be the best" with "winning" within a high-stakes accountability system. Given that teachers' competitive spirits and embrace of high expectations were so closely tethered to their anti-deficit attitudes, teachers interpreted anything but fully embracing the CCSS as a signal that they didn't believe strongly enough in their (EB) students' capacities.

Membership in Playa's *familia*-like culture, and the school's status as "high performing" additionally contributed to teachers' uncritical relationship to the CCSS. Playa teachers valued the sense of *familia* that was central to the principal's leadership approach and that nourished coherence in values, norms, and instruction, such as a schoolwide focus on (bi)literacy, carefully planned instruction, and a sense of community and relational support. However, Playa's *familia*-like culture also inhibited teachers' opportunities and capacities to engage critically with high-stakes accountability policies, including the CCSS. As many teachers shared, the CCSS held special appeal because Playa's highly respected administrators "sold" them as an equity-minded instructional tool that was consonant with critical pedagogy. They also held special appeal because of teachers' view that they represented an improvement over California's ELA standards.

Perhaps most evidently, closeness and coherence among Playa staff meant that while collaborating, teachers rarely entertained conflicting perspectives about the standards. Instead, teachers mostly drew on shared norms and practices to make meaning of the CCSS and decisions about enacting them.

This coherence even proved true during cross-school "collaboration," where teachers, positioned as leaders, brought their "acceptable" ideas about the CCSS to other teachers districtwide. In these spaces, too, discussions privileged Playa teachers' perceptions that the CCSS aligned with principles of equity-minded, bilingual pedagogy. Even with teachers from other schools at the table, Playa's teachers' coherent beliefs and understandings made it difficult for other teachers' perspectives to gain traction. Thus, what could have served as a space for more critical analyses of the CCSS mostly strengthened understandings that Playa teachers already held, and shifted district discourse about the CCSS in the direction of Playa's existing discourse.

Just as important, Playa's status as a high-performing school served to suppress teachers' criticality toward the CCSS. Even though teachers' CCSS-driven instruction was compromised in certain ways, especially when mapped against their stated commitments to critical and bilingual pedagogies, they maintained "high-performing" status, and continued to receive public praise. Given the dynamic nature of activity, and the interconnectedness of any activity system's different elements, these outcomes—and teachers' responses to them—fed back into that very activity system, further contributing to or "mediating" activity therein.

Specifically, receiving so publicly a "high-performing" label, and being treated by the district as a leader, sent an almost incontestable message that whatever Playa's teachers were doing with the CCSS must have been working. This, in turn, served to obscure for teachers those instances when their CCSS-based instruction chipped away at EB students' opportunities for language and literacy learning. That Playa's journey from "low-performing" to "high-performing" seemed to confer an almost post-traumatic accountability stress exacerbated these tendencies, encouraging compliance as a kind of survivor instinct, while discouraging criticality.

Put another way, although teachers thought they were privileging what they named, in CHAT terms, as Playa's core "motive" or motivation for teaching—engaging critical and bilingual pedagogies—they were, in fact, privileging another motive—working to retain their "high-performing" status as determined by students' performance on English-only standardized tests. Because teachers believed they were most driven by Playa's "core" motive, it was challenging for them to see how motives had perhaps been "reordered" and that they were, therefore, mostly privileging policy compliance over equity goals.

In Sum, Ascending and Also Singed and Susceptible

Mythologically speaking, the phoenix is interpreted as knowingly extinguishing itself in a fire (or pyre) it has not itself set, so that a new generation can form and rise from it. Its story of cyclical rebirth positions flying into the flames as a necessary condition for regeneration, for survival.

For Playa, its own survival depended upon leaning into the logic of the accountability climate, treating its "low-performing" label as legitimate, transforming itself accordingly, and charting its progress by the terms of accountability's terrain in order to "fly again" as a bilingual school for the community.

But, fire, while scary in its spectacle, is arguably even sneakier with its scars. It is smoke inhalation, after all, and not burn that accounts for most fire-related death. Rising up from ashes, then, any phoenix—and certainly any school— might reasonably show signs of singeing and carry in its lungs less visible scars and still-lingering irritants. These environmental impacts, in turn, might render it more susceptible to infection or further injury.

In Playa's case, the journey from founding to floundering to failing to feted—and the story of ascendency wrapped around that journey—seemed to leave its teachers, and some more than others, susceptible to a kind of discursive infection—in other words, taking up as their own certain discourses that they weren't fully conscious of or in agreement with, and that stood to impact their practices, too.

As Russian philosopher Mikhail Bakhtin (1981) explains, part of "the ideological becoming of a human being . . . is the process of selectively assimilating the words of others" (p. 341). In this sense, "we speak ourselves into existence within the terms of the available discourses" (Davies, 2000, p. 55). And so on one level, what Playa's teachers were at risk of was simply being human. On another level, being embedded in a school that "spoke" itself into "existence"—or more specifically, out of potential extinction and into positive distinction—using the "terms" of high-stakes accountability, eased for teachers a kind of "assimilation," whereby external "authoritative discourses" become "internally persuasive" ones (Bahktin, 1981, p. 342).

SUPPRESSION OF CRITIQUE: AN UNDERLYING MEDIATOR

Underlying the Playa-specific "mediators" described above is the more general culture of public school teaching—notably a "state-mediated profession"—within which criticality is always at risk of being suppressed. As Ellis (2014) explains, in "state-mediated professions . . . a state organization, acts as a mediator between the profession and its clientele in deciding . . . what should be provided for its clientele through a legal framework" (White, 2006, p. 207, as cited by Ellis, 2014, p. 218). In this case, by imposing "what should be provided"—new standards—and a "legal framework" of policies that enforce their usage, the state disciplines teachers, including Playa's, concerning what—and albeit less directly, how—to teach. Through these disciplinary practices, the state "suppresses" the very creativity essential to teachers engaging as professionals.

Drawing on Vygotsky's work, Ellis (2014) explains that in the context of contemporary schooling, "creativity" should be understood as encompassing an "intellectual interdependency" between individuals (i.e., teachers) and institutions (i.e., schools). This interdependency, Ellis argues, provides opportunities for "transformation," particularly when multiple "intellectual heritages" collide and in the process bring about "disruptions, breakdowns, or contradictions" that need resolving (p. 223). Put another way and applied to teaching, Ellis's Vygotskian ideas about creativity map on to the very best of what we might typically think of as teachers' critical reflection—the kind of reflection that can arise for teachers when one "intellectual heritage" (such critical and bilingual pedagogies) comes into contact with another (such as standards-based reform). Indeed, in Playa's case, we can see how teachers' compliance-oriented responses to the CCSS, and particularly their failure to recognize the CCSS as bringing its own "intellectual heritages" into contact—and perhaps into tension or contradiction—with Playa's embraced "intellectual heritages," represent the kind of creative "suppression" that Ellis describes and cautions against.

Ironically, as part of a "high-performing" school for several years, Playa teachers didn't face the conditions or practices—for example, district surveillance, mandated adoption of scripted (monolingual) curricula and pacing calendars, or imminent threats of closure—that often impose extraordinary (external) pressure on teachers in "low-performing", tight-tight school contexts. Yet, teachers engaged in a kind of "self-disciplining" and internalization of policy discourses (Foucault, 1977)—what teachers referred to as "getting out in front of reforms" and "doing it to ourselves."

At times, this took the form of over-compliance, or going beyond what external entities, such as the state and district, would have expected had they played a more explicit role in shaping teachers' instruction. This was evidenced perhaps most conspicuously in 1st-grade teachers' practice of drawing from the 2nd- and 3rd-grade standards to guide instruction, including their selections of complex texts. Fourth-grade teachers' tendencies to almost every day create from scratch new and exceptionally detailed graphic organizers so that students might master some of the more complicated standards stands as another example. Schoolwide propensities to use the same complex texts with all readers, to normalize excessive struggle, and to address each and every standard likewise point to a sort of self-imposed compliance whereby the CCSS took on a more prominent role than was perhaps even called for by the reform itself. Indeed, it was through this self-discipline and self-surveillance that teachers risked complying with the very "institutionalism" they most sought to challenge.

"Success," Status, and Self-Discipline

Considering the distribution of power and labor and pervasive cultural norms at Playa, these tendencies toward over-compliance can be partially attributed to the principal's interpretations of the CCSS and the role he perceived them playing in relation to broader accountability demands. Yet, these tendencies weren't exclusively the product of teachers following so-called administrative "orders." In some respects, teachers' inclinations to self-comply and even over-comply with the CCSS echo findings from studies that suggest high-stakes accountability demands—because of their pervasiveness and longevity—can shape teachers' identities and conceptions of teaching, making teachers more likely to accept as "normal" those practices that reflect accountability norms (Booher-Jennings, 2005; Buchanan, 2015).

This perceived "normality," in turn, contributed to the suppression of professional creativity that Ellis (2014) describes. That teachers in some ways suppressed themselves made that suppression, and the tensions and contradictions among "intellectual heritages" that such suppression masks, even harder for Playa's teachers to see and to grasp. This, in part, helps explain: why teachers who saw themselves as "critical" nevertheless took up so willingly the language and tools of the mainstream policy discourse; how Playa's "hierarchy of motives" came to be somewhat reordered, somewhat unbeknownst to the teachers themselves; and how the boundaries between divergent "motives" or objects increasingly blurred.

Perhaps most troubling to us was that we gradually came to see the blurring of motives, enabled in part by teachers' tendencies to succumb to discursive "infection" or conflation, as simply part and parcel of what it takes to be a "high-performing" school—even a purportedly equity-minded one—under a high-stakes accountability system. More specifically, teachers' perceptions of congruency between the CCSS and equity pedagogy's core features—including critical social analysis and pedagogical approaches designed to support bilingual/biliteracy development—were instrumental to Playa's "success" in a high-stakes accountability system. Indeed, after conducting this study, we are all the more inclined to argue that it is through the (false) impression that critical pedagogy, bilingual education, and high-stakes accountability can coexist authentically that fundamental threats to educational equity are both justified and obscured.

These explanations for the tendencies of Playa's teachers to overlook instances of compromised practice raise numerous questions, not the least of which is: Is it even possible for schools to uphold and actualize liberatory values while also succeeding in a system of high-stakes accountability? Findings also raise moral questions about which types of schools stand to confer the most benefits for minoritized students, and also about what the contributions of different educational visions and approaches might be in these times. Although this study does not provide answers to these questions, it does raise serious concerns about what is at risk when an equity-minded school is also a "high-performing" one. In particular, it highlights some of the human consequences—excessive struggle, diminished opportunities for play, and unrelenting pressure on teachers and students, to name a few—and the conditions that serve to normalize those consequences and even to frame them as potentially beneficial.

Findings also complicate understandings about how state-mediated suppression manifests in different types of schools. Whereas previous research suggests that teachers in "tight-tight" schools where reforms and surveillance are "tightest" are among the most likely to have their professionalism undermined and to respond to reforms in ways that compromise equity-minded instruction (Gutiérrez, 2006), Playa's story offers evidence that teachers who experience "looser" surveillance of tight reforms (in what we might call "tight-loose" cultures) may be just as vulnerable to these tendencies.

In fact, Playa's story suggests that teachers' de-professionalization and compromised instruction may be more difficult to detect in "high-performing" schools than in "low-performing" ones, where equity-minded teachers have been shown to be aware of and troubled by such tendencies, even if constrained in their capacity to disrupt them (Achinstein & Ogawa, 2006; Picower, 2011). This very idea complicates findings from some of our own earlier research that suggests the protection and autonomy that higher performance affords are critical to teachers' sense of agency and ability to deliver equity-minded instruction despite accountability demands (Stillman, 2011). In this respect, Playa arguably represents a different kind of "tight-tight" school culture: one in which tight reforms are tightly monitored, not directly by outside entities, but by teachers themselves acting in ways that collude with external pressures.

These findings underscore how school contexts shape or "mediate" teachers' work with and learning about policy, including the CCSS, in complex and nontrivial ways. These contexts, however, are never fixed or static; they are always shifting and changing, and as they do, their mediation of teachers' work shifts and changes, too. This is daunting, because of the complexity with which it suggests teachers must grapple; however, it is also comforting to realize the potential for transformation always exists in dynamic systems like schools.

Nowhere was this contextual dynamism more evident during our study than in Playa teachers' responses to the video-mediated interviews we conducted with them approximately halfway through our study. When teachers participated in these interviews, we observed some of them undergo dramatic shifts in how they thought and talked about the CCSS and their enactments of them. In short, as the conditions for policy engagement changed, so did teachers' actual policy engagement.

LIFTING SUPPRESSION THROUGH "CONTEXTS OF CRITICISM"

In Chapter 7 we recount how, 1 year into our 2-year study, we found ourselves perplexed by the frequency with which we were witnessing such dedicated, equity-minded teachers use the CCSS in ways that compromised their literacy instruction and EB students' opportunities to learn. The instruction we were observing contradicted some of our own understandings of equity-minded, culturally and linguistically responsive teaching, while also contradicting what teachers themselves described as essential elements of instruction for Latinx EB students. Also perplexing was that these teachers were mostly overlooking instances of compromised instruction and struggling to notice or raise questions about the role of the CCSS therein.

Assuming—given the caliber of teachers in our study—that it was nothing so simple as teachers just "not getting it," and also hoping to better understand what was transpiring, we asked teachers if we could video their CCSS-based literacy instruction, and then, on an individual basis, watch and engage in conversation with them around selected video clips. (Details about the video-mediated interviewing process can be found in the Appendix, where we describe the study's design and methods.)

Creating Conditions for Creativity and Critique

Throughout this chapter, we have made efforts to illuminate how and why Playa's teachers responded to the CCSS-ELA as they did. In particular, we have focused on various contextual factors, including artifacts such as the CCSS itself, norms such as participants' shared commitments to bilingual education and to a certain brand of high expectations, and a division of labor that mirrored certain familial dynamics. We have shown how these factors mediated teachers' CCSS responses, leading them to police their own over-compliance with the CCSS; to uncritically embrace the CCSS; to assume certain kinds of alignment between the CCSS and their own established equity-minded principles and practices; and to deliver CCSS-based instruction that at times undermined, rather than facilitated, EBs' learning. We've also shown how these same factors contributed to teachers' tendencies to leave somewhat unquestioned their CCSS enactments, and to miss instances when such enactments appeared to disadvantage certain students. In all of this, teachers struggled to see tensions and contradictions between their purported ideologies and preferred practices, and the CCSS and their enactments of them.

During video-mediated interviews, however, teachers began to notice moments when standards-based instruction came into conflict or contradiction with their more equity-oriented visions and expectations. As they watched clips, multiple teachers literally called out moments when academically strong students appeared to struggle with texts that teachers had assumed all students could access. Concerned about what they were seeing, some such teachers began to surface questions and previously unspoken reservations about the text selection process. A few reconsidered administrators' advice, which seemed to imply to them that more difficult texts were necessarily deemed better ones; others began to reflect critically on and question recommendations advanced by the CCSS, including those from the text-complexity staircase and the Lexile, and Playa-adopted CCSS guidebooks. A couple of newer and relatively quiet teachers wondered aloud if they should approach the administration to share what they had seen in watching clips; one among them suggested that teachers come together as a grade-level team to make an argument for using a greater variety of grade-level (rather than above-grade-level) texts, in order to better meet students' needs.

That teachers noticed instructional tensions reminds us that the very suppression that Ellis (2014) identifies as endemic to state-mediated work also has the potential to lift, or be lifted, even if only briefly. Indeed, since we conducted them, we've come to understand our video-mediated interviews as a form of *re-mediation*—that is, as a targeted reorganization of teachers' learning conditions that served to scaffold policy-related learning and critical reflection.

By offering teachers video clips of their own CCSS-based instruction, we introduced into their activity system new mediating artifacts, specifically, concrete and varied representations of their own standards-based practice. The spirit with which these interviews were conducted likewise seemed to play a re-mediating role in relation to the prevailing norms around engaging with the CCSS. Video-mediated interviews were not task- or compliance-oriented; rather, they offered time and other resources for reflection. Although we considered preliminary findings and teachers' own preferences while selecting clips, interviews remained relatively unstructured. We played clips, offered opportunities for teachers to notice what was happening, and gave them license to shape the focus and tone of the ensuing exchanges. This combination of artifacts and norms re-mediated teachers' thinking, leading a good number of them to note instances of compromised CCSS-based instruction, to acknowledge that not everything was working as well as they had assumed (and had been told), and to voice concerns and questions about how the CCSS and their enactments of them might be constraining, rather than expanding, EBs' opportunities to learn. Put succinctly, for the first time since we had arrived at Playa, teachers identified and began discussing tensions and contradictions between their CCSS-driven practice and their equity-minded instructional ideals.

Enabling Learning

Framed this way, we can see how video-mediated interviews embodied some of the very conditions that sociocultural theorists identify as crucial for deep and "expansive" learning. Video-mediated interviews diverged from the interactions that Playa teachers typically had around policy and practice and mirrored in several ways Engeström's (1991) ideas about the learning-rich spaces he calls "contexts of criticism" where "transformations in consciousness" occur when participants engage around their "current activity and its inner contradictions" (p. 252). From this perspective, the existence of tensions and contradictions in any activity is inevitable; what learners do in relation to them, however, is what varies, and can either cultivate or impede learning.

As they watched clips of their own CCSS-based practice, Playa teachers had opportunities to identify, analyze, and reflect upon their "current activity" of enacting the CCSS. In doing so, evidence suggesting that the CCSS might not be an inherently equity-minded tool, or that the rewards of "high performance" might mask when things aren't working for minoritized youth, began to shape or "mediate" teachers' interactions with us and with themselves (and their practice). By identifying these tensions and contradictions, teachers planted seeds for future critical engagement—engagement that may or may not lead to expansive learning.

Video-mediated interviews also reflected the idea that learners' identification of tensions and contradictions, and their authentic desire to resolve them, can cultivate opportunities for learners' understandings to "ascend from the abstract to the concrete" (Davydov, 1999; Engeström, 1991). By engaging with us around clips of their CCSS-based instruction and by identifying instances of tension and contradiction between their own critical and bilingual pedagogy ideals and their enactments of the CCSS, teachers took initial steps toward bringing their more abstract ideas about teaching Latinx EBs—such as their language-as-resource ideologies and anti-deficit attitudes—to bear on "concrete" examples of their own practice. For example, after watching clips they felt offered evidence of some texts being overly complex, especially for use with the whole class, teachers drew on their previously theoretical knowledge about reading development among EBs and emergent readers to voice concerns about how their instructional choices might be negatively affecting students.

In this sense and others, video-mediated interviews arguably functioned as a modest "change laboratory" wherein some of the suppression of critique (of policy mandates, especially) that teachers regularly experienced was alleviated, thereby helping to activate and even stoke their "professional creativity" (Ellis, 2011, 2014; Engeström, 1987, 2007). Although we didn't initially view video-mediated interviews as a form of design research aimed at facilitating expansive learning among teachers, the approach ended up seeming quite well suited to that task. To be sure, we don't want to overstate the outcomes of teachers' learning about CCSS that emerged during video-mediated interviews. Yes, in each one, though to different degrees, teachers identified tensions and contradictions between their notions of equity-minded teaching and their CCSS enactments, and they voiced concerns and questions about their standards-driven instruction they hadn't prior. In that respect, the interviews did seem to help unmask tensions and contradictions that Playa's existing context had, until that moment, rendered invisible.

In light of this, it is accurate to describe the interviews as indicative of *potential* for transformative teacher learning about policy and for such interviews as a tool in enabling it. It is likewise accurate to frame Playa teachers' responses to video-mediated interviews as *laying groundwork* for future expansive learning—or the sort of deep learning that CHAT theorists suggest results from the reconciliation of conflicts or tensions that arise as learners pursue a meaningful object or motive (Cole & Levitin, 2000; Roth & Lee, 2007). We can imagine, for example, Playa's teachers coming together in grade-level meetings to share problems of practice (perhaps identified during video-mediated interviews), to recognize patterns, and to work together to reconcile tensions between their CCSS enactments and their more concrete (less abstract/theoretical) notions of equity-minded teaching. Drawing on our own earlier research (Stillman & Anderson, 2015), we can also imagine how, as part of their efforts to address contradictions and tensions, teachers might begin to *appropriate* the standards—in other words, bring their own equity-minded identities and ideas to bear more powerfully on the CCSS and transforming them in the process. Importantly, in both of these imaginings, teachers get to move beyond uncritical "horizontal interaction" (Engeström, 1991), where harmony prevails and alternative perspectives tend not to surface, and begin to engage in more critical, solution-oriented exchanges.

We frame these above scenarios as "imaginings," not only because they didn't actually occur during our time at Playa, but also because the mere presence of tensions and contradictions does not guarantee that (expansive) learning will, in fact, occur. Teachers' working and learning conditions have everything to do with whether tensions and contradictions become "productive" for teachers' learning, or "unproductive" in the sense of hampering learning and, in some cases, increasing teachers' feelings of demoralization and powerlessness (Stillman, 2011).

We also frame these scenarios as imaginings because doing so helps underscore the complexity and contextual sensitivity of teachers' policy-related work and learning. Based on earlier research conducted in schools with "low-performing" labels, we've argued that the tensions and contradictions that emerge when equity-minded teachers' commitments and/or expertise conflict with educational policies can serve as fodder for learning and critical agency, and that administrators have a crucial role to play in creating enabling conditions. Building on and complicating these findings, this study indicates that contextual conditions present in "high-performing" schools may obscure from teachers' view these very tensions and contradictions. Indeed, in such contexts, teachers may require policy-related learning support on two levels: (1) at the level of noticing tensions and contradictions, and (2) at the level of addressing tensions and contradictions once identified. This is not to suggest that all teachers in schools with "low-performing" labels require certain kinds of learning conditions, and those in schools with "high-performing" labels require others. Our point, rather, is to suggest that the conditions teachers most need depend largely on who they are and the contexts within which their learning is occurring, in much the same way as K–12 students.

RUMINATIONS AND RECOMMENDATIONS

This study highlights the multiple ways that allegedly race- and language-neutral educational policies like the CCSS stand to disadvantage minoritized students, through their general governance of teachers' instruction and corollary undermining of the specific expertise that teachers bring to their work with specific students. Departing from our own previous research, our study indicates that these disadvantages may be just as likely to manifest in schools labeled "high performing" as they are in those labeled "low performing."

Teachers working across a range of different school contexts face daunting tasks when it comes to reversing systemic inequities. Nevertheless, we recognize that actionable steps are crucial, and so we close with some pragmatic recommendations for advancing more equitable schooling conditions and practices for teachers and Latinx EB students, like those at the heart of our inquiry.

First and foremost, we add our voices to those many proponents of *high-quality bilingual programs* who have long advocated for sustained investments in such programs' maintenance, expansion, and improvement. One need only spend a few minutes at Playa to realize that so much of what's happening there, in terms of linguistic and cultural preservation and innovation/hybridity, represents the future at its brightest. Because our study was not intended to gauge the merits of a particular bilingual model, especially vis-à-vis other models that are not the subject of this book's inquiry, we will holster our thoughts on the specifics of implementing a dual-immersion program grounded in language separation, except to say that being at Playa, whatever its flaws, only convinced us further of the importance of enabling bilingual educators like Playa's to establish programs that draw on the best research, alongside their unbridled passions and principled professionalism, to realize the beauty and power of biliteracy and bilingualism.

Second, the anti-deficit attitudes and humanizing behaviors that Playa's faculty—mostly bilingual teachers of color—directed toward their Latinx, EB, and immigrant students, even in the face of potentially constraining policy demands, leads us to add our voices to the chorus already singing clearly about the need to diversify the teaching force, and to create pipelines into the profession for bilingual teachers of color, especially (Neal, Sleeter, & Kumashiro, 2016; U.S. Department of Education, 2016; Valenzuela, 2016). Whereas students of color are now the majority of U.S. schoolchildren, teachers of color represent roughly 18% of teachers overall (NCES, 2012). Among the teaching force, Latinx bilingual teachers remain particularly underrepresented vis-à-vis students, a dynamic further exacerbated by declines in the already inadequate number of credentialed bilingual teachers that have emerged following the passage of restrictive language policies in various states (Hopkins, 2013).

Among those teachers who displayed the strongest relational ties with their Latinx EB students and who were their most vocal advocates were those who hailed from Playa's neighboring communities, and who were heritage Spanish speakers themselves. These teachers demonstrated deep knowledge of EBs' cultural experiences and served as community-oriented, accomplished role models. That they had such a powerful presence at Playa without question contributed to the very best, most loving, most affirming, and more achievement-enabling aspects of Playa's overall school culture. These teachers, especially, raised the standard of respect and care for all teachers, including those whose backgrounds differed from their students'. In all these respects, their presence and the anti-deficit, affective labor they engaged in at Playa mitigated some of the more negative dimensions of CCSS implementation.

There is so much to remember about Playa, and yet there are also certain images that stick out as somehow reflecting the essence of the place and its people. In our case, the image that always comes to mind is from one of our first visits to the school. In it, Paco is crouched down and conferencing with one of his 4th-graders. Both are leaning toward one another, eyes locked. In the physical space between them is one of the many graphic organizers that Paco and his colleagues have designed. But there is also, clearly, so much more; there is reciprocal respect, trust, common culture and language, and evident love. With one hand pointing back toward his own chest, Paco is telling the student to be brave and "*escribe lo que salga de tu corazón*" ("write from the heart"). The student, listening intently and engrossed in this mutual engagement, is almost literally expanding before our eyes. It struck us then and strikes us still that we were seeing something that went far beyond any simplistic notion of cultural match to deeper founts of intersubjective experience; it also struck us and still does that if such exchanges, where students can look to their teachers to see their best selves and vice versa, are to be made available to the increasingly diverse children in U.S. schools, then we need a teaching force that can make that possible, demographically speaking and otherwise.

Third, all that said, we recognize that we cannot do right by EB students just by bringing them into contact with teachers who love them, look like them, and speak their languages. Nor can we do right by teachers in suggesting that those dimensions of teaching are enough. Certainly, they matter profoundly. But they do not matter exclusively. Professional knowledge is essential, too; and this is an especially crucial point in the face of proliferating and arguably de-professionalizing programs—a hallmark of the neoliberal reform environment—that fast-track candidates into teaching, often without the requisite content and pedagogical knowledge needed for meeting learners' needs (Hopkins & Heineke, 2013; Jameson & DeMarrais, 2015).

Much has been written about the necessary knowledge base for effective teaching, which includes knowledge of learners, content, and pedagogy (Darling-Hammond & Bransford, 2005). Within this broad base, extensive scholarship delineates the kinds of knowledge that teachers need in order to understand and respond to linguistically diverse learners, specifically (e.g., Lucas & Villegas, 2013; Wong Fillmore & Snow, 2002). Given projected demographic shifts, including increasing numbers of "English learners" in schools throughout the United States (Gándara & Hopkins, 2011), it is increasingly important to frame these kinds of knowledge as *particular*—as representing areas of potentially deep *specialization*—and also as *foundational*. All teachers—teachers of color and bilingual teachers, included—need to develop such knowledge if they are to teach today's students well.

As our study attests, teaching EBs in today's educational climate is a complex undertaking, the success of which depends in no small part upon teachers possessing requisite and complex knowledge. Indeed, when Playa teachers were most able to use the CCSS to support equity-minded instruction, it was usually in part the result of them tapping into such knowledge—some acquired in preservice preparation and some acquired on the job—about effective, culturally responsive, language-affirming, equity-minded teaching for EBs.

Ensuring that preservice teacher education and inservice professional development opportunities treat this complex knowledge as foundational to the general knowledge base for teaching and prioritize its development accordingly, in turn, holds promise for ensuring that teachers are equipped to serve linguistically diverse students well. Because this will require recognizing and developing this kind of expertise among teacher educators, too, this is no small shift (Faltis & Valdés, 2016); still, it is essential and thankfully under way in various programs, professional development initiatives, and practitioner communities nationwide (e.g., *La Cosecha*, Understanding Language, Bilinguals United for Education and New Opportunities [The BUENO Center], and the Grow Your Own Teacher Education Institutes [GYO-TEI] sponsored by the National Latino/a Education Research and Policy Project, etc.).

Fourth, the kind of expertise just described, though crucial for teachers of EBs and other linguistically diverse learners, will also not be adequate to ensure equitable opportunities to learn. Simply put, diversifying the teaching force and making certain that teachers know how to teach EBs well do not protect against school and policy conditions that threaten to compromise equity-minded teaching and undermine EBs' learning. Thus, it is all the more crucial to support teachers to develop critical competencies for policy navigation.

Based on this study and our prior research, we contend that such competencies warrant explicit attention and cultivation as part and parcel of broader efforts to nurture ideological clarity among teachers, particularly but not exclusively concerning what it means to teach EBs in this historical moment. Indeed, it is ideological clarity that enables teachers to analyze different aspects of "the system" —everything from the way schooling is structured, to the discrete practices employed in classrooms, to the policies that seek to govern those practices—and to understand (and potentially to interrupt) their implications for Latinx EB students (Arellano, Cintrón, Flores, & Berta-Ávila, 2016; Bartolomé & Trueba, 2000; Valenzuela, 2016).

Some of the struggles Playa's teachers faced as they engaged with the CCSS reflected a lack of concrete knowledge about, and experience responding adaptively (rather than compliantly) to, educational policies, especially those that might appear on their surface to be equity-minded yet might still threaten equity-minded teaching and learning. In essence, although teachers were comfortable applying a critical lens to monolingualism and to (restrictive) language policies, they struggled to apply such a lens to their work with broader instructional policies, especially when trusted colleagues framed such policies positively. Potential harms imposed by the CCSS were thus obscured from their view—clouded over, rather than clear as day.

This study captures some of the ways that policy can, under particular conditions, lead teachers, even those as knowledgeable and capable as Playa's, to compromise their practices and curtail their activism in students' interests (Achinstein

& Ogawa, 2011). It also underscores the importance of teachers of Latinx EBs developing ideological clarity in relation to policy demands and in tandem with pedagogical clarity concerning how they might respond with agency to those demands (Heineke, Ryan, & Tocci, 2015; Valenzuela, 2016). Latinx teachers because of their own life experiences—including schooling and language learning experiences—may be particularly well positioned to develop ideological clarity about EBs' needs and rights, as well as about the ways that policy stands to impact EBs' development if not interrupted (Athanases, Banes, & Wong, 2015). That said, like any other teachers, they also stand to benefit from formal learning experiences that press them to imagine and practice navigating policies with agency and in ways that align with their expertise about EBs.

Calls to focus more on policy in teacher education aren't new. Scholars have long acknowledged the shortcomings of emphasizing "ideal conceptualizations of what teachers need to know about language," when policies constrain teachers' freedom to apply those conceptualizations in real classrooms (Baca & Escamilla, 2002, p. 71). Ironically, calls to focus more on practice, which are currently quite prominent in the popular discourse, potentially collide with the kind of policy-pertinent and practice-informing teacher education for which we would advocate most vociferously. These calls often advance a vision of practice-based teacher education that risks emphasizing practice at the expense of theory (Lemov, 2010; Sawchuk, 2013), and making it less likely that teachers will receive the support needed to teach in pedagogically sound ways.

What we envision as most critical in teacher education is not a discarding of theory, but an effort to develop political and ideological clarity in tandem with pedagogical clarity, such that the latter is tethered to the former and both inform teachers' policy engagement. This kind of teacher education would involve, among other things, opportunities for teachers to bring (typically) decontextualized knowledge about the technical dimensions of language learning into conversation with concrete policies like the CCSS. It would support them to identify aspects of policy that might undermine EBs' language and literacy learning. It would engage them in relation to questions like: What sorts of language demands do this particular policy or policy-related tool present? Given these demands and your knowledge base, including all you know about your EB students, how might you scaffold their learning? Most important, it would assist them in becoming comfortable with this kind of collaborative, action-oriented critical analysis.

Fifth, there are many ways to deepen teachers' knowledge, nurture their ideological clarity, and support them to make informed, even activist, decisions in the interest of EBs' learning. In this regard, we argue that *contexts of criticism* hold special power. As illustrated earlier, video-mediated interviews provided supportive conditions for learning about teachers' policy enactments and their implications for EB students. Given their actual and potential benefits for Playa's teachers— for example, that video-mediated interviews enabled them to identify moments when the CCSS were perhaps disadvantaging students, to begin applying a more critical lens to their policy navigation, and to take steps toward activism—we feel compelled to advocate for the creation of such contexts for preservice and practicing teachers alike.

At the preservice level, this might involve designing learning experiences that help trigger—as video-mediated interviews did—the identification of tensions and contradictions—for example, between teacher-education-sanctioned knowledge and policy mandates, and then designing assignments to help candidates collectively address and even reconcile them. In this respect, "contexts of criticism" represent an important departure from expecting that future teachers—regardless of challenges presented by their school contexts—will, on their own, be able to apply their teacher-education learnings forward.

Although preservice teacher education has an important role to play, it can also only do so much, developmentally speaking, when it comes to learning about responsive teaching (Lucas & Villegas, 2013). Practicing teachers need robust professional learning experiences, too. At the inservice level, "contexts of criticism" stand to provide opportunities for teachers to recognize and reconcile tensions and contradictions between their ideals, their practices, and the policy prescriptions intended to govern their work. Such opportunities might involve engaging them, alone or together, around video clips of their teaching in order to help them notice—as the teachers did in this study—how policy enactments, and instructional moves more generally, are impacting students (Sherin & van Es, 2009). In addition, given the somewhat ironic constraining effect on learning that Playa's teachers' coherent perspectives appeared to have, "contexts for criticism" would likely benefit from outside, and potentially "triggering," perspectives. These could, for example, be introduced through artifacts such as readings, presentations, or insights from teachers' own action research.

Sixth, navigating policies in equity-minded ways, particularly for new and less-practiced teachers—even within "contexts of criticism"—is very hard work to which different people bring different knowledge and experience. To say that scaffolding matters should not be interpreted as a lowering of expectations or a knock on teachers' capacities for powerful intellectual work.

Thoughtful *scaffolding for teacher learning*—much like thoughtful scaffolding for student learning—must take into account teachers' varied expertise, as well as their strengths, needs, prior knowledge, core commitments, and interests. As Playa's case also reminds us, such consideration likely needs to occur in relation to teachers as individuals, and as learning collectives. The 1st-grade teachers, for example, well prepared and full of amazing potential, were nevertheless mostly new to the profession, and so, as expected, struggled more than the other grade-level teams to use the CCSS to serve their students well. Notably, they also had to wrestle against a particularly wide gap between what research suggests were their student needs, in early childhood and as emergent readers, and what the CCSS calls for (Fitzgerald et al., 2015, 2016; Hiebert, 2012).

Yet, the support the 1st-grade team received—for example, an administrator offering abstract encouragement for them to "support" rather than "guide" students—mostly mirrored the types of support that teachers with more experience and expertise received. Being so committed to treating all teachers as equally power-ful intellectuals and avoiding status distinctions based on simple things like years teaching meant that even relatively new teachers were called to do much on their own. Undifferentiated support, in turn, made suboptimal outcomes more likely—for example, the 1st-grade teachers struggled to translate the abstract feedback they received into the kind of learning they hoped to facilitate. Though research on the characteristics of effective professional learning communities suggests that clustering teachers with similar degrees of experience might not be the best option (Kardos & Johnson, 2007), it is also the case that Playa's 1st-grade team worked tremendously well together and perhaps could have simply benefited from more targeted scaffolding that met them where they were, and helped move them for-ward from there.

Seventh, and finally, we want to close with some comments about research, including why we have tossed and turned over the writing of this book. When we embarked on this research project we were, as Britzman (2003) wrote about her seminal study of learning to teach, interested in understanding "what teach-ers make happen because of what happens to them and what it is that structures their practices" (p. 70). Initially, we were particularly interested in Playa teachers, because of who and how they were and what they brought with them to teaching insofar as shared commitments, knowledge and expertise, dogged work ethic, and abundant love and respect for students. We were interested in Playa as a site for research, almost secondarily, because we believed it to be a place where teachers like these just might be able to spread their wings and soar—to access and activate and amplify for learning all of the assets that they and their students possess. Who among us would not want to be there to see that? Having worked in education—primarily in and around urban, high-poverty schools that serve students of color, many of them EBs, that bear the burden of "low-performing" labels among other slights—we wanted so much to tell a positive story about what teachers could do with policies, like the CCSS, that inherently impinge on their practice. And so, we joyfully seized what seemed like, for us too, a "dream."

Circling back to the dream metaphor feels right for the final gasps of this book, and for admission of some nights spent tossing and turning. We saw many moments like the ones we imagined. But we saw other things, too, and in some ways those things were the ones that flew to the fore, because they stood in such stark contrast with our sense of what could have gone otherwise. It is the project of research to try as hard as possible to answer the questions asked, and we would argue, with as much honesty and humility as possible.

To be sure, many things "happened" during our time at Playa, but in relation to our research questions, what "happened" most especially to teachers was that the accountability systems and school conditions within which they were working made it quite difficult for them to engage consistently in the kind of equity-minded teaching they espoused, even in a context where we expected that constraints might be more peripheral than in bilingual schools bearing "low-perform-ing" labels. That these teachers were so susceptible to discursive infection and compromised practice suggests that we—all of us who want to support equity-minded teaching and expansive learning for EB students—really do have our work cut out for us. In some ways, it feels rather empty to end this book by saying that we need more and better research, because there is already so much that exists and sometimes it seems so far from serving the public good—and by public, we mean explicitly our increasingly diverse, multicultural, and multilingual public. That said, to the extent that research can assist in demonstrating how amazing some teachers are, how hard they work, and how difficult it is even for them to practice in equity-minded ways; to the extent that research can exert much-needed counterpressure on pressure-generating accountability systems and thereby impress upon policymakers the importance of better policies for practice; and to the extent that research can contribute to the construction of conditions within which teachers like Playa's can truly soar, unsinged, in their students' interests and their own, then *more and better research* is certainly useful and just.

Research Methods

The study reported on in this book aimed to capture equity-minded teachers' contextualized sensemaking and enactment of the Common Core State Standards (CCSS). Given previous research, we were especially interested in generating understandings about how these teachers, working with emergent bilingual (EB) students, were navigating new national standards in a "high-performing" context where conditions for teaching and learning were likely to differ from those in schools bearing "low-performing" labels.

STUDY DESIGN AND SITE AND PARTICIPANT SELECTION

We constructed our inquiry around the following questions:

- What meaning do teachers make of the CCSS, particularly in language arts/literacy? What does that meaning-making entail?
- How do teachers use the CCSS in their language arts/literacy teaching practice? How does their meaning-making shape their instruction and vice versa?
- What role does context play in teachers' responses to the CCSS? Which mediating factors matter most, and with what implications for students' opportunities to learn?

To pursue these questions, we designed a nested qualitative case study that unfolded over 2 academic years, from October 2012 through May 2014, at our research site, which we called "Playa." We chose this site, which employed a dual-immersion, "50/50" Spanish and English bilingual model, because it provided a unique and generative context for investigating how equity-minded teachers of EBs made sense of and responded to new monolingual standards. The school's K–8 campus (Playa) represented the overarching case, with individual teachers ($n = 10$), grade-level teams ($n = 3$), and administrators ($n = 3$) representing cases within that case (Yin, 2003).

Once administrators granted us permission to conduct the research, we presented the project at a faculty meeting and invited all teachers to join. All who expressed interest—10 teachers across three grade-level teams—were chosen to participate. These teachers included, at the start of the study, four in 1st grade, three in 4th grade, and three in middle school (6th, 7th, and 8th grade). Reflecting the school's language separation model, four taught exclusively in Spanish, while six taught exclusively in English. Although four school-based administrators also agreed to participate, as did several people connected to but not employed by Playa, our research centered around the 10 teachers.

DATA SOURCES AND COLLECTION

Data collection occurred over 11 visits and across 2 academic years. During visits, between two and five research team members spent consecutive full days at Playa. Visits were typically organized around weeklong "cycles of learning" and thus lasted 4 to 5 days (Greene, 1994).

During the study's first year, we conducted 90 to 150-minute semi-structured interviews with each of the teachers, in which we sought to elicit details about their biographies; their understandings of various topics, including literacy, language arts instruction, and bilingual education; their perspectives on the school and community; and their experiences navigating policy, especially related to high-stakes accountability. We also sought to uncover teachers' knowledge about the CCSS and views on the role they believed standards played (and should and would play) in their literacy instruction.

Early in the study we also conducted 90 to 150-minute focus group interviews with each of the three grade-level teams to elicit more collective understandings and accounts of how the CCSS were being taken up schoolwide; how teachers were working together across classrooms, subject areas, languages, and grade levels to respond to policy demands; and how school conditions were influencing collaboration.

We additionally interviewed three school-based administrators. Through formal interviews specifically, we sought to elicit administrators' perspectives on literacy, language arts instruction, bilingual education, teacher learning, and standards' ideal and actual role in instruction. We also asked questions that we thought would help us learn about Playa's leadership structure, working and learning conditions, and policy's role schoolwide. Toward the end of the study, we also interviewed a key administrator of the local district to better understand the context within which Playa was situated, and how its positioning shaped teachers' CCSS engagement.

All interviews were audio-recorded and transcribed.

To triangulate self-reported data, we conducted 11 approximately week-long school visits, during which we clustered observations by grade level and by teacher. Thus, not every teacher was observed at every visit. However, every teacher was observed for roughly 10 days—or two 4- to 5-day observation cycles.

During observations, we focused on the structure, content, and language of literacy instruction; the role of the CCSS and other resources therein; and the materials utilized throughout. We also focused on the relationship between teachers' knowledge and espoused beliefs about teaching and learning, on one hand, and the expectations imposed by the CCSS, on the other.

Because of administrators' generosity and trust, we mostly enjoyed an open-door policy during visits. This enabled us to observe grade-level meetings, schoolwide meetings, instructional leadership team meetings, on- and off-site professional development sessions, and family/community meetings. In keeping with our ethnographic approach, we also observed in the school's shared spaces such as the dropoff and pickup area, courtyard, library, cafeteria, playground, front office, and teachers' lunchroom area. In these beyond-the-classroom observations, we hoped to glean a better understanding of the school as a context for teaching and learning, and the presence and role of the CCSS therein. During and after observations, we wrote field notes, which aimed to capture through "thick description" people's actions in context (Geertz, 1973).

During most observation cycles, we collected as many relevant documents as possible, including teachers' instructional materials, such as standards-based unit and lesson plans; student work samples; standards-related resources, such as benchmark assessments; meeting agendas; and so forth. We regularly documented photographically various aspects of the spaces where we conducted observations and the interactions that unfolded therein.

Worth noting here is that the ratio of participation to observation was always in flux for research team members (Bogden & Biklen, 1998). In consultation with teachers, participant observation sometimes included supporting students who required extra assistance, working with small groups, escorting students to classrooms or activities, and making photocopies. These parameters were appropriate and embraced by research team members, all of whom are teacher educators with significant classroom teaching experience and expertise. At times, though rather rarely, participants solicited feedback from us about the instruction we observed. In these instances we took seriously our role as critical friends (e.g., offering teachers accounts of student performance that we had seen and they had not, suggesting possible texts and lessons, offering alternative methods for addressing content or skills, etc.). Because this didn't occur with frequency, and because we documented carefully whenever it did occur, we are not concerned that we influenced our findings in ways that are not already reported outright in the book.

EXPERIMENTING WITH VIDEO-MEDIATED INTERVIEWING

About a year or so into the study, we began experimenting with video-mediated interviewing. This proved highly productive. In generating our approach, we drew on our theoretical framework and on the structure of stimulated recall interviewing (e.g., Kagan & Krathwohl, 1967). In stimulated recall interviewing, interviewers present participants with a "stimulus" to "elicit verbal commentaries about the cognitions (typically thoughts or decision-making)" occurring therein (Borg, 2006, p. 209).

For our study, we adapted this structure in alignment with cultural-historical activity theory (CHAT), and our research questions and epistemological concerns. Specifically, we departed from a focus on stimulation and recall, which we considered to be too behaviorist and positivist in their underlying logics;

methodologically compromised given the limits of memory; and more focused on retrospective accuracy than what we intended—namely, to scaffold detailed discussion of teaching practice and policy navigation.

Our video-mediated interviews were designed with several related purposes. First, we wanted to document via video, for closer analysis, teachers' instruction. Second, we hoped to prompt teachers to speak with specificity about the backstage labor involved in making sense of and navigating policy in practice, particularly concerning aspects of CCSS-aligned instruction that emerged as central and that we hoped to understand better from teachers' perspectives (e.g., close reading of complex text). Third, we sought to position video-mediated interviewing as an invitation to reflection, which we know to be of value to teachers and also under assault as time for rumination has diminished under increasing policy demands.

For the research team, video-mediated interviewing involved the following: (1) recording and re-watching stretches of instruction; (2) identifying 2 to 3-minute focal clips, often based on criteria developed through preliminary analysis; (3) screening clips for teachers; and (4) asking teachers to comment and/or respond to questions before, during, and/or after screenings.

Prescreening questions typically prompted teachers to recall the process that led to the recorded instruction (e.g., What can you tell us about the process that led to the plan you put in place today? How do you feel about the way things unfolded?). Questions during screening and/or post-screening questions were more open-ended by design:

- How would you describe what's happening in this clip?
- As you _____ (example: monitor students engaging with materials during this part of the lesson and stop to check in with some of them), what's going through your mind? What are you paying attention to, looking for, and why?
- How are you deciding _____ (example: when to intervene in students' dialogue)?
- This seems like one of those times for which a teacher can't really plan in advance (example: when a student says something on the fly)—can you talk us through why you responded the way you did?
- How would you explain to someone else the connection between this segment of classroom life and the CCSS?

The screenings and ensuing discussion were recorded and transcribed and then subjected to further analysis.

DATA ANALYSIS

Preliminary data analysis began once data were collected and, in keeping with the tenets of the constant comparative method, was ongoing throughout the project (Glaser & Strauss, 1967). Analysis was "joint" and "interpretive," in the sense that we engaged as co-analysts (Wasser & Bressler, 1996). Our process began with open coding, during which we analyzed data inductively, noted core themes, and focused on patterns and ruptures in how teachers were engaging the CCSS. Doing this necessitated bringing into conversation different data sources—those that captured what teachers were saying about the standards, doing with the standards, and noticing about their own standards-based instruction.

Our first round of analysis indicated that although teachers were at times able to use the CCSS efficaciously, there were also numerous instances when teachers' instruction seemed to fall short of or even contradict their espoused beliefs, evident expertise, and equity-oriented goals. To understand why and how this might be occurring, we drew on CHAT to develop and revise coding schemes and to write an array of analytical memos addressing themes that emerged as we engaged around the data in different ways. Ultimately, CHAT helped us home in on mediating factors—such as particular school conditions and cultural norms—that were shaping participants' understandings and practices in especially consequential ways. The fruits of that analysis are the findings reported throughout this book.

Notes

Introduction

1. Although the term *Latinx* has been the subject of some debate, we use it in lieu of *Latina/o*. We recognize that some may view the term, for example, as critical of the Spanish language and/or of Latino culture. We do not take up the term as a critique, but rather because it represents the most established gender neutral and nonbinary option at this time.

2. Throughout the book we refer to students who are developing two languages as *emergent* or *emerging bilinguals* (EBs). Like others (Escamilla & Hopewell, 2010; García, 2015; Palmer & Martinez, 2013), we use this term to signal the importance of viewing such students through a lens of potential, rather than a lens of deficiency, as terms used historically to describe EBs (i.e., limited English proficient [LEP], English learner [EL]) have done. The term *emergent bilingual* also frames the overall goal for students' learning as bilingualism/biliteracy, instead of positioning monolingualism/monoliteracy, specifically in English, as schooling's primary goal. Referring to students as emergent bilinguals additionally reflects a *holistic* view of language. This means that linguistic activities in different languages are not considered as distinct sets of language practices; instead, these practices are viewed as part of a dynamic, evolving, and unified language/translanguaging system. Finally, we employ this term because it reflects Playa teachers' anti-deficit orientations toward their students, and it is the term they use to refer to their students in public-facing materials and documents (García, 2015; García & Wei, 2014).

3. All names, including the name of the school, are pseudonyms. In addition, there are a few places where we have opted to tweak some specifics to protect the site's and participants' identities.

4. Throughout this book we use the term *minoritized* rather than *minority*. This terminology reflects our understanding that the condition that certain groups in the United States experience of being (or being named as) a "minority" is rooted in histories of colonization, genocide, and linguistic hegemony (i.e., who gets to name whom, how, and with what language). The term *minoritized* likewise reflects the contemporary racial discrimination that accompanies any group being labeled a "minority," even when that group has become the numerical majority in the population.

Chapter 3

1. While SDAIE (Specially Designed Academic Instruction in English) approaches were/are designed to support "ELs" in accessing academic content across disciplines, SEI (Structured English Immersion) approaches emphasize language over academic content. As

proponent Clark (2009) writes, "the English language *is* the main content of SEI instruction. Academic content plays a supporting, but subordinate, role. . . . The operant principle is that students must have a strong understanding of the English language *before* they can be expected to learn grade-level content" (p. 44, italics are our own). Teaching English absent academic content counters extensive research demonstrating that language and content are most effectively learned together and through one another (August, Goldenberg, & Rueda, 2011). Importantly, in California (and elsewhere) no plans have been put into place to assist students in "catching up" on content after being held in SEI until they test into "mainstream" English classrooms (Matas & Rodriguez, 2014).

2. Although we use the term *emergent bilingual* throughout much of the book and in this chapter, we revert to the phrase "English learner" in instances like this one where it reflects the historical context and/or mainstream policy language and discourse under discussion; we put quotation marks around the phrase to signal that it is not the language we would choose ourselves, but rather the phrasing we believe makes the most sense in context.

3. These credentials—previously called Crosscultural, Language and Academic Development (CLAD) credentials—signaled expertise in language structure, first and second language acquisition and teaching methodologies, and cross-cultural competencies, generally. Bilingual, Crosscultural, Language and Academic Development (BCLAD) credentials signaled competency in primary language acquisition and instruction, alongside deep knowledge of a particular culture and language.

4. We changed the word *daddy* to *dad* because we thought that better captured, in writing, the spirit of the utterance, which might be read otherwise as more flippant or loaded with meaning the speaker did not intend.

Chapter 4

1. Because there is no 1st-grade (or 2nd-grade) standard specifically requiring that students compare number sentences as Rocio had them do, the work that Rocio's students did went beyond the grade-level standard concerning comparison and ended up addressing an amalgamation of 1st- through 3rd-grade standards.

Chapter 5

1. The Lexile Framework lists *The Circuit* as having a Lexile level of 880L, which is above the typical range they offer for 4th grade (480L–830L), at the high end of the range for 5th grade, and within the typical range for grades 6 through 9.

References

Achinstein, B., & Ogawa, R. (2006). (In)fidelity: What the resistance of new teachers reveals about professional principles and prescriptive educational policies. *Harvard Educational Review, 76*(1), 30–63.

Achinstein, B., & Ogawa, R. T. (2011). *Change(d) agents: New teachers of color in urban schools.* New York, NY: Teachers College Press.

Akkerman, S. F., & Bakker, A. (2011). Boundary crossing and boundary objects. *Review of Educational Research, 81*(2), 132–169.

Alcoff, L. (1988). Cultural feminism versus post-structuralism: The identity crisis in feminist theory. *Signs, 13*(3), 405–436.

Allen, C. D., & Penuel, W. R. (2015). Studying teachers' sensemaking to analyze teachers' responses to professional development focused on new standards. *Journal of Teacher Education, 66*(2), 136–149.

Alliance for Childhood. (2010, March 2). *Joint statement of early childhood health and education professionals on the Common Core Standards Initiative.* Retrieved from http://www.edweek.org/media/joint_statement_on_core_standards.pdf

Allington, R. L. (2002). You can't learn much from books you can't read. *Educational Leadership, 60*(3), 16–19.

Allington, R. L., & Gabriel, R. E. (2012). Every child, every day. *Educational Leadership. 69*(6), 10–15.

Almasi, J., & McKeown, M. (1996). The nature of engaged reading in classroom discussions of literature. *Journal of Literacy Research, 28*(1), 107–146.

Alvermann, D., Young, J. P., Weaver, D., Hinchman, K., Moore, D., Phelps, S., Thrash, E. C., & Zalewkis, P. (1996). Middle and high school students' perceptions of how they experience text-based discussions: A multicase study. *Reading Research Quarterly, 31*(3), 244–267.

American Association of School Librarians (AASL). (2011). *Position statement on labeling books with reading levels.* Retrieved from http://www.ala.org/aasl/advocacy/resources/statements/labeling

Anderson, L. (2014, March 14). Grit, Galton and eugenics. *Education Week.* Retrieved from http://blogs.edweek.org/teachers/living-in-dialogue/2014/03/lauren_anderson_grit.html

Anderson, L., & Stillman, J. (2013). Making learning the object: Using cultural historical activity theory to analyze and organize preservice field placements in urban, high-needs schools. *Teachers College Record, 115*(3), 1–36.

Anderson, M. D. (2015, November 10). The economic imperative of bilingual education. *The Atlantic.* Retrieved from http://www.theatlantic.com/education/archive/2015/11/bilingual-education-movement-mainstream/414912/

Appatova, V., & Hiebert, E. H. (2013). Reconciling college and career readiness with lifelong reading. *American Reading Forum Annual Yearbook* [Online] (Vol. 33). Retrieved from http://americanreadingforum.org/yearbook/13_yearbook/documents/CollegeCareerReadiness.Appatova.2013.pdf

Arellano, A., Cintrón, J., Flores, B., & Berta-Ávila, M. (2016). Teaching for critical consciousness: Topics themes, frameworks, and instructional activities. In A. Valenzuela (Ed.), *Growing critically conscious teachers* (pp. 39–66). New York, NY: Teachers College Press.

Artiles, A. J. (2013). Untangling the racialization of disabilities: An intersectionality critique across disability models. *Du Bois Review: Social Science Research on Race, 10*(2), 329–347.

Artiles, A. J., Kozleski, E. B., Trent, S. C., Osher, D., & Ortiz, A. (2010). Justifying and explaining disproportionality, 1968–2008: A critique of underlying views of culture. *Exceptional Children, 76*(3), 279–299.

Athanases, S., Banes, L. C., & Wong, J. W. (2015). Diverse language profiles: Leveraging resources of potential bilingual teachers of color. *Bilingual Research Journal, 38*(1), 65–87.

Au, K. (1998). Social constructivism and the school literacy learning of students of diverse backgrounds. *Journal of Literacy Research, 30*(2), 297–319.

Au, W. (2007). High-stakes testing and curricular control: A qualitative metasynthesis. *Educational Researcher, 36*(5), 258–267.

Au, W., & Waxman, B. (2015). The four corners not enough: Critical literacy, education reform and the shifting instructional strands of the Common Core State Standards. In K. Winograd (Ed.), *Critical literacies and young learners: Connecting classroom practice to the Common Core* (pp. 14–32). New York, NY: Routledge.

August, D., Goldenberg, C., & Rueda, R. (2011). Restrictive state language policies: Are they scientifically based? In P. Gándara & M. Hopkins (Eds.), *Forbidden language: English Learners and restrictive language policies* (pp. 139–158). New York, NY: Teachers College Press.

August, D., & Shanahan, T. (2015). What are the language demands for English language arts in the Common Core State Standards? In G. Valdés, K. Menken, & M. Castro (Eds.), *Common Core bilingual and English language learners: A resource for educators* (pp. 155–156). Philadelphia, PA: Calston Publishing.

Baca, L., & Escamilla, K. (2002). Educating teachers about language. In C. T. Adger, C. E. Snow, & D. Christian (Eds.), *What teachers need to know about language* (pp. 71–84). Washington, DC: Delta Systems Co., Inc., and The Center for Applied Linguistics.

Bakhtin, M. M. (1981). *The dialogic imagination: Four essays.* Austin, TX: University of Texas Press.

Ball, S. (2003). The teacher's soul and the terrors of performativity. *Journal of Educational Policy, 18*(2), 215–228.

Banks, C. A. M., & Banks, J. (1995). Equity pedagogy: An essential component of multicultural education. *Theory Into Practice, 34*(3), 152–158.

Bartolomé, L. I. (2004). Critical pedagogy and teacher education: Radicalizing prospective teachers. *Teacher Education Quarterly, 31*(1), 97–122.

Bartolomé, L. I., & Trueba, H. T. (2000). Beyond the politics of schools and the rhetoric of fashionable pedagogies: The significance of teacher ideology. In E. T. Trueba & L. I. Bartolomé (Eds.), *Immigrant voices: In search of educational equity* (pp. 277–292). Oxford, UK: Rowman & Littlefield Publishers, Inc.

Beltramo, J., & Stillman, J. (2015). Why should students *want* to do a close reading? *Voices from the Middle, 22*(4), 9–14.

Berliner, D. C. (2013). Effects of inequality and poverty vs. teachers and schooling on America's youth. *Teachers College Record, 115*(12), 1–26.

Berliner, D. C., & Biddle, B. J. (1995). *The manufactured crisis: Myths, fraud, and the attack on America's public schools.* Cambridge, UK: Perseus Books.

Bhattacharjee, Y. (2012, March 17). Why bilinguals are smarter. *The New York Times.* Retrieved from http://www.nytimes.com/2012/03/18/opinion/sunday/the-benefits-of-bilingualism.html?_r=0

Bogden, R., & Biklen, S. K. (1998). *Qualitative research in education: An introduction to theory and methods.* Boston, MA: Allyn & Bacon.

Booher-Jennings, J. (2005). Below the bubble: "Educational triage" and the Texas accountability system. *American Educational Research Journal, 42*(2), 231–268.

Borg, S. (2006). *Teacher cognition and language education: Research and practice.* London, UK: Continuum.

Britzman, D. P. (2003). *Practice makes practice* (Rev. ed.). Albany, NY: State University of New York Press.

Brown, A. L. (1992). Design experiments: Theoretical and methodological challenges in creating complex interventions in classroom settings. *The Journal of the Learning Sciences, 2*(2), 141–178.

Brisk, M. E. (2005). Bilingual education. In E. Hinkel (Ed.), *Handbook of research in second language teaching and learning* (pp. 7–24). Mahwah, NJ: Lawrence Erlbaum Associates.

Brisk, M. E., & Proctor, C. P. (2015). What do the Common Core State Standards mean for bilingual education? In G. Valdés, K. Menken, & M. Castro (Eds.), *Common Core bilingual and English language learners: A resource for educators* (pp. 15–16). Philadelphia, PA: Calston Publishing.

Buchanan, R. (2015). Teacher identity and agency in an era of accountability. *Teachers and Teaching: Theory and Practice, 21*(6), 700–719.

Budde, R. (1988). *Education by charter: Restructuring school districts.* Andover, MA: The Regional Laboratory for Educational Improvement of the Northeast and Islands.

Bunch, G. C. (2013). Pedagogical language knowledge: Preparing mainstream teachers of English learners in the new standards era. *Review of Research in Education, 37*(1), 298–341.

Bunch, G. C. (2015). What are the language demands for English language arts in the Common Core State Standards. In G. Valdés, K. Menken, & M. Castro (Eds.), *Common Core bilingual and English language learners: A resource for educators* (pp. 161–162). Philadelphia, PA: Calston Publishing.

Bunch, G., Kibler, A., & Pimentel, S. (2012, January). *Realizing opportunities for English Learners in the Common Core English Language Arts and Disciplinary Standards.* Paper presented at the Understanding Language Conference, Stanford University. Retrieved from http://ell.stanford.edu/sites/default/files/pdf/academic-papers/01_Bunch_Kibler_Pimentel_RealizingOpp%20in%20ELA_FINAL_0.pdf

Burris, C., & Murphy, J. (2013, November 9). Why young kids are struggling with Common Core math. *The Washington Post.* Retrieved from https://www.washingtonpost.com/news/answer-sheet/wp/2013/11/09/why-young-kids-are-struggling-with-common-core-math/

Butvilofsky, S., Hopewell, S., & Escamilla, K. (2015). What are the role of bilingual education teachers and bilingual content classes in Common Core Standards implementation?

In G. Valdés, K. Menken, & M. Castro (Eds.), *Common Core bilingual and English language learners: A resource for educators* (pp. 139–141). Philadelphia, PA: Calston Publishing.

California Ballot Measure. (1998). Proposition 227, English Language in Public Schools. Retrieved from http://vigarchive.sos.ca.gov/1998/primary/propositions/227text.htm

California Department of Education. (2015). *CalEdFacts: Charter schools.* Retrieved from http://www.cde.ca.gov/sp/cs/re/cefcharterschools.asp

California Environmental Protection Agency (Cal/EPA) & the Office of Environment Health Hazard Assessment (OEHHA). (2013). *CalEnviroScreen 1.1 statewide ZIP code results.* Retrieved from http://www.oehha.ca.gov/ej/ces11.html

Calkins, L., Ehrenworth, M., & Lehman, C. (2012). *Pathways to the Common Core.* Portsmouth, NH: Heineman.

Callahan, R. (2005). Tracking and high school English learners: Limiting opportunities to learn. *American Educational Research Journal, 42,* 305–328.

CAST. (2011). *Universal design for learning guidelines version 2.0.* Wakefield, MA: Author. Retrieved from http://www.udlcenter.org/aboutudl/udlguidelines

Chubb, J. E., & Moe, T. M. (1990). *Politics, markets and America's schools.* Washington, DC: The Brookings Institute.

Clark, K. (2009). The case for structured English immersion. *Educational Leadership, 66*(7), 42–46.

Coburn, C. E. (2001). Collective sensemaking about reading: How teachers mediate reading policy in their professional communities. *Educational Evaluation and Policy Analysis, 23*(2), 145–170.

Coburn, C. E. (2004). Beyond decoupling: Rethinking the relationship between the institutional environment and the classroom. *Sociology of Education, 77*(3), 211–244.

Cochran-Smith, M. (1991). Learning to teach against the grain. *Harvard Educational Review, 51*(3), 279–310.

Cohen, D. K., & Hill, H. C. (2001). *Learning policy: When state education reform works.* New Haven, CT: Yale University Press.

Cohen, R. M. (2015, June 18). When charters go union. *The American Prospect.* Retrieved from http://prospect.org/article/when-charters-go-union

Cole, M., & Engeström, Y. (1997). A cultural-historical approach to distributed cognition. In G. Salomon (Ed.), *Distributed cognitions: Psychological and educational considerations* (pp. 1–46). New York, NY: Cambridge University Press.

Cole, M., & Levitin, K. (2000). A cultural-historical view of human nature. In N. Roughley (Ed.), *Being humans: Anthropological universality and particularity in transdisciplinary perspectives* (pp. 64–80). New York, NY: De Gruyter.

Coleman, D., & Pimentel, S. (2012). *Revised publishers' criteria for the Common Core State Standards in English language arts and literacy, grades 3–12.* Retrieved from http://www.corestandards.org/assets/Publishers_Criteria_for_3-12.pdf

College Board Access and Diversity Collaborative. (2009). *Access and diversity toolkit.* Reston, VA: College Board. Retrieved from https://diversitycollaborative.collegeboard.org/sites/default/files/document-library/09b_588_diversitytoolkit_web_091123.pdf /

Collins, P. H. (1998). *Fighting words: Black women and the search for justice.* Minneapolis, MN: University of Minnesota Press.

Common Core State Standards Initiative. (2010a, June). *Common Core State Standards for English Language Arts & Literacy in History/Social Studies, Science and Technical Subjects.* Retrieved from http://www.corestandards.org/wp-content/uploads/ELA_Standards1.pdf

Common Core State Standards Initiative. (2010b, June). *Common Core State Standards for Mathematics.* Retrieved from http://www.corestandards.org/wp-content/uploads/Math_Standards1.pdf

Council on Foreign Relations. (2012, March). *U.S. education reform and national security.* Retrieved from http://www.cfr.org/united-states/us-education-reform-national-security/p27618

Craig, M. A., & Richeson, J. A. (2015). On the precipice of a "majority-minority" America: Perceived status threat from the racial demographic shift affects White Americans' political ideology. *Social Psychological and Personality Science, 6*(2), 210–218.

Crocco, M. S., & Costigan, A. T. (2007). The narrowing of curriculum and pedagogy in the age of accountability: Urban educators speak out. *Urban Education, 42*(6), 512–535.

Crosland, K., & Gutiérrez, K. (2003). Standardizing teaching, standardizing teachers: Educational reform and the deprofessionalization of teachers in an English-only era. *Educators for Urban Minorities, 2*(2).

Cummings, R. A., & Lau, A. L. D. (2003). Community integration or community exposure? A review and discussion in relation to people with an intellectual disability. *Journal of Applied Research in Intellectual Disabilities, 16,* 145–157.

Dalton, B., Proctor, C. P., Uccelli, P., Mo, E., & Snow, C. E. (2011). Designing for diversity: The role of reading strategies and interactive vocabulary in a digital reading environment for fifth-grade monolingual English and bilingual students. *Journal of Literacy Research, 43*(1), 68–100.

Daniel, S. M., & Pacheco, M. B. (2015). Translanguaging practices and perspectives of four multilingual teens. *Journal of Adolescent & Adult Literacy, 59*(6), 653–663.

Darder, A. (2015, August 20). Facing the complexities of the charter school debate. *Truthout.* Retrieved from http://www.truth-out.org/opinion/item/32435-facing-the-complexities-of-the-charter-school-debate

Darling-Hammond, L. (1998). Teacher learning that supports student learning. *Educational Leadership, 55*(5), 6–11.

Darling-Hammond, L. (2001). *The right to learn: A blueprint for creating schools that work.* San Francisco, CA: Jossey-Bass.

Darling-Hammond, L., & Bransford, J. (Eds.). (2005). *Preparing teachers for a changing world: What teachers should learn and be able to do.* San Francisco, CA: Jossey-Bass.

Davies, B. (2000). *A body of writing.* Oxford, UK: Rowan & Littlefield.

Davydov, V. (1999). The content and unsolved problems of activity theory. In Y. Engeström, R. Miettinen, & R. Punamaki (Eds.), *Perspectives on activity theory* (pp. 39–52). New York, NY: Cambridge University Press.

Duckworth, A. (2013, April). *Grit: The power of passion and perseverance* [TED Talk]. Retrieved from http://www.ted.com/talks/angela_lee_duckworth_the_key_to_success_grit?language=en

Duncan, A. (2013). Arne Duncan remarks at the American Society of News Editors Annual Convention. Retrieved from https://www.ed.gov/news/speeches/duncan-pushes-back-attacks-common-core-standards

Dutro, E., Fisk, M. C., Koch, R., Roop, L. J., & Wixson, K. (2002). When state policies meet local district contexts: Standards-based professional development as a means to individual agency and collective ownership. *Teachers College Record, 104*(4), 787–811.

Echevarría, J. J., Vogt, M., & Short, D. J. (2016). *Making content comprehensible for English learners: The SIOP model* (5th ed.). Boston, MA: Pearson.

Edwards, A., & Kinti, I. (2010). Working relationally at organisational boundaries: Negotiating expertise and identity. In H. Daniels, A. Edwards, Y. Engeström, T. Gallagher, & S. R. Ludvigsen (Eds.), *Activity theory in practice: Promoting learning across boundaries and agencies* (pp. 126–139). New York, NY: Routledge.

Ellis, V. (2011). Reenergising professional creativity from a CHAT perspective: Seeing knowledge and history in practice. *Mind, Culture, and Activity, 18*(2), 181–193.

Ellis, V. (2014). Professional creativity: Toward a collaborative community of teaching. In A. Sannino & V. Ellis (Eds.), *Learning and collective creativity: Activity-theoretical and sociocultural studies* (pp. 216–233). New York, NY: Routledge.

Engeström, Y. (1987). *Learning by expanding: An activity theoretical approach to developmental research.* Helsinki, Finland: Orienta Konsultit.

Engeström, Y. (1991). Toward overcoming the encapsulation of school learning. *Learning and Instruction, 1,* 243–259.

Engeström, Y. (1999a). Introduction. In Y. Engeström, R. Miettinen, & R. Punamaki (Eds.), *Perspectives on activity theory* (pp. 1–18). New York, NY: Cambridge University Press.

Engeström, Y. (1999b). Activity theory and individual and social transmission. In Y. Engeström, R. Miettinen, & R. Punamaki (Eds.), *Perspectives on activity theory* (pp. 19–38). New York, NY: Cambridge University Press.

Engeström, Y. (1999c). Innovative learning in work teams: Analyzing circles of knowledge creation in practice. In Y. Engeström, R. Miettinen, & R. Punamaki (Eds.), *Perspectives on activity theory* (pp. 377–405). New York, NY: Cambridge University Press.

Engeström, Y. (2007). Putting activity theory to work: The change laboratory as an application of double stimulation. In H. Daniels, M. Cole, & J. V. Wertsch (Eds.), *The Cambridge companion to Vygotsky* (pp. 363–382). Cambridge, UK: Cambridge University Press.

Engeström, Y. (2009). The future of activity theory: A rough draft. In A. Sannino, H. Daniels, & K. Gutiérrez (Eds.), *Learning and expanding with activity theory* (pp. 303–327). New York, NY: Cambridge University Press.

Escamilla, K., Chavez, L., & Vigil, P. (2005). Rethinking the "gap": High-stakes testing and Spanish-speaking students in Colorado. *Journal of Teacher Education, 56*(2), 1–13.

Escamilla, K., & Hopewell, S. (2010). Transitions to biliteracy: Creating positive academic trajectories for emerging bilinguals in the United States. In J. E. Petrovic (Ed.), *International perspectives on bilingual education: Policy, practice and controversy* (pp. 69–94). Charlotte, NC: Information Age Publishing.

Faltis, C., & Valdés, G. (2016). Preparing teachers for teaching in and advocating for linguistically diverse classrooms: A vade mecum for teacher educators. In D. Gitomer & C. Bell (Eds.), *The handbook of research on teaching* (5th ed., pp. 549–592). Washington, DC: American Educational Research Association.

Fine, M. (2002). *The psychological and academic effects on children and adolescents of structural facilities' problems, exposure to high levels of under-credentialed teachers, substantial teacher turnover, and inadequate books and materials.* Expert report prepared for *Williams v. California.* Retrieved from www.decentschools.org

Fink, J. L. W. (2014, November 13). Parents, educators coping with Common Core as best they can. *Hot Chalk Education Network.* Retrieved from http://www.hotchalkeducationnetwork.com/parents-educators-coping-with-common-core/

Fisher, D., & Frey, N. (2013). *Common Core English language arts in a PLC at work: Grades 6–8.* Bloomington, IN: International Reading Association.

Fisher, D., Frey, N., & Lapp, D. (2012). *Text complexity: Raising rigor in reading.* Bloomington, IN: International Reading Association.

Fitzgerald, J., Elmore, J., Hiebert, E. H., Koons, H. H., Bowen, K. Sanford-Moore, E. E., & Stenner, A. J. (2016). Examining text complexity in the early grades. *Phi Delta Kappan, 97*(8), 60–65.

Fitzgerald, J., Elmore, J., Koons, H., Hiebert, E. H., Bowen, K., Sanford-Moore, E. E., & Stenner, A. J. (2015). Important text characteristics for early-grades text complexity. *Journal of Educational Psychology, 107*(1), 4–29.

Flores, N., & García, O. (2015). What do the Common Core State Standards mean for bilingual education? In G. Valdés, K. Menken, & M. Castro (Eds.), *Common Core bilingual and English language learners: A resource for educators* (pp. 16–17). Philadelphia, PA: Calston Publishing.

Foucault, M. (1977). *Discipline and punish: The birth of the prison.* New York, NY: Pantheon Books.

Freire, P. (1970). *Pedagogy of the oppressed.* New York, NY: Continuum.

Freire, P. (2005). *Teachers as cultural workers: Letters to those who dare teach* (Expanded ed.). Boulder, CO: Westview Press.

Frey, W. H. (2014). *Diversity explosion: How new racial demographics are remaking America.* Washington, DC: Brookings Institute.

Friedman, M. & Friedman, R. (1980). *Freedom to choose: A personal statement.* New York, NY: Houghton Mifflin Harcourt Publishing.

Galton, F. (1869). *Hereditary genius.* Retrieved from http://galton.org/books/hereditary-genius/text/pdf/galton-1869-genius-v3.pdf

Gándara, P., & Hopkins, M. (Eds.). (2011). *Forbidden language: English learners and restrictive language policy.* New York, NY: Teachers College Press.

Gándara, P., Rumberger, R., Maxwell-Jolly, J., & Callahan, R. (2003). English learners in California schools: Unequal resources, unequal outcomes. *Education Policy Analysis Archives, 11*(36), 1–52.

Garcia, E. E. (2005). *Teaching and learning in two languages: Bilingualism and schooling in the United States.* New York, NY: Teachers College Press.

García, O. (2015). How should we refer to students who are acquiring English as an additional language? In G. Valdés, K. Menken, & M. Castro (Eds.), *Common Core Bilingual and English language learners: A resource for educators* (pp. 23–24). Philadelphia, PA: Calston Publishing.

García, O., & Flores, N. (2013). Multilingualism and common core state standards in the U.S. In S. May (Ed.), *The multilingual turn: Implications for SLA, TESOL, and bilingual education* (147–166). New York, NY: Routledge.

García, O., Flores, N., & Woodley, H. H. (2015). Constructing in-between spaces to "do" bilingualism: A tale of two high schools in one city. In J. Cenoz & D. Gorter (Eds.), *Multilingual education: Between language learning and translanguaging* (pp. 199–224). Cambridge, UK: Cambridge University Press.

García, O., & Hesson, S. (2015). Translanguaging frameworks for teachers: Macro and micro perspectives. In A. Yiacoumetti (Ed.), *Multilingualism and language in education: Current sociolinguistic and pedagogical perspectives from commonwealth countries* (pp. 221–242). Cambridge, UK: Cambridge University Press.

García, O., & Menken, K. (Eds.). (2010). *Negotiating language policies in schools: Educators as policymakers.* New York, NY: Routledge.

García, O., & Wei, L. (2014). *Translanguaging: Language, bilingualism and education.* New York, NY: Palgrave Macmillan.

Garfinkel, H. (1967). *Studies in ethnomethodology.* Malden, MA: Blackwell Publishers, Inc.

Geertz, C. (1973). *The interpretation of cultures.* New York, NY: Basic Books.

Gibbons, P. (2002). *Scaffolding language, scaffolding learning.* Portsmouth, NH: Heinemann.

Gibbons, P. (2003). Mediating language learning. *TESOL Quarterly, 37*(2), 247–273.

Gibbons, P. (2006). *Bridging discourses in the ESL classroom: Students, teachers and researchers.* London, UK: Continuum.

Gibbons, P. (2008). "It was taught good and I learned a lot": Intellectual practices and ESL learners in the middle years. *Australian Journal of Language and Literacy, 31*(2), 155–173.

Glaser, B. G., & Strauss, A. L. (1967). *The discovery of grounded theory.* Chicago, IL: Aldine.

Golding, W. (1954). *Lord of the flies.* London, UK: Faber & Faber.

Goldman, S. R., & Lee, C. D. (2014). Text complexity: State of the art and the conundrum it raises. *The Elementary School Journal, 115*(2), 290–300.

Gonzalez, N., Moll, L., & Amanti, C. (Eds.). (2005). *Funds of knowledge: Theorizing practices for households, communities and classrooms.* New York, NY: Routledge.

Greene, J. C. (1994). Qualitative program evaluation: Practice and promise. In N. K. Denzin & Y. S. Lincoln (Eds.), *Handbook of qualitative research* (pp. 530–544). Thousand Oaks, CA: Sage.

Guthrie, J. T. (2015). Growth of motivations for cognitive processes of reading. In P. D. Pearson & E. H. Hiebert (Eds.), *Research-based practices for teaching Common Core literacy* (pp. 107–122). New York, NY: Teachers College Press.

Guthrie, J. T., Rueda, R. S., Gambrell, L. B., & Morrison, D. A. (2009). Roles of engagement, valuing, and identification in reading development of students from diverse backgrounds. In L. Morrow & R. S. Rueda (Eds.), *Handbook of reading and literacy among students from diverse backgrounds* (pp. 195–215). New York, NY: Guilford Press.

Guthrie, J. T., & Wigfield, A. (2000). Engagement and motivation in reading. In M. J. Kamil, P. B. Mosenthal, P. D. Pearson, & R. Barr (Eds.), *Handbook of reading research* (Vol. 3, pp. 406–424). Mahwah, NJ: Erlbaum.

Gutiérrez, K. (2006). White innocence: A framework and methodology for rethinking educational discourse. *International Journal of Learning, 12*, 1–11.

Gutiérrez, K., Asato, J., Santos, M., & Gotanda, N. (2002). Backlash pedagogy: Language and culture and the politics of reform. *Review of Education, Pedagogy, and Cultural Studies, 24*(4), 335–351.

Gutiérrez, K., Asato, J., Zavala, M., Pacheco, M., & Olson, K. (2003). *The effects of educational reforms on English learners.* Paper presented at the Annual Meeting of the American Educational Research Association, Chicago, IL.

Gutiérrez, K., Baquedano-López, P., & Asato, J. (2000). English for the children: The new literacy of the old world order. *Bilingual Research Journal, 24*(1–2), 87–105.

Gutiérrez, K., & Rogoff, B. (2003). Cultural ways of learning: Individual traits or repertoires of practice. *Educational Researcher, 32*(5), 19–25.

Gutiérrez, K., & Stone, L. (2002). Hypermediating literacy activity: How learning contexts get reorganized. In O. Saracho & B. Spodek. (Eds.), *Contemporary perspectives in early childhood education* (pp. 25–51). Greenwich, CT: Information Age Publishing.

Gutstein, E. (2010). Commentary: The Common Core State Standards Initiative: A critical response. *Journal of Urban Mathematics Education, 3*(1), 9–18.

Hamilton, L. S., Stecher, B. M., Marsh, J. A., McCombs, J. S., Robyn, A., Russell, J. L., et al. (2007). *Standards-based accountability under No Child Left Behind: Experiences of teachers and administrators in three states.* Santa Monica, CA: RAND.

Hargreaves, A. (1992). Cultures of teaching: A focus for change. In A. Hargreaves & M. Fullan (Eds.), *Understanding teacher development* (pp. 216–240). London, UK: Cassell.

Hargreaves, A., Earl, L., Moore, S., & Manning, S. (2001). *Learning to change: Teaching beyond subjects and standards*. San Francisco, CA: Jossey-Bass.

Haskins, G., & Huber, J. J. (2015). *Students with dual labels: English language learners with disabilities*. Phoenix, AZ: Arizona Department of Education. Retrieved from http://www.azed.gov/english-language-learners/files/2015/09/pell-students-with-dual-labels-09-09-15.pdf

Heineke, A. J., Ryan, A. M., & Tocci, C. (2015). Teaching, learning, and leading: Preparing teachers as educational policy actors. *Journal of Teacher Education, 66*(4), 382–394.

Hiebert, E. H. (2012). The Common Core's staircase of text complexity: Getting the size of the first step right. *Reading Today, 29*(3), 26–27.

Hiebert, E. H. (2013a). The case for reader friendly articles. *Educational Leadership, 71*(3). Retrieved from http://www.ascd.org/publications/educational_leadership/nov13/vol71/num03/The_Case_for_Reader-Friendly_Articles.aspx

Hiebert, E. H. (2013b). Supporting students' movement up the staircase of text complexity. *The Reading Teacher, 66*(6), 459–468.

Hiebert, E. H. (2014). *Knowing what's complex and what's not: Guidelines for teachers in establishing text complexity*. Santa Cruz, CA: Text Project & University of California, Santa Cruz. Retrieved from http://textproject.org/assets/library/papers/Hiebert-2014-Knowing-whats-complex-and-whats-not.pdf

Hiebert, E. H., & Mesmer, H. E. (2013). Upping the ante of text complexity in the common core state standards: *Examining its potential impact on young readers*. *Educational Researcher, 42*(1), 44–51.

Hirsch, E. D. (1987). *Cultural literacy: What every American needs to know*. New York, NY: Houghton Mifflin.

Hoffman, J. V., & Pearson, P. D. (2000). Reading teacher education in the next millennium: What your grandmother's teacher didn't know that your granddaughter's teacher should. *Reading Research Quarterly, 35*(1), 28–44.

Hopewell, S., & Escamilla, K. (2014). Struggling reader or emerging bilingual student? Reevaluating the criteria for labeling emerging bilingual students as low achieving. *Journal of Literacy Research, 46*(1), 68–89.

Hopewell, S., & Escamilla, K. (2015). How does a holistic perspective on (bi/multi) literacy help educators address the demands of the Common Core State Standards for English language learners/emerging bilinguals? In G. Valdés, K. Menken, & M. Castro (Eds.), *Common Core bilingual and English language learners: A resource for educators* (pp. 39–41). Philadelphia, PA: Calston Publishing.

Hopkins, M. (2013). Building on our teaching assets: The unique pedagogical contributions of bilingual teachers. *Bilingual Research Journal, 36*(3), 350–370.

Hopkins, M., & Heineke, A. J. (2013). Teach for America's preparation for English language learners: Shortcomings of the organization's teacher training model. *Critical Education, 4*(12), 18–36.

Horowitz, R. (2015). Oral language: The genesis and development of literacy for schooling and everyday life. In P. D. Pearson & E. H. Hiebert (Eds.), *Research-based practices for teaching Common Core literacy* (pp. 57–78). New York, NY: Teachers College Press.

Hynde, C. (1999). Instructional considerations in middle and secondary schools. In J. Guthrie & D. Alvermann (Eds.), *Engaged reading: Processes, practices, and policy implications* (pp. 81–104). New York, NY: Teachers College Press.

Jameson, T. J., & DeMarrais, K. (2015). *Teach for America counter-narratives: Alumni speak up and speak out*. New York, NY: Peter Lang.

Jones, B., Chang, S., Heritage, M., & Tobiason, G. (2014). *Supporting students in close reading*. Los Angeles, CA: National Center for Research on Evaluation, Standards, and Student Teaching.

Kagan, N., & Krathwohl, D. R. (1967). *Studies in human interaction: Interpersonal process recall*. Washington, DC: U.S. Department of Health, Education, and Welfare.

Kaptelinin, V. (2005). The object of activity: Making sense of the sense-maker. *Mind, Culture and Activity, 120*(1), 4–18.

Kapur, M. (2008). Productive failure. *Cognition and Instruction, 26*(3), 379–424.

Kardos, S., & Johnson, S. (2007). On their own and presumed expert: New teachers' experience with their colleagues. *Teachers College Record, 109*(9), 2083–2106.

Kibler, A. K. (2015). How can language arts teachers meet the challenge and expectations of language arts in the Common Core State Standards when working with English language learners/emergent bilinguals? In G. Valdés, K. Menken, & M. Castro (Eds.), *Common Core bilingual and English language learners: A resource for educators* (pp. 184–185). Philadelphia, PA: Calston Publishing.

Kibler, A. K., Walqui, A., & Bunch, G. C. (2015). Transformational opportunities: Language and literacy for English language learners in the Common Core era in the United States. *TESOL Journal, 6*(1), 9–35.

Kincheloe, J. L. (2008). *Knowledge and critical pedagogy: An introduction*. New York, NY: Springer. Retrieved from http://www.springer.com/us/book/9781402082238

King, B. J. (2013, November 14). New study shows brain benefits of bilingualism. National Public Radio. Retrieved from http://www.npr.org/sections/13.7/2013/11/14/244813470/new-study-shows-brain-benefits-of-bilingualism

Kohn, A. (2014, April 6). The downside of "grit:" What really happens when kids are pushed to be more persistent. *The Washington Post*. Retrieved from http://www.alfiekohn.org/article/downside-grit/

Kostogritz, A. (2012). Accountability and the affective labour of teachers: A Marxist-Vygotskian perspective. *The Australian Educational Researcher, 39*(4), 397–412.

Kraatz, M. S. (2009). Leadership as institutional work: A bridge to the other side. In T. B. Lawrence, R. Suddaby, & B. Leca (Eds.), *Institutional work: Actors and agency in institutional studies of organizations* (pp. 59–91). Cambridge, UK: Cambridge University Press.

Krashen, S. D. (1987). *Principles and practice in second language acquisition*. Englewood Cliffs, NJ: Prentice-Hall International.

Kumashiro, K. (2012). When billionaires become educational experts. *Academe, 98*(3). Retrieved from http://www.aaup.org/article/when-billionaires-become-educational-experts#.VzyyGGPSOHc

Lampert, M. (1985). How do teachers manage to teach: Perspectives on problems in practice. *Harvard Education Review, 55*(2), 178–194.

Lave, J., & Wenger, E. (1991). *Situated learning: Legitimate peripheral participation*. New York, NY: Cambridge University Press.

Lektorsky, V. A. (2009). Mediation as a means of collective activity. In A. Sannino, H. Daniels, & K. Gutiérrez (Eds.), *Learning and expanding with activity theory* (pp. 75–86). New York, NY: Cambridge University Press.

Lemov, D. (2010). *Teach like a champion: 49 techniques that put students on the path to college (K–12)*. San Francisco, CA: Jossey Bass.

Lennon, C., & Burdick, H. (2014). *The Lexile Framework as an approach for reading measurement and success*. MetaMetrics, Inc. Retrieved from https://lexile-website-media-2011091601.s3.amazonaws.com/resources/materials/The_Lexile_Framework_ for_Reading.pdf

Leontiev, A. N. (1978). *Activity, consciousness, and personality.* Englewood Cliffs, NJ: Prentice Hall.

Levin, J. R., & Pressley, M. (1981). Improving children's prose comprehension: Selected strategies that seem to succeed. In C. M. Santa & B. L. Hayes (Eds.), *Children's prose comprehension: Research and practice* (pp. 44–71). Newark, DE: International Reading Association.

Lichter, D. T., Parisi, D., & Taquino, M. C. (2015). Toward a new macro-segregation? Decomposing segregation within and between metropolitan cities and suburbs. *American Sociological Review, 80*(4), 843–873.

Little, J. W. (1993). Teacher professional development in a climate of educational reform. *Educational Evaluation and Policy Analysis, 15*(2), 129–151.

Lucas, T., & Villegas, A. M. (2013). Preparing linguistically responsive teachers: Laying the foundation in preservice teacher education. *Theory into Practice, 52*(2), 98–109.

MacGillivray, L., Ardell, A., Curwen, M., & Palma, J. (2004). Colonized teachers: Examining the implementation of a scripted reading program. *Teaching Education, 15*(2), 131–144.

Masuda, A. M. (2010). The teacher study group as a space for agency in an era of accountability and compliance. *Teacher Development, 14*(4), 467–481.

Matas, A., & Rodriguez, J. L. (2014). The education of English learners in California following the passage of Proposition 227: A case study of an urban school district. *Perspectives on Urban Education, 11*(2), 44–56.

Mausethagen, S. (2013). A research review of the impact of accountability policies on teachers' workplace relations. *Educational Research Review, 9,* 16–33.

Maxwell, L. A. (2012, June 1). Raising Latino achievement seen as "demographic imperative." *Education Week.* Retrieved from http://www.edweek.org/ew/ articles/2012/06/07/34overview.h31.html

McLaren, P. (2000). *Che Guevara, Paulo Freire, and the pedagogy of revolution.* New York, NY: Rowman & Littlefield Publishers.

Menken, K. (2008). *English learners left behind: Standardized testing as language policy.* Clevedon, UK: Multilingual Matters.

Menken, K. (2010). No Child Left Behind and English language learners: The challenges and consequences of high-stakes testing. *Theory into Practice, 49*(2), 121–128.

Menken, K. (2015). What have been the benefits and drawbacks of testing and accountability for English language learners/emergent bilinguals under No Child Left Behind, and what are the implications under the Common Core State Standards? In G. Valdés, K. Menken, & M. Castro (Eds.), *Common Core bilingual and English language learners: A resource for educators* (pp. 246–247). Philadelphia, PA: Calston Publishing.

Mesmer, H. E., Cunningham, J. W., & Hiebert, E. H. (2012). Toward a theoretical model of text complexity for the early grades: Learning from the past, anticipating the future. *Reading Research Quarterly, 47*(3), 235–258.

Meyer, A., Rose, D. H., & Gordon, D. (2014). *Universal design for learning: Theory and practice.* Wakefield, MA: CAST.

Miller, E., & Carlsson-Paige, N. (2013, January 29). A tough critique of the Common Core on early childhood education. *The Washington Post.* Retrieved from http:// www.washingtonpost.com/blogs/answer-sheet/wp/2013/01/29/a-tough-critique-of-common-core-on-early-childhood-education/

Milone, M. (2015). *Development of the ATOS Readability Formula.* Wisconsin Rapids, WI: Renaissance Learning, Inc. Retrieved from http://doc.renlearn.com/KMNet/R004250827GJ11C4.pdf

National Association for Bilingual Education. (2013). Position statement on Common Core Standards. Retrieved from http://www.nabe.org/Resources/Documents/Home%20page/NABE_Position_Statement_Core_Standards_2013.pdf

National Black Education Agenda. (2012). *For Black America: We are "still a nation at risk." The National Black Agenda responds to the Common Core State Standards.* Retrieved from http://blackeducationnow.org/id17.html

National Council of Teachers of English (NCTE). (2012). Reading instruction for all students. National Council of Teachers of English. Retrieved from http://www.ncte.org/library/NCTEFiles/Resources/Journals/CC/0221-sep2012/Chron0221PolicyBrief.pdf

National Education Association. (2010). *Common Core State Standards: A tool for improving education.* Retrieved from http://www.nea.org/assets/docs/HE/PB30_CommonCoreStandards10.pdf

National Governors Association, Council of Chief State School Officers, & Achieve. (2008). *Benchmarking for success: Ensuring U.S. students receive a world-class education.* Retrieved from http://www.achieve.org/files/BenchmarkingforSuccess.pdf

Neal, D., & Schanzenbach, D. W. (2010). Left behind by design: Proficiency counts and test-based accountability. *The Review of Economics and Statistics, 92*(2), 263–283.

Neal, L. I., Sleeter, C., & Kumashiro, K. K. (2016). Introduction: Why a diverse teaching force must thrive. In C. Sleeter, L. I. Neal, & K. K. Kumashiro (Eds.), *Preparing and retaining highly effective teachers* (pp. 1–16). New York, NY: Routledge.

Nelson, H. (2013). *Testing more, teaching less: What America's obsession with student testing costs in money and lost instructional time.* Washington, DC: American Federation of Teachers. Retrieved from http://www.aft.org/sites/default/files/news/testingmore2013.pdf

Nichols, S. L., & Berliner, D. C. (2007). *Collateral damage: How high-stakes testing corrupts America's schools.* Cambridge, MA: Harvard Education Press.

Oakes, J. (2004). Investigating the claims in *Williams v. State of California*: An unconstitutional denial of education's basic tools? *Teachers College Record, 106*(10), 1889–1906.

Oakes, J., Lipton, M., Anderson, L., & Stillman, J. (2013). *Teaching to change the world* (4th ed.). Boulder, CO: Paradigm.

O'Day, J. A., & Smith, M. S. (1993). Systemic reform and educational opportunity. In S. H. Fuhrman (Ed.), *Designing coherent education policy: Improving the system* (pp. 250–312). San Francisco, CA: Jossey-Bass.

O'Donnell, C. L. (2008). Defining, conceptualizing, and measuring fidelity of implementation and its relationship to outcomes in K–12 curriculum intervention research. *Review of Educational Research, 78*(1), 33–84.

Orfield, G., & Ee, J. (2014). *Inequality and its alternative: 60 years after Brown v. Board of Education.* Los Angeles: Civil Rights Project/Proyecto Derechos Civiles. Retrieved from https://civilrightsproject.ucla.edu/research/k-12-education/integration-and-diversity/segregating-california2019s-future-inequality-and-its-alternative-60-years-after-brown-v.-board-of-education/orfield-ee-segregating-california-future-brown-at.pdf

Pacheco, M. (2010). English learners' reading achievement: Dialectical relationships between policy and practices in meaning-making opportunities. *Reading Research Quarterly, 45*(3), 292–317.

Pajares, M. F. (1992). Teachers' beliefs and educational research: Cleaning up a messy construct. *Review of Educational Research, 62*(3), 307–332.

Palmer, D., & Martinez, R. (2013). Teacher agency in bilingual spaces: A fresh look at preparing teachers to educate Latino/a bilingual children. *Review of Research in Education, 37*(1), 269–297.

Palmer, D., & Rangel, V. S. (2011). High stakes accountability and policy implementation: Teacher decision making in bilingual classrooms in Texas. *Educational Policy, 25*(4), 614–647.

Pearson, P. D. (2013). Research foundations of the Common Core State Standards in English language arts. In S. Neuman & L. Gambrell (Eds.), *Quality reading instruction in the age of Common Core State Standards* (pp. 237–262). Newark, DE: International Reading Association.

Pearson, P. D., & Gallagher, M. (1983). The instruction of reading comprehension. *Contemporary Educational Psychology, 8*(3), 317–344.

Pease-Alvarez, L., & Samway, K. D. (2012). *Teachers of English learners negotiating authoritarian policies.* Dordrecht, The Netherlands: Springer.

Pease-Alvarez, L., Samway, K. D., & Cifka-Herrera, C. (2010). Working within the system: Teachers of English learners negotiating a literacy instruction mandate. *Language Policy, 9*(4), 313–334.

Penuel, W., Phillips, R. S., & Harris, C. J. (2014). Analysing teachers' curriculum implementation from integrity and actor-oriented perspectives. *Journal of Curriculum Studies, 46*(6), 751–777.

Peterson, J. L. (2014). For education entrepreneurs, innovation yields high returns. *Education Next, 14*(2). Retrieved from http://educationnext.org/for-education-entrepreneurs-innovation-yields-high-returns/

Picower, P. (2011). Resisting compliance: Learning to teach for social justice in a neoliberal context. *Teachers College Record, 113*(5), 1105–1134.

Porter, A. C. (2005). Getting the content of instruction right. *Orbit, 35*(3), 11–13.

Quinn, H., Lee, O., & Valdés, G. (2012). *Language demands and opportunities in relation to next generation science standards for English language learners: What teachers need to know.* Paper presented at the Understanding Language Conference, Stanford University. Retrieved from http://ell.stanford.edu/sites/default/files/pdf/academic-papers/03-Quinn%20Lee%20Valdes%20Language%20and%20Opportunities%20in%20Science%20FINAL.pdf

Ravitch, D. (1990a). *The American reader: Words that moved a nation.* New York, NY: HarperCollins.

Ravitch, D. (1990b). Diversity and democracy: Multicultural education in America. *American Educator, 14*(1), 16–20, 46–48.

Reville, P. (2014, April 21). How to create a new K–12 engine. *Education Week.* Retrieved from http://www.edweek.org/ew/articles/2014/04/23/29reville_ep.h33.html

Roth, W. M., & Lee, Y. J. (2007). "Vygotsky's neglected legacy": Cultural historical activity theory. *Review of Educational Research, 77*(2), 186–232.

Roth, W. M., & Tobin, K. G. (Eds.). (2005). *Teaching together, learning together.* New York, NY: Peter Lang.

Roth, W. M., Tobin, K., & Zimmermann, A. (2002). Coteaching/cogenerative dialoguing: Learning environments research as classroom praxis. *Learning Environments Research, 5*(1), 1–28.

Ruiz, N. T. (1996). *The OLE curriculum guide: Creating optimal learning environments for students from diverse backgrounds in special and general education.* Sacramento, CA: California Department of Education.

Ruiz, R. (1984). Orientations in language planning. *National Association for Bilingual Education Journal, 8*(2), 15–34.

Samson, J., & Lesaux, N. (2009). Language-minority learners in special education. Rates and predictors of identification for services. *Journal of Learning Disability, 43*(2), 148–162.

Sannino, A., Daniels, H., & Gutiérrez, K. D. (2009). Activity theory between historical engagement and future-making practice. In A. Sannino, H. Daniels, & K. Gutiérrez (Eds.), *Learning and expanding with activity theory* (pp. 1–17). New York, NY: Cambridge University Press.

Santoro, D. A. (2011). Good teaching in difficult times: Demoralization in the pursuit of good work. *American Journal of Education, 118*(1), 1–23.

Santoro, D. A., & Morehouse, L. (2011). Teaching's conscientious objectors: Principled leavers of high-poverty schools. *Teachers College Record, 113*(12), 2670–2704.

Sawchuk, S. (2013, March 25). Teacher-prep programs zero in on effective "practice." *Education Week.* Retrieved from http://www.edweek.org/ew/articles/2013/03/27/26practice_ep.h32.html?r=668878791

Schlesinger, A. M., Jr. (1992). *The disuniting of America.* New York, NY: Norton.

Seiler, G. (2011). Reconstructing science curricula through student voice and choice. *Education and Urban Society, 45*(3), 362–384.

Seltzer, K., & Ibarra Johnson, S. (2015). What are the roles of bilingual education teachers and bilingual content classes in Common Core State Standards implementation? In G. Valdés, K. Menken, & M. Castro (Eds.), *Common Core bilingual and English language learners: A resource for educators* (pp. 141–142). Philadelphia, PA: Calston Publishing.

Semuels, A. (2015, July 30). White flight never ended. *The Atlantic.* Retrieved from http://www.theatlantic.com/business/archive/2015/07/white-flight-alive-and-well/399980/

Sergiovanni, T. J. (2000). *The lifeworld of leadership: Creating culture, community, and personal meaning in our schools.* San Francisco, CA: Jossey-Bass.

Shah, N. (2011). Combating anti-Muslim bias. *Teaching Tolerance, 11.* Retrieved from http://www.tolerance.org/magazine/number-39-spring-2011/feature/combating-anti-muslim-bias

Sherin, M. G., & van Es, E. A. (2009). Effects of video club participation on teachers' professional vision. *Journal of Teacher Education, 60*(1), 20–37.

Sleeter, C. E. (2005). *UnStandardizing the curriculum: Multicultural teaching in the standards-based classroom.* New York, NY: Teachers College Press.

Sleeter, C. E., & Stillman, J. (2005). Standardizing knowledge in a multicultural society. *Curriculum Inquiry, 35*(1), 27–46.

Sleeter, C. E., & Stillman, J. (2007). Navigating accountability pressures. In C. E. Sleeter (Ed.), *Facing accountability in education: Democracy and equity at risk* (pp. 13–29). New York, NY: Teachers College Press.

Smith, M. S., & O'Day, J. (1991). Systemic school reform. In S. H. Fuhrman, & B. Malen (Eds.), *The politics of curriculum and testing, 1990 yearbook of the Politics of Education Association* (pp. 233–267). Washington, DC: Falmer Press.

Snow, C. E. (2013). Cold versus warm close reading: Building students' stamina for struggling with text. *Reading Today, 30*(6), 18–19.

Solano-Flores, G. (2008). Who is given tests in what language by whom, when, and where? The need for probabilistic views of language in the testing of English language learners. *Educational Researcher, 37*(4), 189–199.

Solórzano, D. G., & Yosso, T. J. (2002). Critical race methodology: Counter-storytelling as analytical framework for education research. *Qualitative Inquiry, 8*(1), 23–44.

Solórzano, R. W. (2008). High stakes testing: Issues, implications, and remedies for English language learners. *Review of Educational Research, 78*(2), 260–329.

Solórzano, R. W. (2015). What are the challenges of test based accountability for English language learners/emergent bilinguals? In G. Valdés, K. Menken, & M. Castro (Eds.), *Common Core bilingual and English language learners: A resource for educators* (pp. 247–249). Philadelphia, PA: Calston Publishing.

Spillane, J. P. (2002). Local theories of teacher change: The pedagogy of district policies and programs. *Teachers College Record, 104*(3), 377–420.

Spillane, J. P. (2004). *Standards deviation: How schools misunderstand education policy.* Cambridge, MA: Harvard University Press.

Spring, J. H. (2007). *Deculturalization and the struggle for equality: A brief history of the education of dominated cultures in the United States.* Boston, MA: McGraw-Hill.

Stillman, J. (2009). "Taking back the standards": Equity-minded teachers' responses to accountability-related instructional constraints. *The New Educator, 5*(2), 135–160.

Stillman, J. (2011). Teacher learning in an era of high-stakes accountability: Productive tension and critical professional practice. *Teachers College Record, 113*(1), 133–180.

Stillman, J., & Anderson, L. (2015). From accommodation to appropriation: Teachers, identity, and authorship in a tightly coupled policy context. *Teachers and Teaching: Theory and Practice, 21*(6), 720–744.

Subban, P. (2006). Differentiated instruction: A research basis. *International Education Journal, 7*(7), 935–947.

Taylor, P. (2014, April 10). *The next America.* Washington, DC: Pew Research Center. Retrieved from http://www.pewresearch.org/next-america/#Two-Dramas-in-Slow-Motion

Texeira, R., Frey, W. H., & Griffin, R. (2015). *States of change: The demographic evolution of the American electorate, 1974–2060.* Washington, DC: Center for American Progress. Retrieved from https://www.americanprogress.org/issues/progressive-movement/report/2015/02/24/107261/states-of-change/

Thomas, W. P., Collier, V. P., & Collier, K. (2011). *English learners in North Carolina, 2010.* Raleigh, NC: North Carolina Department of Public Instruction. Retrieved from http://gled.ncdpi.wikispaces.net/DLI+Research

Tomlinson, C. (2004). Differentiation in diverse settings. *School Administrator, 61*(7), 28–33.

Tough, P. (2012). *How children succeed: Grit, curiosity, and the hidden power of character.* New York, NY: Houghton Mifflin Harcourt.

Tuck, E. (2009). Suspending damage: A letter to communities. *Harvard Educational Review 79*(3), 409–427.

Turley, J. (2005, November 10). Chicago's segregated schools. *Chicago Tribune.* Retrieved from http://articles.chicagotribune.com/2005-11-10/news/0511100182_1_gay-high-black-male-students-segregation

U.S. Department of Education. (2016). *The state of racial diversity in the educator workforce.* Retrieved from https://www2.ed.gov/rschstat/eval/highered/racial-diversity/state-racial-diversity-workforce.pdf

U.S. Department of Education, National Center for Education Statistics (NCES). (2015). English language learners in public schools. In *The Condition of Education 2015* (NCES 2015-144). Retrieved from https://nces.ed.gov/fastfacts/display.asp?id=96

Valdés, G., Kibler, A., & Walqui, A. (2014, March). *Changes in the expertise of ESL professionals: Knowledge and action in an era of new standards.* Alexandria, VA: TESOL International Association.

Valencia, S. W. & Wixson, K. K. (2013). Suggestions and cautions for implementing the reading standards. *The Reading Teacher, 67*(3), 181–185.

Valencia, S. W., Wixson, K., & Pearson, P. D. (2014). Putting text complexity in context: Refocusing on comprehension of complex text. *The Elementary School Journal, 115*(2), 270–289.

Valenzuela, A. (1999). *Subtractive schooling: U.S.-Mexican youth and the politics of caring.* Albany, NY: State University of New York Press.

Valenzuela, A. (2016). True to our roots: NLERAP and grow your own teacher education institutes initiative. In A. Valenzuela (Ed.), *Growing critically conscious teachers* (pp. 1–23). New York, NY: Teachers College Press.

Valli, L., & Chambliss, M. (2007). Creating classroom cultures: One teacher, two lessons, and a high-stakes test. *Anthropology & Education Quarterly, 38*(1), 57–75.

van Lier, L., & Walquí, A. (2012). Language and the Common Core State Standards. Paper presented at the Understanding Language Conference, Stanford University. Retrieved from http://ell.stanford.edu/sites/default/files/pdf/academic-papers/04-Van%20Lier%20Walqui%20Language%20and%20CCSS%20FINAL.pdf

Vescio, V., Ross, D., & Adams, A. (2008). A review of research on the impact of professional learning communities on teaching practice and student learning. *Teaching and Teacher Education, 24*(1), 80–91.

Vygotsky, L. (1978). *Mind in society.* Cambridge, MA: Harvard University Press.

Walqui, A. (2006). Scaffolding instruction for English language learners: A conceptual framework. *International Journal of Bilingual Education and Bilingualism, 9*(2), 159–180.

Walqui, A. (2015). What do educators need to know about language as they make decisions about Common Core State Standards implementation? In G. Valdés, K. Menken, & M. Castro (Eds.), *Common Core bilingual and English language learners: A resource for educators* (pp. 49–50). Philadelphia, PA: Calston Publishing.

Wasser, J., & Bressler, L. (1996). Working in the interpretive zone: Conceptualizing collaboration in qualitative research teams. *Educational Researcher, 25*(5), 5–15.

Watanabe, T. (2011, May 8). Dual-language immersion programs growing in popularity. *Los Angeles Times.* Retrieved from http://articles.latimes.com/2011/may/08/local/la-me-bilingual-20110508-63

Wertsch, J. V. (1991). *Voices of the mind: A sociocultural approach to mediated action.* Cambridge, MA: Harvard University Press.

White, V. (2006). *The state of feminist social work.* Abingdon, UK: Routledge.

Wiley, T. G. (2015). In what ways are the Common Core State Standards de facto language education policy? In G. Valdés, K. Menken, & M. Castro (Eds.), *Common Core bilingual and English language learners: A resource for educators* (pp. 10–11). Philadelphia, PA: Calston Publishing.

Winograd, K. (2015). Critical literacy and the Common Core: Resolving tensions and enhancing student engagement. In K. Winograd (Ed.), *Critical literacies and young learners: Connecting classroom practice to the Common Core* (pp. 205–210). New York, NY: Routledge.

Winstead, L. (2011). The impact of NCLB and accountability on social studies: Teacher experiences and perceptions about teaching social studies. *The Social Studies, 102*(5), 221–227.

Wong Fillmore, L., & Fillmore, C. J. (2012, January). What does text complexity mean for English learners and language minority students? Paper presented at the Understanding Language Conference, Stanford University. Retrieved from http://ell.stanford.edu/sites/default/files/pdf/academic-papers/06-LWF%20CJF%20Text%20Complexity%20FINAL_0.pdf

Wong Fillmore, L., & Martinez, R. B. (2015). What are the language demands for English language arts in the Common Core State Standards? In G. Valdés, K. Menken, & M. Castro (Eds.), *Common Core bilingual and English language learners: A resource for educators* (pp. 156–161). Philadelphia, PA: Calston Publishing.

Wong Fillmore, L., & Snow, C. E. (2002). What teachers need to know about language. In C. T. Adger, C. E. Snow, & D. Christian (Eds.), *What teachers need to know about language* (pp. 7–54). Washington, DC: Delta Systems Co., Inc., and the Center for Applied Linguistics.

Wong Fillmore, L., & Valadez, C. (1986). Teaching bilingual learners. In M. C. Wittrock (Ed.), *Handbook of research on teaching* (3rd ed., pp. 648–685). New York, NY: Macmillan.

Yin, R. K. (2003). *Case study research, design and methods* (3rd ed.). Newbury Park, CA: Sage Publications.

Yolen, J. (1996). *Encuentro* (Trans. Alma Flor Ada). Orlando, FL: Harcourt.

Yosso, T. (2005). Whose culture has capital? A critical race theory discussion of community cultural wealth. *Race, Ethnicity and Education, 8*(1), 69–91.

Index

About the Authors

Jamy Stillman is an associate professor of educational equity and cultural diversity at the University of Colorado Boulder and a former K–5 public school bilingual teacher.

Lauren Anderson is an associate professor of education at Connecticut College and a former K–5 public school teacher.

John Luciano Beltramo is an assistant professor of education at Regis University in Denver, Colorado, and a former middle school English language arts teacher and vice principal.

Kathryn Struthers is an instructor of literacy and elementary methods courses at Bank Street Graduate College of Education and Barnard College and a former K–5 public school teacher.

Joyce Gomez-Najarro is an assistant professor in the Department of Teacher Education at Azusa Pacific University and a former K–5 public school teacher and literacy coach.